INSIDE EDUCATION

To learn more about learning – *what it is* and *how it works* – it is necessary to look inside education. *Inside Education* takes the reader on a journey of four 'live' education projects: the first all Irish-speaking, mixed-gendered, multi-faith primary school in Ireland (based in Cork; ideally suited to exploring learning identity); an alternative post-primary school for those who leave (or are left behind by) the formal education system (based in Waterford, Ireland; ideally suited to exploring personal learning); an early college school that enables students to simultaneously sit their high-school diploma and college exams (based in Queens, New York; ideally suited to exploring learning success) and an adult education training centre that works with 'landless' movement members (based in Pernambuco state, Brazil; ideally suited to exploring learning power).

Using a critical ethnography approach, each research narrative naturally unfolds/ enfolds to tell a more complete learning story. By (re-) viewing their own learning outlook, they may begin to advance deeper critical ideas and debates in education. They may come to (re-) represent education, reminding public consciousness of its human stories, as well as its curious, intricate and powerful qualities. And they may (re-) discover 'other' roads to raise a scholar. Teachers, educational researchers, parents and guardians will be particularly interested readers.

Stephen O'Brien is a lecturer in the School of Education, University College Cork, Republic of Ireland.

'Steve O'Brien's work is characterised by a fascinated social curiosity and a strong sense of moral purpose. In these changing economic times it is important that his work should be read widely.'

Ivor Goodson, Professor of Learning Theory, University of Brighton, England; and International Research Professor, University of Tallinn, Estonia.

'This is a thought-provoking, challenging and revealing journey inside the world of education and learning. Its exploration of school and classroom practices in a range of different settings provides important insights into how we learn – a central aspect of our education system which remains overlooked and understudied. In doing so, it lays down a challenge to policy-makers and educators everywhere to think differently about the way we learn and, ultimately, help students fulfil their real potential.'

Carl O'Brien, Chief Reporter for *The Irish Times*.

...le Education is a stunning example of passionate scholarship that nonetheless ...ses a redemptionist stance. The ethnography captures people and contexts and ..s the reader into the four sites of learning in fluent and lyrical prose. This is ...tated by the extensive use of research notes deploying historical, comparative, ...ry, artistic and scholarly sources.'

Denis O'Sullivan, Emeritus Professor of Education, University College Cork, Ireland.

...ng a critical lens to document learning stories, O'Brien weaves a web of ideas, ...ry, experience around each narrative, giving breadth and depth to the learning ...s of children and adults in Ireland, New York City, and Brazil ... Rich ...tives encapsulate details of learning in each setting within significant theoretical ...historical underpinnings that illuminate the inconsistencies and intricacies of ...learning process.'

Francine P. Peterman, Dean of the College of Education and Human Services, Montclair State University, New Jersey.

'... the micro-macro ethnographic educational journey narrated here is at once refreshing, engaging, challenging and thought provoking. While the story teller's art is much in evidence, its subtle yet subversive flow belies its more critical edge that makes its message and meaning all the more apposite and rewarding. The cumulative impact of the book's trans-cultural cases provides a most timely read for those seriously engaged with the significance of learning in our lives beyond the performative agenda.'

Ciaran Sugrue, Professor of Education, University College Dublin, Ireland.

INSIDE EDUCATION

Exploring the art of good learning

Stephen O'Brien

Routledge
Taylor & Francis Group

LONDON AND NEW YORK

First published 2016
by Routledge
2 Park Square, Milton Park, Abingdon, Oxon OX14 4RN

and by Routledge
711 Third Avenue, New York, NY 10017

Routledge is an imprint of the Taylor & Francis Group, an Informa business

British Library Cataloguing in Publication Data
A catalogue record for this book is available from the British Library

Library of Congress Cataloging in Publication Data
A catalog record for this book has been requested

ISBN: 978-0-415-52919-8 (hbk)
ISBN: 978-0-415-52920-4 (pbk)
ISBN: 978-1-315-66896-3 (ebk)

Typeset in Bembo and Stone Sans
by Florence Production Ltd, Stoodleigh, Devon, UK

Printed and bound in Great Britain by
Ashford Colour Press Ltd, Gosport, Hampshire

For A, A and T.

CONTENTS

INTRODUCTION

About this book

It's something we all do. We do it both in and out of school. We do it formally and informally. We do it naturally. Yet we seldom reflect on this thing that we do the most – *learning*. This book is a response to our inattentive attitude. With a particular focus on schooling, it reveals, in the most ordinary of circumstances, how learning appears. Stories from different educational settings tell of its more subtle, covert, creative qualities. And research observations expose how learning works in diverse ways, along cultural, historical, social, personal, political and economic lines.

To learn more about learning – *what it is* and *how it works* – it is necessary to look *inside* education. Too often school and classroom practices are overlooked by capricious *outside* 'interests'. While these dominate the production and circulation of education symbols and practices, 'lived' learning becomes increasingly misplaced. This is particularly true in the case of education projects that 'stand for something different', that seek to secure 'other' representations. These stories take centre stage in this book. In themselves, the projects are worthy of storytelling and their unique 'messages' offer us valuable learning lessons. Collectively, as empirical and conceptual elements gradually unfold and envelop, they tell a more complete *learning* story. This emergent learning journey informs the structure of the book. Each chapter corresponds to a different education project that speaks to a particular learning theme: *Learning identity, personal learning, learning success* and *learning power*.[1] The reader is taken on a journey of 4 'live' education projects: the first all Irish-speaking, mixed-gendered, multi-faith primary school on the island of Ireland (based in Cork, Ireland; ideally suited to exploring *learning identity*); an alternative post-primary school for those who leave (or are left behind by) the formal education system (based in Waterford, Ireland; ideally suited to exploring *personal learning*);

an early college school that enables students to simultaneously sit their high-school diploma and college exams (based in Queens, New York; ideally suited to exploring *learning success*) and an adult education training centre that works with 'landless' movement members (based in Pernambuco state, Brazil; ideally suited to exploring *learning power*). As the reader partakes in this learning tour and reaches some fleeting endpoints, he/she learns more about learning. This challenges what we already know. Almost every one of us has experienced some form of formal education that continues to shape, in some significant way, our views. But, in truth, we remain disengaged from learning; we rarely appreciate its uniqueness or contemplate its meaningful existence. Experience and knowledge gaps lead to incomplete accounts of education, misrepresentations and an associated lack of common public under-standing. Much of what we know needs to be 'unlearned'. This book attempts to recast education's image, to remind public consciousness (as achieved in the promotion of some science, for example) of its human stories, as well as its curious, intricate and powerful qualities.

For whom is this book written?

Inside Education is a collection of short learning stories. Its motivation is twofold: to elevate our knowledge of learning from the inside-out, and to critically support those 'on the ground' – especially educators, educational researchers and parents/ guardians. The more we learn about learning, it is advanced, the better learners (and teachers) we may become. The very success of learning, then, depends on our knowledge of it. And the best way we may come to know good learning is through exploring, and putting into effect, its practice. The book's title is thus inspired by a journey metaphor and by an elevated learning purpose.[2] In setting out on 4 different paths, the journey is valued more than any destination. This, in itself, is an important learning lesson.[3] It was always envisaged that the book's main readers would be *teachers*. As one of the most important learner groups (charged with a duty to share learning), this book naturally appeals to them. Student teachers, teacher professionals, support practitioners and educational leaders will be particularly interested readers. The book bears testimony to their work and demonstrates how certain individuals can make extraordinary things happen in the most ordinary of ways. But it also challenges them. Taken-for-granted school practices, cultural norms, pedagogical values and approaches are seriously critiqued. The learning journey naturally involves self-questioning, developed understanding and renewed personal/professional positioning. Teachers change who they are, as much as what they do. So this book speaks to teachers across primary, post-primary and adult education divides. It seeks to inspire them with new learning ideas, values and goals. And it seeks to help them find new ways to resolve very practical learning problems in their work.

Educators may be particularly attracted by critical insights into project activities. And their professional development needs may be well-served by punctuated (theoretical) commentary and (conceptual) critique. *Educational researchers* too may be interested in this study's critical narratives and the different research methods employed, while other social scientists may appreciate the messy, multifarious and unsettled features of educational milieus. Many questions are posed for the reader throughout the book. Their purpose is to enlighten – to raise/generate hypotheses in line with informed theoretical perspectives and understandings. Questions are intended to move away from theoretical 'certainties' or 'theory-driven' approaches that merely assign their own labels to 'findings'. Instead, in promoting theory-practice connections, questions help the reader move between the 'big picture' (often 'invisible' to the eye) and the 'specific' (which appears immediately 'obvious'). Indeed, prominence is given to bottom-up analysis – where the reader moves more from the 'concrete' to the 'abstract'. Above all, questions facilitate reader-communication and self-dialogue; we make sense together, and make sense for ourselves,[4] as and when learning appears.

In addition to professional roles, it takes significant others to raise a scholar. *Parents and guardians* routinely escort their children along affective, social and learning journeys. As important learning models, their ideas, values and goals greatly influence their children's learning path. But beyond surface indicators (see Chapter 3), how much do they really know about their child's learning in school? In this book parents/guardians may find the projects' events, activities and commentaries most valuable. They offer them (and adult learners generally) an opportunity to learn more about learning, to communicate good learning habits to their children. They offer an opportunity too for adults to reciprocate modelling relations, to learn as much from their children. Parents/guardians are often left out of *critical* debates on education. Many find educational jargon forbidding and critical ideas impenetrable. In playing its (inclusive) part, this book differs from conventional academic texts. It hopes to present as more 'user-friendly', its material may read as more 'accessible', its writing 'lighter'. In this fashion, the book seeks to appeal to *a wider reader base*. At the same time, it's important to stress that some learning struggle is necessary. The reader may experience this progressively throughout the book. Thus, while the learning journey is made 'easier', this doesn't mean that it *is* easy.

Why this book?

Learning thrives on challenge, especially if it's interesting, worthwhile and enjoyable. But 'learning about learning' doesn't always inspire or challenge. Why do discussions on education fail to stimulate more debate? Why do they not advance greater knowledge and practice? Why are they not aired more regularly? The media, it seems, is saturated with trivial coverage. 'Big' educational ideas and debates give way to talk of 'crisis', latest 'reforms', expediency 'measures' and 'success' stories. Statisticians clamour over the latest test results; policymakers and managers rush to direct new bureaucratic tasks; private 'interests' grind out their competitive position; politicians take credit for 'improvements' and, simultaneously, impose strict 'value for money' rulings. While these groups drive the 'education-economy' relation, there's little room for disturbance. 'Human capital' values abound. Education is seen as something to be captured (objectified/commodified in tightly prescribed curricula), to be measured (by learning outcomes and standardised tests), to be desired and transferred (via 'upskilling' and 'accreditation'). The disconnect between wider social structures and practice places inordinate pressure on teachers to 'bridge the gap'. Together with their students, they are subjected to more normative measures of performance (student against student, teacher against teacher, school against school, country against country). We are in the throes of learning intensification, in the business of 'product' ('end-game') education. There's less and less freedom to explore learning as a contested science, to faithfully question *what it is* and *how it works*. And as education as a 'process' is downgraded, there are fewer 'learning about learning' moments. This book is written within this context. Ultimately, it is a written testimony against this context.[5] This volume takes the time to tell some new stories. It consciously recites against the clamour of quantitative noise, against the rush of managerial directives, 'innovations', political intrusions and economic rules. It consciously makes space to energise, animate and authenticate real learning practices. And it consciously re-presents the *inherent value* of education.

We need 'other' stories in education – ones that focus on the here-and-now, not ones fixed on some limited future state that speak of predictive targets, learning outcomes or 'products'. This book has this existential thrust. Its stories focus on human experiences, authentic learning events and cognitive, perceptual and affective responses. In everyday schooling, learning is 'lived'. Teachers and students exercise learning freedoms, limits, responsibilities and contradictions that effectively (and affectively) channel new learning paths. There is a depth and richness to learning that is worked out in ways that are contextual, personal, social, creative and powerful. But there is an ordinariness to learning too. As John McGahern (2005) guides, much of life's journey is 'lived quietly', unnoticed, as a matter of course.[6] This is where 'precious life' resides; this is where we find, in the words of Michel de Certeau (1984), 'the practice of everyday life'. We need to explore and understand everyday practice, not least because this brings to light people's repetitive, 'tactical' activities (much of which remains unseen, unpredictable and unconscious). In this regard, de Certeau's plunging view from the 110th floor down to Manhattan's streets is a powerful illustration of how:[7] Strategists (like city planners or educational policy-makers) are elevated, distanced viewers ('voyeurs' of practice) focused on generating and regulating simulacrum ('fictional') representations; while practitioners (like walkers or teachers) make different use of the spaces designed ('tactically' speaking) and hurriedly navigate hidden, 'plural' pathways (e.g. by taking alternative routes, creative short-cuts and qualitative journeys that leave no real trace).[8] de Certeau's commanding perspective embodies the current educational landscape – functional organisation appears to be the order of the day, but it's rarely ordered in practice. A parallel case is now made for the unseen world of learning to be revealed. We need to relocate our viewpoint. We need to take a closer look at the world of learning from *tactical* as well as strategic perspectives.

About this research

Analogous to de Certeau's (1984, 98) idea of 'walking as a space of enunciation', this book makes room for teachers, students and school parents to articulate *their* learning views. This 'grounded' position opposes a rigid, dominant, panoptic structure that orders learning 'from above' and produces normalised meanings everywhere. And it challenges us to find a fitting methodology to capture (as far as possible) actors' *qualitative* locations. *Ethnography* is chosen for this purpose.[9] This is a particular research approach that traces what people *do* in their 'familiar' cultural settings. Everyday life in schools is captured (as far as possible) by paying close attention to individuals' thoughts, feelings and actions and connecting these to specific cultural historical contexts.[10] The focus, therefore, is on becoming familiar with teachers', students' and parents' practices at a particular time, within a particular cultural site. In order to 'know' cultural actors in their site (and vice versa), we need to read beyond their stories. Specifically, for the purpose of inductive analysis, we must learn to interpret observed rituals and behaviours. We are obliged, therefore, to *make the familiar unfamiliar*. This is not an easy task, especially if one is already 'immersed' as an actor and/or reader. Thus, teachers are challenged to make teaching unfamiliar, researchers have to detach themselves from familiar participants and settings and parents/guardians have to 'unlearn' much of their own learning experiences.

While this learning journey is certainly challenging, it doesn't have to be daunting, less still dull. I have long admired the work of cultural theorists whose real-life studies exude a stimulating, attentive quality, and whose links between the cultural, social, political and economic are communicated more plainly and imaginatively. I'm thinking here of the work of Raymond Williams, Stuart Hall and Paul Willis,[11] amongst others. Narrative enquiry[12] is also an inspirational guide. Narratives focus on meaningful ways in which we can learn from others' life histories, characteristics, thoughts, values and patterns of practice. In the course of engaging others' stories, we can begin to create our own. We can self-learn. Of course narratives are unencumbered by academic mores. We are more likely to encounter learning, including philosophical kinds, in simple everyday stories. These can be unassuming in tone, yet beautifully composed; they can describe routines, which echo with rhythmic power; they can proclaim, yet still question; and they can provide portals to the past, which speak to future revival. People relate to stories, such as those handed down by 'common' histories. This book draws on these. It draws too on the visual arts, poetry, literature, music and film to communicate culturally and connect with the more sensory features of learning. In this way, an 'aesthetic sensibility' (Willis, 2000) helps illuminate more complex, concealed elements of the human condition (Heidegger, 1927/1996). While (expressive) art plays on all the senses (and not just the intellect), it can still motivate deeper thoughts and change actions. Through the arts we can announce, question, critique, resist and renew everyday practices.

The stories in this book help us to see that learning is historically, socio-culturally situated. Learning rituals and practices are interpreted from a number of critical perspectives, namely from political, economic, class, gender, racial and ability standpoints. As new critical understandings emerge, we are faced with changing our learning ways. In setting out this transformative journey, this book consciously draws upon the traditions of critical theory and critical social research. 'Big' critical theorists feature in the book, such as Karl Marx, Hannah Arendt, Jean Baudrillard, Pierre Bourdieu, Michel Foucault, Paulo Freire, Friedrich Nietzsche, Lev Vygotsky, amongst others. Of course each thinker has different ideas, but all may find common purpose in their questioning of power relations, 'normalised' language and signs, and oppressive practices. These critical theorists help us to 'see' research findings as being connected to hidden political and ideological power structures. In this way, they caution against education being seen as an isolated field of social and cultural production. And they challenge *scholars* of education (scholar teachers, scholar researchers, learner scholars) to critically empower themselves by refusing passivity, embracing complexity, developing power literacies, advancing new practices and being self-critical and open to further change. Ethnographic research that applies critical theory or takes on a 'political purpose' (Thomas, 1993) may be more accurately described as *critical ethnography*.[13] This critical ethnography study focuses on education and so it naturally draws upon *critical pedagogy* theories.[14] The work of Paulo Freire is particularly influential here (see Chapter 4), but other critical educators and social theorists are drawn upon.[15] These theorists make us think seriously (reflexively) about the 'bigger' education connections that may be gleaned from seemingly ordinary rehearsal. They present new learning insights in opposition to dominant status quo meanings. And they sustain scholarly dialogue and offer up new possibilities. The *critical narratives* presented in this book, then, describe not just what is, but what can (gradually) be.[16] Reciprocally, critical pedagogy is enacted *through* critical narratives. We learn more about ourselves and learning as we revise ('re-story') our lives and gradually identify as learner scholars, scholar teachers (see Goodson *et al*, 2010; Goodson and Gill, 2011, 2014).

The critical narratives in this book perform as learning stories. By organically revealing themselves, these stories ease intellectual struggle and relieve creative expression. In stories, we look for 'sense' (perceptiveness, reasoning, evidence) and 'sensibility' (responsiveness, feelings, emotions). Critical ethnography captures much of the latter but so too does it shape the former. Specifically, critical ethnography informs the range and types of research methods chosen to tell a more complete learning story. In this study, the research methods chosen vary according to each cultural site and each learning theme addressed. Thus, in Chapter 1 (*learning identity*), visual (photographic) methods are employed to facilitate pupils' self-expressions of 'who we are'; in Chapter 2, we are given access to the teacher's autobiographical writings and poetry in order to enrich this *personal learning* story; in Chapter 3, a focus group enquiry with parents/guardians is employed to investigate their understandings of *learning success*; and in Chapter 4 (*learning power*), historical documentary sources are reviewed to contextualise and elucidate Brazil's complex relationship with the land. Furthermore, a range of interviews, focus groups and conversations are employed with different groups of teachers, students and parents/guardians. In all cases, classroom and school observations were conducted, field notes were recorded, a research diary/journal was kept and, once each story was written, participants were given an opportunity to review it. These research methods were used throughout the course of site visits;[17] they were not entirely 'pre-planned', nor did they present as merely 'procedural'. In keeping with the fluid, organic nature of storytelling, these methods emerged: In part through iterative analysis and a developing 'sense' of evidence, and in other part through moment-by-moment observation and 'sensibility'.

On reading this book

In storytelling, there is a unique bond between *writer-researcher and reader*. Roland Barthes (1968/1977) claims that a book's purpose is realised in its moment of being read,[18] and that the 'birth of the reader' is delivered at the precise moment of the book being written (Barthes refers to this instant as the 'Death of the author', *La mort de l'auteur*).[19] Indeed, Barthes queries any real authorial presence, reasserting that "it is language which speaks, not the author" – that the author's 'voice' really consists "of several indiscernible voices" (Barthes 1968/1977, 2, 3). I think it's right to authenticate ideas at the point of their reading: Readers make sense of learning for themselves and there can be no written 'conclusion'. I think it's also right to destabilise the 'expertise' and 'authority' of the writer-researcher: 'My own' voice merely echoes many others' re-citing. But this is not to deny 'the author function', as Michel Foucault puts it (Foucault, 1969/1977). While the sovereign author doesn't exist, he/she still performs a (necessary) creative purpose (ibid.). The author puts (back) in the public domain language and ideas that are rarely used. He/she helps bring a distorted picture, which may otherwise be unobserved, (back) into focus.[20] And he/she exercises an ethical purpose that (once more) says something about our time, however disagreeable. In doing critical ethnography, the writer-researcher performs certain challenging tasks, including co-constructing learning stories with/for 'others'; telling people's stories, whilst being immersed; making meaning (gradually) from new information and critical ideas; and demonstrating (not overstating) hidden power relations. *Writing* critical ethnography is particularly challenging.[21] But it's also very rewarding. Intuitively, I always felt that readers might benefit more from an accessible text[22] – one that is no less 'deep', no less 'political' and no less 'contentious'. At the same time, there was always the danger that the book would 'fall between 2 stools', that it would be seen as neither popular nor academic. In truth, I'm not sure if either seat is secure. I'd like to think that *scholarly* work is more stable. In any case, readers (lay and academic) have the final say.[23]

Readers will have their 'own' thoughts on these learning stories. By encountering 'others', they can encounter them*selves*. And they can begin to inspect their own *learning* outlook. *Guiding research* notes are liberally provided at the end of each chapter for the purpose of 'deeper' scholarly enquiry. I hope that these notes don't unduly frustrate the reader and/or take from their reading 'flow'. Some readers may choose to consult these *after* the main text. Others may choose to refer to them simultaneously or they may draw upon them selectively. In any case, *guiding research* notes are not intended as merely informational and/or auxiliary points, nor are they exclusively directed towards 'academic' readers. It is genuinely hoped that they facilitate 'deeper' research into learning. Readers may appreciate that such analysis demands greater time and space than is afforded in this book. Even so, they may appreciate that this book's material demands constant re-reading. To illustrate, many learning categories re-emerge *within and across* stories that relate to 'identity', 'time', 'memory', 'spirituality', 'space', 'success', 'power' and more. There is little point in extending these connections now in advance (and in isolation) of the stories. Much like a writer who later re-drafts an introduction, the reader may re-consider these learning connections at the 'end'. Indeed, since the stories organically unfold and enfold, this 'inverse reading' may make more 'sense' and 'sensibility'. With no 'conclusion' offered then, readers are encouraged to continually seek out unique and generic features of learning, and coherent ways in which *they* might renew learning in their daily personal/professional lives. This is no easy learning task, but it is an important one. As a society, we have a responsibility to understand what is being done to education in the name of learning. We are personally responsible too for how education is enacted, for the ways in which *we* name learning. In this spirit of educational accountability, I invite you now to join the collective narrative and to question throughout: *How does learning appear to me?*

Guiding research (notes)

1 Of course there are many more education stories that could tell a more complete *learning* story. One can think, for example, of education projects that speak to these learning themes: *Learning independence, learning experience, learning technology*, and *learning culture*.
2 This exploratory direction is poetically captured in the old Gaelic phrase, *go n-éirí an bóthar leat*. Often misinterpreted as 'may the road rise up to meet you', *go n-éirí an bóthar leat* more accurately translates as 'may the journey be successful for you'. Ultimately, it is hoped that new learning pathways are created in this book, enabling various educators (and students) to become more successful *learners*.
3 A destination could not exist without the journey. Consider how this value order is inverted in contemporary educational policy and discourse. Destination is given priority – it even determines the journey e.g. 'teaching to the test', 'learning outcomes', 'performativity targets', measures of professional 'competency' and 'successful' learning.
4 Making sense for ourselves is an *existential* responsibility. In the context of this learning journey, readers are responsible for authentic self-questioning and self-creating. Only *they* can produce their own learning responses.
5 The introduction to this book was, as is customary, written lastly. Having completed Chapters 1–4, I am affirmed in my opposition to neoliberal forms of education. It is up to readers to make up their own minds; to take this journey and reflect on their own learning response to this question (see Note 4 above).
6 ". . . the best of life is life lived quietly, where nothing happens but our calm journey through the day, where change is imperceptible and the precious life is everything." (McGahern, 2005, 80).

7 See Chapter VII, entitled 'Walking in the city', in de Certeau (1984, 91–110).

8 From a strategic perspective, teachers' and students' lives are evermore *quantitatively* captured e.g. longitudinal surveys of attitudes and behaviours or, more crudely, 'performance' indicators. We come to 'know' more about exam results, learner participation rates, professional development indicators, student attrition rates, etc. But how can these ever inform us of the 'journey' of success, the 'act' of participation, the 'authenticity' of professional development, dropout 'causes', etc.? A quantitative (even a quasi-qualitative) focus on learning may do nothing more than draw a 'totalizing line', causing *qualitative* meanings to be forgotten. Thus, to extend de Certeau's (1984, 97) spatial analogy (he speaks here of worn pathways with no walkers in sight): "These fixations constitute procedures for forgetting. The trace left behind is substituted for the practice."

9 For further reading on ethnography, see: Hammersley and Atkinson, 1983; Ager, 1996; Denzin, 1997; Marcus, 1998; Denscombe, 2007; Fetterman, 2009; Van Maanen, 2011. Here the reader will find much more detail about this specific research approach, particularly in relation to: Researcher/Authorial positioning; research ethics; participant sampling; complementary research methods; data analysis procedures; and research limitations.

10 Each story in this book pays close attention to individuals' thoughts, feelings and actions and connects these to specific cultural historical contexts (one can add the particular importance of social, personal, political and economic contexts). In the case of Chapter 1, for example, it was important to highlight the school's wider struggle for (identity) recognition upfront and in conjunction with its own identity work with pupils. In the case of Chapter 2, it was important to briefly profile Nuala Jackson's personal life before examining her personal relations with the students. In the case of my visit to New York (Chapter 3), it was important to 'set the scene' of (American cultural) 'success' alongside my investigation into one particular 'successful' school. And in the case of my visit to Brazil (Chapter 4), it was important to highlight 'land' legacy issues from colonial times and explore their on-going effects on Brazilian attitudes to 'protest' and 'power'. In each education project, therefore, cultural historical contexts are both reflected and (re)made.

11 See, for example: Williams, 1958/1983a, 1983b; Hall, 1973, 1997; Willis, 1977, 2000.

12 See, for example: Clandinin and Connell, 2000; Ritchie and Wilson, 2000; Goodson et al, 2010.

13 For further reading on critical ethnography, see: Mead, 1932/2002; Anderson, 1989; Thomas, 1993; Carspecken and Walford, 2001.

14 For further reading on critical pedagogy, see: Steinberg, 2001; Kincheloe, 2008; Giroux, 2011.

15 This list includes: Judith Butler; Diane Ravitch; Diane Reay; Annette Lareau; Beverley Skeggs; and Naomi Klein.

16 While critical theory informs ethnography (this is known as 'critical ethnography'), it ought not to be an end in itself; meaning critical theory 'can't tell the whole story'. Thus, while this study is consciously informed by critical theory and while critical narratives reflect influential concepts and values (e.g. from critical pedagogy), the story must also (gradually) 'speak for itself'.

17 In keeping with the main ethnographic principle of 'familiarity' (of cultural historical actors within site and vice versa), I visited each education project a number of times. It was not feasible to standardise the frequency of visits, as practical concerns dictated e.g. I was committed to my 'day job'; there were distance issues (e.g. New York and Brazil); research access rights were restricted, etc. But suffice to say that each education project was visited for a minimum duration of 2 full working weeks. I visited the primary school (described in Chapter 1) regularly over a 2 month Summer period in 2012; the post-primary school (described in Chapter 2) regularly during the months of January and February in 2013; the New York high school between Monday 15th April, 2013 and Friday 26th April, 2013; and the adult education training centre in Brazil from April 11–27, 2014.

18 Barthes (1968/1977, 6) notes: ". . . the unity of a text is not in its origin, it is in its destination; but this destination can no longer be personal: The reader is a man [sic.] without history, without biography, without psychology; he [sic.] is only that someone who holds gathered into a single field all the paths of which the text is constituted."

19 Barthes (1968/1977, 6) states: ". . . we know that to restore to writing its future, we must reverse its myth: The birth of the reader must be ransomed by the death of the Author."

20 I often thought about this writer-researcher function when taking pictures of the various education sites (see photographic figures in each chapter). For example, in Chapter 3 I take a picture of a 'successful' high school in New York. To a number of 'passers-by' (literally), I may have presented as someone just taking a picture of a school. But there's more to this picture than meets the eye. As I wrote in Chapter 3: "Many will be unsighted to the *sources* of 'success' that lie well beyond the school gates; including socio-economic foundations that matter the most (e.g. Berliner, 2013). Many will not see beyond a narrow vista of 'teacher quality'; nor recognise that there are simultaneous, inter-related 'success' factors at play. And many, whose sights are set on 'outcomes', will not observe *learning success* in rehearsal." The writer-researcher function, especially within the critical tradition, is surely to help bring this (bigger) picture into focus; at least for critical discussion and debate.

21 See Gary Anderson's (1989) paper that highlights some of the more challenging and contested features of critical ethnography.

22 I certainly have benefitted from accessing ('reading' and 'telling') others' stories. Not least, this learning has challenged my relatively stable beliefs and identity. As a 'system worker' (university lecturer), I follow certain (academic) conventions. Many are worthy of pursuit; some need to be circumvented; others obstructed. My own learning journey navigates this tricky path.

23 I was always conscious to prioritise research participants' feedback, while a few trusted 'lay' readers were also asked to give their views on the stories as they progressed. Once the book was written, a select group of academic colleagues were consulted for their thoughts and guidance.

References

Agar, M. (1996). *The professional stranger: An informal introduction to ethnography*. New York. Academic Press.

Anderson, G. (1989). Critical ethnography in education: Origins, current status and new directions. *Review of Educational Research*, Fall, 59, no. 3, 249–270.

Barthes, R. (1968/1977). *The death of the author*. Translated into English by Stephen Heath (New York). *Image, Music, Text*, 142–48. Page numbers cited in the main text from 2015 internet source, February 19. Retrieved from www.tbook.constantvzw.org/wp-content/death_authorbarthes.pdf

Berliner, D. (2013). Effects of inequality and poverty vs. teachers and schooling on America's youth. *Teachers College Record*, 115, no. 2. Retrieved from www.tcrecord.org/Print Content.asp?ContentID=16889 on January 8, 2014.

Camus, A. (1949). *Les Justes*. Act III. Reprinted in 1999. New York. French and European Publications.

Carspecken, P. F. and Walford, G. eds. (2001). *Critical ethnography and education*. Volume 5 of *Studies in Educational Ethnography*. Amsterdam, New York, Oxford. JAI Press.

Clandinin, D. J. and Connelly, F. M. (2000). *Narrative inquiry: Experience and story in qualitative research*. San Francisco. Jossey-Bass.

de Certeau, M. (1984). *The practice of everyday life*. Translated by Steven Rendall. Berkeley, Los Angeles and London. University of California Press.

Denscombe, M. (2007). *The good research guide: For small-scale and social research projects.* 3rd edn. Maidenhead, England. Open University Press.

Denzin, N. (1997). *Interpretive ethnography: Ethnographic practices for the 21st Century.* California, London, New Delhi. Sage Publications.

Fetterman, D. (2009). Ethnography. In L. Bickman and D. J. Rog, eds (543–588). *The SAGE handbook of applied social research methods.* 2nd edn. California, London, New Delhi, Singapore. Sage Publications.

Foucault, M. (1969/1977). What is an author? In D. F. Bouchard, ed. (113–138). *Language, counter-memory, practice: Selected essays and interviews by Michel Foucault.* Ithaca, New York. Cornell University Press.

Giroux, H. A. (2011). *On critical pedagogy.* New York. Continuum.

Goodson, I. F., Biesta, G., Tedder, M. and Adair, N. (2010). *Narrative learning.* London and New York. Routledge.

Goodson, I. F. and Gill, S. R. (2011). *Narrative pedagogy: Life history and learning.* New York. Peter Lang.

Goodson, I. F. and Gill, S. R. (2014). *Critical narrative as pedagogy.* New York, London, New Delhi and Sydney. Bloomsbury.

Hall, S. (1973). *Encoding and decoding in the television discourse.* Birmingham. Centre for Contemporary Cultural Studies Publication.

Hall, S. ed. (1997). *Representation: Cultural representations and signifying practices.* Milton Keynes. The Open University.

Hammersley, M. and Atkinson, P. (1983). *Ethnography: Principles in practice.* London. Tavistock.

Heidegger, M. (1927/1996). *Sein und Zeit/Being and Time.* New York. State University of New York Press.

Kincheloe, J. L. (2008). *Critical pedagogy primer.* New York. Peter Lang.

Marcus, G. E. (1998). *Ethnography through thick and thin.* Princeton, New Jersey. Princeton University Press.

McGahern, J. (2005). *Memoir.* London. Faber and Faber.

Mead, G. H. (1932/2002). *The philosophy of the present.* Amherst, New York. Prometheus Books.

Richie, J. and Wilson, D. (2000). *Teacher narrative as critical inquiry: Rewriting the script.* New York. Teachers College Press.

Thomas, J. (1993). *Doing critical ethnography.* Thousand Oakes, California. Sage Publications.

Van Maanen, J. (2011). *Tales of the field: On writing ethnography.* 2nd edn. Chicago and London. University of Chicago Press.

Williams, R. (1958/1983a). *Culture and society.* New York. Columbia University Press.

Williams, R. (1983b). *Writing in society.* London. Verso.

Willis, P. (1977/1981). *Learning to labor: How working class kids get working class jobs.* Morningside Edition. Introduction by Stanley Aronowitz. New York. Columbia University Press.

Willis, P. (2000). *The ethnographic imagination.* Cambridge. Polity.

ACKNOWLEDGEMENTS

My sincere thanks are due to many people. For their professional support in producing this book, I would like to thank Kathy Hall, Angela Desmond, Deirdre McGlynn, Leah Neville, Patrick O'Donovan and the committee members that serve on the *College of Arts, Celtic Studies and Social Sciences Research and Innovation Committee* and the *College Sabbatical Research Leave Committee* in University College Cork. I wish to honour the commitment of, and express my deepest gratitude to, all the teachers, students and parents/guardians of *Gaelscoil an Ghoirt Álainn*, the XLC school project, Queens School of Inquiry (QSI) and the *Centro de Formação Paulo Freire*. I am always grateful to my university colleagues in the School of Education and to scholarly friends who are elsewhere scattered. I would like to acknowledge those mentors and colleagues from the very beginning, including Denis Burns, Francis Douglas, Marian Elders, Rosarii Griffin, Des Hourihane, Hannah Joyce, Fiachra Long, Agnes McMahon, Tom Mullins, Martín Ó Fathaigh, Denis O'Sullivan, Sally Power, Brid Ronaghan, Regina Sexton, Willie Weir and all my school tutor colleagues. Many others positively contributed to this book and have been generous with their time and their ideas. They include Paul Conway, Maura Cunneen, Alfredo Gomes, Edward Fuller, Ivor Goodson, Kathy Hall, Elizabeth Kiely, Karl Kitching, Rosaleen Murphy, Carl O'Brien, James O'Malley, Denis O'Sullivan, Francine Peterman, Tim Rudd and Ciaran Sugrue. I am grateful to all those learners – post-primary pupils, student teachers, Masters and PhD students – who I have had the pleasure to work with over the years. We still struggle to make sense of learning. In preparing the book, I have depended on the wise counsel and professional backing of Anna Clarkson and her editorial, marketing and publication teams at Routledge – most notably, Christopher Byrne – and George Warburton at Florence Production. Thank you for your kind forbearance and support. During some three-and-a-half years of writing, I needed the sustenance of family and friends. Special mention goes to my Dad, Seán. Thank you to Alain, Janine, my brothers and their families, Margaret and Kathleen and Paul and Maureen for your continued encouragement, and to Elizabeth, neighbour, friend and first 'lay' critic of the book. Thank you too to Alfredo, Niall and Rory for putting me up (and putting up with me) on my research visits, and to Gary, Fiachra, John, Des, Don and Jim for keeping me away from the office. Finally, very special thanks are due to you Amélie, Anna and Tom. Albert Camus (1949) says it far more eloquently: . . . *c'est cela l'amour, tout donner, tout sacrifier sans espoir de retour.*

1

LEARNING IDENTITY

It's a wet May Monday morning in Cork. Despite the artificial allure of its southernmost location, Cork city is no stranger to bad weather – and that Irish summer of 2012 would be heralded as the worst in 50 years. People were to be heard recording their own views on the weather, drawing on their rich store of familiar experience and language inventory. It is said that the Irish have as many words to portray 'rain' as the Inuit have to describe 'snow'. Thus, not accounting for particular forms of jargon, the day may be 'soft', 'misty', 'showery', 'heavy' or 'torrential'. This particular Monday morning is 'lashing' [very heavy rain] and I am stationed in my car outside Gaelscoil an Ghoirt Álainn, north of the city. Ireland has two official languages – English and Irish ('Gaeilge') – both of which are uniquely spoken by its populace.[1] While 'Hiberno-English' may arguably be more accessible (e.g. rain descriptors), Gaeilge (the indigenous language of Ireland) may not be so. Thus, a brief interlude for 'translation': *Gaelscoil* means 'Irish (speaking) school' and *an Ghoirt Álainn* literally means 'the beautiful field' (or colloquially, 'Mayfield'). On this very wet morning, then, I am waiting outside Mayfield's (Irish-speaking) primary school. I have come to visit with an open mind; though what has been written about this particular school, and Gaelscoileanna (the plural of Gaelscoil, denoting 'Irish language schools') in general, commonly presupposes the research scene. Mindful of this supposed narrative, which I hope to share with you shortly, my primary desire is to learn more about this school. What, I ask myself, is the identity of this place and how is learning so connected to this identity? Officially, Gaelscoil an Ghoirt Álainn is the first mixed-gendered, all-Irish-speaking, multi-faith school on the island of Ireland.[2] My thoughts drift to how a child that attends this school might identify differently, that is, become a different person and a different learner than he/she would if attending a single-sex, all-English-speaking, Catholic school (for example). While I do not wish to compare school-type identities,

I start to speculate how *this* particular community shapes (and is shaped by) notions of identity. I also begin to wonder how a child learns an identity and how this might influence his/her learning character. My thoughts, as heavy as the rain, find relief in the stirring of people from all directions.

The school is set back from an open public green area, known locally as the 'tank field', so named because a water tower once stood on its grounds. This common area is used by Brian Dillon's GAA (Gaelic Athletic Association[3]) sports club, which has permanently erected goalposts for hurling and Gaelic football matches and regularly organises training sessions for its young male and female members. The field is also used by local people of all ages for jogging, strolling, 'hanging out' and walking their dogs, as well as by local schools for matches, fêtes and sports days. There is always some activity in the tank field. On school mornings just before 8.45 AM, it is the turn of the pupils and guardians of Gaelscoil an Ghoirt Álainn to provide the bustle. The vast majority are headed towards the narrow road behind the far-end goalpost that leads to the gates of Brian Dillon's sports pavilion. The school is housed on the right-hand side of the club within its gated arena. At busy times of the school day, parents and guardians are asked to keep the roadway clear and desist from entering the grounds by car. Many park on the main road alongside the walled perimeter of the field and make their way by foot towards the gated entrance. They form a long column. A few brave souls choose to hurdle the walled border and forge their path across the sodden pitch towards a side entrance further up. The bravest few choose to walk the fullest length of the pitch from the southern (old 'tank') position. It is strangely touching to see so many youngsters struggle in their efforts to come to school. An hour or so ago they had been tucked up in their beds, cosily protected from the elements. Now, as they make their way towards the school gates, some stop to greet their friends, while others jockey and jostle in the rain. The parents and guardians are less enthusiastic about the prospect of a journey delay. I sympathise and eventually make my own brisk way – not via pasture.

The children's uniforms, barely visible beneath the layers of weather proof clothing, mark community membership. But wider impressions of Gaelscoil membership presuppose this assembly. The media has been instrumental in generating these. Writing in *The Irish Times*, Louise Holden (2007) asks if the rise of the Gaelscoil owes much to "real engagement with the Irish language and culture", or if it constitutes "old fashioned snobbery and elitism." The impression given is that Gaelscoileanna confer unfair 'advantage' on its members. Kate Holmquist (2008) is more assertive in her article in *The Irish Times*, which is provocatively (regrettably) entitled 'Language of Educational Apartheid':[4]

> Not only will your [Gaelscoil] child be surrounded by mostly middle-class children and get 10 per cent bonus,[5] but he or she will also be likely to have smaller classes, aiding performance in other subjects.

Sarah Carey (2008) goes further in another *Irish Times* article entitled 'Gaelscoil parents want to have their cake and eat it':

> In practice, it's a class issue. Whether the motivating force is middle-class liberalism or heartfelt nationalist ideology, you won't find too many immigrants and local ruffians at the Gaelscoil. Parents are entitled to make every effort to improve their children's chances in this world and Gaelscoileanna with their smaller class sizes and self-selecting participants are a good mechanism for that. But do me two favours: Stop pretending that this is all about the Irish language and don't expect the rest of us to pay for it.

In counter argument, proponents of Gaelscoileanna, such as Foras na Gaeilge (the Irish Language Organisation) and Gaelscoileanna Teoranta (a national voluntary organisation that supports the development of Irish-medium schools), point to the important role such schools play in celebrating national culture, identity and language. While they would certainly argue that the 'elitist' tag is unfair, they might concede that some of their schools are 'advantaged', particularly those that are predominantly white, Irish and middle class and are deemed to intellectually perform. Overall, and by design, they argue an *inclusive* case, highlighting a network of primary and secondary Gaelscoileanna in disadvantaged areas of Ireland, a non-fee paying school structure and a universal 'open' enrolment policy. Moreover, they point to widespread parental support for their schools.[6] Undoubtedly influenced by market and state support for 'school choice' (see Chapter 4), this has translated to a rapid rise in Gaelscoileanna in Ireland over the past 3 decades: From a total of 16 schools in 1972, to 175 Irish-medium primary schools and 41 post-primary schools in 2012.[7]

The Gaelscoil I'm about to visit has made its own impression. It is aesthetically unpleasing with adjoining prefabs shaping its higgledy-piggledy structure. The latest supplement bears down on earlier prototypes that once housed younger tenants. Such aesthetics tell a bigger story. These 'temporary' prefabs have been home to the Gaelscoil since 1998. Up to this time, the school community had been searching for a permanent residence, a pursuit that's still ongoing and not without controversy. In 2006, Cork City Council, which had acquired the 'tank field' by statutory powers in 2001, offered to sell the land to the Department of Education to build a new Gaelscoil. In response, representatives of the local residential community formed a 'Save Our Tank Field' campaign. A bitter battle ensued, with both sides ('for' and 'against' the school) claiming legitimacy. Why, asked opponents, were there proposals to build a school on a designated green field site in a district that is already well served by primary schools? Why, asked proponents, were there objections to build a school that planned to maintain large parts of the green field site and ameliorate the substandard accommodation of its pupils and teachers? Oft heated and emotionally charged, such arguments (among others) regularly appeared on blog sites that debated the future of Gaelscoil an Ghoirt Álainn.

These blog sites frequently underscored irreconcilable differences and intractable positions. Associated slogans accommodated political attachment, with little room for elasticity. It appeared that you were either for 'Save Our Tank Field' or 'All We Want Is a School'.

Around the time of this school dispute, David McWilliams (2006) – celebrity economist, broadcaster and author – had just written a bestselling book entitled *The Pope's children: Ireland's new elite*. Written at a time when the country appeared to prosper economically,[8] it presents itself as an entertaining and informative description of Ireland and its people. Replete with populist discourse, caricature descriptors and essentialising arguments, the book sets out to 'capture' what it means to be Irish. In one such depiction, McWilliams offers a profile of 'Hibernian Cosmopolitans' (or 'HiCos'):

> They want to be both special and rich, they want the Gaelscoil and the fancy double-doored fridge, they want Kila [an Irish band that fuses Irish and world music] and the Killers [an American rock band], they want the connectedness of spirituality and the freedom of liberty, they want to belong and yet lose themselves. They are Hibernians but they want cosmopolitan goodies.
>
> (McWilliams, 2006, 146)

Such unproblematic 'blending' of capital and culture is perhaps unsurprising from an economist's standpoint; nevertheless, identity labelling is eagerly advanced. Hence, the typification of Gaelscoil parents:

> The aim of the HiCos is not to turn themselves into Gaeilgeoirí [Irish speakers] but to get the best for their family. As with everything they do, Gaelscoileanna [sic] allows them to pick the best bit from what the Hibernian menu has to offer and move on. It is an economic free lunch, spiced with the virtue of authenticity [. . .] People who send their children to Gaelscoileanna display great taste. They are erudite, refined and concerned. Twenty first Century Gaelscoil parents are in a class of their own. They are both cosmopolitan and Hibernian.
>
> (McWilliams, 2006, 236)

I wondered if parents of Gaelscoil an Ghoirt Álainn identified with this description of themselves – if they saw their school as "the breeding ground for the new sophisticated elite" (McWilliams, 2006, 240). Undoubtedly, impressions had been made of them by an author whose Gaelscoil research appears to have been conducted *outside* a certain school's gates.[9] However artificial/overstated, impressions have real effects, whether these emerge/coalesce via celebrity writing, newspaper articles or select oppositional claims to a Gaelscoil's establishment. I am very mindful of these now, not least because they form a key context to the identity of Gaelscoil an Ghoirt Álainn. Here is a school literally fighting for its identity. And I am about to step *inside*.

Figure 1.1 Gaelscoil an Ghoirt Álainn

Identity signals

As with all schools, organised chaos reigns first thing in the morning. Here, wet bodies cloud the narrow corridors, with teachers on hand to steer their safe passage. Criss-crossing trails eventually fade as pupils disperse into classroom warrens. Further activity centres on the reception area. Sick notes are handed in, children make unexpected phone calls home, parents inform of imminent family events, lunchboxes are belatedly dropped off, appointments are secured and more. A level of stillness returns to the office some twenty minutes later. Lisa, the school's administrator, will soon be available to speak with me but first she has a number of notices to forward to teachers. She apologises for the inconvenience, though I feel responsible for discommoding her. I am keen to speak with Lisa and am happy to wait. It is often said that school administrators are its 'eyes and ears'. They are visibly the first point of contact between home and school and are intimately attuned to communal interests and demands. They are knowledgeable of, and engage with, a variety of educational supports, including counsellors, home liaison officers and health professionals. They understand the personal/professional character of the school principal as they work in tandem on organisational tasks. They enable extracurricular[10] activities (such as field trips and sporting events), communiqués (including school reports and newsletters) and the smooth operation of management systems (including school policies and pastoral supports). Lisa, as I am about to find out, performs all of these functions. She literally communicates school culture.

We head to the newest 'upstairs' prefab that is suspended at the back of the school complex. This, the quietest part of the building, now serves as the staffroom.

Next door, sixth class pupils (12 year olds) settle down to work and the faint sounds of busy Irish can be heard through thin walls. I first ask Lisa what she thinks about impressions of Gaelscoil elitism. Maybe a number of years ago, she states, most parents would have been working. But now almost 1 in 4 families is suffering from unemployment. Some come in confidence to the school to communicate their financial difficulties, and an increasing number cannot afford to pay the voluntary school contribution.[11] It may be the case that approximately half the school's constituency is made up of middle-class families, with the remaining half almost equally split between high and low socio-economic groups.[12] Yet, as Lisa maintains, the recession has adversely affected all social groups.[13] The school too is sited within a disadvantaged area of the city[14] and the parental profile reflects this diverse locale:

> We have lone parents, we have very young parents, we have middle-aged parents, we have parents that have their own business, we have doctors, solicitors, manual workers, cleaners. You know we have everything and our school is really unique. It's just like one big family, different to anything else out there. Well I personally think so because I have a child in another school and it's nothing like this.

Lisa's use of 'family' is interesting here. It signifies a type of 'community spirit', a concept so ingrained in many a 'school ethos' statement. Typically all-embracing and occasionally ephemeral, a school's 'ethos' intends to capture its essence (literally its 'character'). Its bona fide worth is in recital. Here, Lisa offers tangible insights. For some parents, she explains, "school is from 9 to 3 – a place where children go to learn and then get collected." This, in the main, did not describe the 'interested' parents of Gaelscoil an Ghoirt Álainn:

> No matter what you ask our parents, they are always there. I could send out a notice today saying I needed 20 people to come in Friday and paint the school. And I'd have my 20 people by 10 O'clock in the morning.

She adds that the school's parents are "very hands-on" in assisting and leading: School maintenance/repairs, parking supervision, reading programmes, knitting classes, homework support, fundraising events, music tuition, sporting occasions, creative arts events and Irish-medium instruction to other parents (including, for the first time in 2012, Irish instruction to non-Irish national parents).

Is the Irish language, I ask, of particular appeal to parents? In relation to this Gaelscoil, as I'm finding out, this does not present as a straightforward question. It may be the case, explains Lisa, that the Irish language is a particular lure but the multi-denominational character of the school could equally appeal to parents. It may *appear*, I reflect later, that the primary draw of the Irish language is its entrée to traditional forms of national identity. And it may *appear* that the primary appeal of multi-denominational schooling is its entrée to (post)modern forms of multi-cultural identity. Both allures *appear* to indicate oppositional identities, yet the contrary may apply. It is possible, for example, to see both as equivalent – to envisage an Irish-speaking, multi-faith citizenry as now signalling 'all things Irish'. It is also possible to picture a reciprocal fit – to imagine identity sites where distinctions of 'Irishness' and 'worldliness' companionably convene. Certainly, parental reasons for school membership are not simple. Nor are they reducible to McWilliams's (2006) economic narrative that portrays parents as rational choice agents operating singularly for cultural and material profit. What I learn later from Lisa, the teaching staff and parents' representatives is that families reflect carefully on the ethos of Gaelscoil an Ghoirt Álainn. From diverse entry points, they elect to 'buy in' to its character. Perhaps in doing so parents grapple with, what Anthony Giddens (1991) calls, 'reflexive modernity'. This describes individuals in a post-traditional society who are evermore obliged to be consciously meditative. Consequent choices/decisions may be liberating and troubling – liberating because individuals have greater freedom from the 'traditional order'; troubling since greater self-analysis is linked to risky, emotional and uncertain outcomes. While parents may not articulate their reasons for school membership in such complex and discerning ways, a scale of sophistication remains at play. Decisively, the school encapsulates identity transformation in Irish society. It is hard, for example, to imagine how its quest for identification could ever have been realised in an Ireland that was, until relatively recently, governed by theocentric values (O'Sullivan, 2005). Then, self-oriented forms of identity were uncommonly greeted and expressed. Present 'conditions of possibility', to use Michel Foucault's phrase, are such that identity change may now be desirable and achievable.[15]

The school's struggle for recognition of *its* difference mirrors (and is endorsed by) broader inclusive efforts in Irish society.[16] Notwithstanding information challenges and impression effects, the Gaelscoil does attract non-Irish and Irish families for whom the goal of diversity represents an analogous appeal. The former remain a minority in the school,[17] though teachers forecast increasing numbers as the Gaelscoil's culture becomes gradually 'communicated'. Lisa reminds that non-Irish parents (indeed, many Irish parents) can fret over their own lack of Gaeilge. This often centres on their perceived incapacity to help with their children's schoolwork. In Lisa's experience, however, parental worry dissipates upon a child's encounter with 'everyday Irish'. Breaking down language barriers, she explains, is key to communicating with the school's parent body. Indeed, the school appears ever mindful of its 'inclusive' messages to parents. Lisa demonstrates how this begins at the point of entry:

> This school is open, first come first served regardless of background, religion, sex, nationality. And we don't have a sibling policy.[18]

Lisa is keen to elaborate upon the school's inclusive mission but our chat is interrupted by break-time. Later in the day, she hands me some school newsletters. These, she assures me, will tell me more about 'who we are'. I am struck by the inclusive messages in these bilingual communiqués. Here, a host of visual and print entries celebrate the achievements of the football, hurling, tennis and swimming teams. There are entries too that offer congratulations ('comhghairdeas') to individuals and groups who have excelled at athletic competitions, creative arts competitions and cookery practice. To encourage musical talent, an array of traditional and world instruments are advertised for tuition, including violin, concertina, flute, bodhrán, céilí drums, banjo, accordion, fiddle and guitar. All this communicates an interest and commitment to widening the criteria for learning 'success' (see Chapter 3). Still, there are exemplars of elevated academic achievement on show. Literacy and numeracy practices are clearly visible, echoing fashionable concerns for raising standards in these 'priority' areas. Competition between classes is also encouraged via a 'carta buí' ('yellow card') prize system that aims to nurture and consolidate an Irish-speaking culture. Those classes that amass most yellow cards in a month are photographed celebrating their success – in pizza restaurants, cinema theatres and dance studios. All these messages signal an attempt to marry the more assiduous and pleasurable ingredients of learning. I am reminded of Lisa's earlier words that "balancing work and fun" makes this "a school that learns happily." Learning, it seems, is incomplete without a sense of enjoyment and achievement, even if both materialise as good old-fashioned, behaviourist rewards. This sentiment resonates with an old Irish proverb that I later see printed in one of the school's newsletters: *Mol an óige agus tiocfaidh sí* ('Praise youth and she will follow').

Newsletters communicate 'in-group' membership, with teachers, parents and pupils seen as mutual educational partners. Parents' extensive voluntary contributions are publicly praised and they are notified of forthcoming school events and the latest policies (e.g. new child protection procedures). Notably, parents are informed of the school's Ethical Education Curriculum (*Croí na Scoile*), which includes an exploration of the major belief systems in the world. This programme of study enables children to learn about many faiths and beliefs without endorsing any one as religious truth. Frequent communication on the programme's substance (subtly) reminds parents of their collective recruitment to this core value system. More routine messages also appear. These have a more discernible regulatory focus with prompts to park responsibly, enable the timely attendance of well-dressed children, pack healthy school lunches, etc. All of these messages accentuate the twin ideals of community membership and responsibility. Faith in their union is encapsulated in a favourite newsletter phrase: *Ní neart go cur le chéile* ('There is no strength without unity'). I am informed that TJ, the school principal, instigated and coordinates newsletters. I begin to wonder now about his role in modelling the school's identity. As lead teacher, it is he who is officially tasked with inspiring all partners to subscribe to, and act upon, a common educational purpose. I question if this exceptional task is reasonable – if, alongside this, it is fair to portray the principal as a proto-typical practitioner, as someone who literally personifies school culture.

Up to this point, I had known TJ as a PhD scholar. On the many occasions we met in thesis preparation, I was always struck by his erudite passion for the Irish language and culture. His innovative study, now completed, investigates effective forms of Irish language instruction. This scholarly interest complements

his extensive professional portfolio – as an immersion school principal, teacher/
mentor at school and university levels, international online tutor, advocate and
representative of the Irish language. I am conscious that I am about to meet TJ
the 'school principal', a role that is unfamiliar to me. I am mindful too of my research
responsibility, especially the need to strike a balance between detachment, familiarity
and openness of exchange. As I wander the corridors, I unexpectedly bump into
TJ. With characteristic warmth and verve, he offers me a *céad míle fáilte* (literally
'a hundred thousand welcomes') and invites me to exchange a *cúpla focal* ('a few
words') in Irish. I stumble upon some from memory and self-consciously excuse
myself from further effort. Recognising signs of my discomfort, he reverts to English
but not before encouraging me on my (limited) Gaeilge. I sense that he appreciates,
much like a French person might, any efforts at dialogue. En route to the staffroom,
he effortlessly switches between the two languages, sharing school day events with
me and stopping to chat with some teachers and pupils. We soon settle over a cup
of coffee. I want to explore his thoughts on the character of this school.

TJ instantly highlights its inclusive and diverse qualities. As a multi-
denominational organisation,[19] this school is likely to attract "certain types of families
who are very open in their thinking" and have "a particular understanding about
the world." It is an especially welcoming environment for alternative family
structures that include a number of same-sex parent relations. The Ethical Education
Curriculum (*Croí na Scoile*) offers a formal opportunity to celebrate diversity. Each
classroom, from junior infants (4–5 year olds) to sixth class (12 year olds), spends
time exploring and engaging the realms of moral and spiritual enquiry, equality
and justice, wider belief systems, as well as ethics and the environment.[20] TJ suggests that this work goes beyond formal instruction or even a collective creed.
Importantly, it embraces "a learning experience" where children and adults discover
new things together and become "intrigued" by one another's lives. Akin to viewing
Irish as a communicative language, this relational 'way of being' appears as a speech
act, as a form of cultural script where actors share a language of 'difference'.
Sometimes script lines are openly rehearsed (e.g. formal curriculum instruction)
but, more often than not, it is in the ether or, as TJ puts it, it is "natural." In
educational jargon, this is the stuff of the 'hidden curriculum'. This is not to say,
TJ reminds, that diversity is implicitly shared. It's okay to have different opinions
and "we might not all agree." "Conflict", he adds, "is healthy." Later, I consider
these words. In a university setting, one expects an education that formalizes and
naturalizes a curiosity to question and a desire to self-author in the midst of multiple
meanings and identities. This methodological approach aims to foster learners'
capacity for 'critical literacy'. Yet, while it may be expected of university students
to exercise critical faculty, it appears more problematical for younger students to
write themselves in to this cultural script. This presents as a particular *learning identity*
challenge for schools.

TJ's scholarly interest in, and experience of, the Irish language provides him
with an unequivocal position on its role in schools and society. He acknowledges
its historical legacy, such as its association with Republican politics and ideals,

symbolically captured by *Ní tír gan teanga* ('There is no nation without a language'). He also acknowledges that, for some Irish adults, Gaeilge has an emotive connection with negative school practices. TJ aspires to present the Irish language as a "way of interacting", "a medium through which we all learn." This notion of 'medium' is interesting. While it signifies a common tongue where particular meanings are created, it also implies a network of social relations that generate distinct identity arrangements. This alludes to the sociocultural power of language.[21] TJ exemplifies this when he refers to the children speaking to each other *as Gaeilge* ('in Irish') outside of school, such as when they 'code-switch' at birthday parties or when they meet in town.[22] He also refers to how he has come to know his colleagues "through Irish and only Irish." This is partly an expression of professional identity where teachers are keen to present themselves as language role models. But it also appears to express deeper personal/social identification with the language. This highlights the important influences of language on one's individual character and shared relations. With a focus on children and young people, TJ elaborates on this point:

> Just the whole idea of being bilingual and biliterate from a very young age opens up other opportunities. You know, it gives people a sense of self-confidence, self-esteem. Having access to another language and using a language that mam or dad or the family may not use at home leads to a greater sense of self-identity. That sense of self-confidence in a child leads to development not just with respect to character, but in relation to better communicative ability.

Intergenerational communication is markedly present in bilingual family settings. While children tend to receive "constant scaffolding and encouragement", parents/guardians get a chance to (re)connect with the Irish language. Having access to another language also generates positive cognitive effects. Here, TJ highlights how 'code-switching' enables divergent and creative ways of thinking.[23] He also observes that children who are bilingual at a very young age tend to thrive at other languages. Indeed, it is established that a 'second' language can benefit the learner at no cost to the 'first' language – a learning effect known as 'additive bilingualism' in the research literature.[24] Even at an older age this effect is felt, as evidenced by Anna Maria's (the language teacher's) encouraging accounts of pupils' introduction to Italian.[25]

The conversation now turns to the school's political struggle for identity. TJ knows how much it means to have a new school building. His constituency continues to endure dismal, unsanitary conditions and he is quietly resolved in his leadership response. There is a photograph in one of the school's newsletters of the visit of Cork's Lord Mayor in September 2011. This shows the first citizen being presented with a junior infant's portrait of her dream school. It is a strikingly symbolic act, expounding reach to a wider political constituency. This reach extends to the local community. Beyond attempts at political foothold, I sense that there is an earnest desire to communicate 'who we are' to others. TJ accepts that people from the outside genuinely wonder about this; after all, here's a multi-faith, all-Irish-speaking group seeking to acquire a green field site that is "much loved and steeped in rich history." And, for TJ, there's work to be done "to be more proactive in the community and get recognized as a local school." All his communicative skills are summoned here: Writing school newsletters, penning articles for the local newsletter, working closely with community and voluntary organisations and liaising with resident youth projects. Most of these interactions have been "extremely positive" with, he adds intriguingly, "a few hiccups." While he doesn't elaborate, I don't press. Rather characteristically, he emits quiet resoluteness:

> I suppose the organisations realize that we're here to stay in the community as a school, that we're not going anywhere, that we have a very strong school population [. . .] We're not coming to the table expecting, with our hands out. We've a part to play and we realize that, but the community has an awful lot to gain from us as well.

Ultimately, the political struggle for identity is "more than securing a school site." It's about "a way of teaching and learning", the validation and expression of one's educational ethos. At this point, and with usual vigour, TJ steers discussions towards his role as educator. Still, it is difficult to circumvent political connections. After all, this head teacher must habitually perform an educator's role each time he dons his political hat.

School leaders are expected to be 'head' or 'principal' teachers and TJ articulates a clear learning vision. This aims to encourage children "to be unique, to develop their learning interests and talents within a collective." Alluding to the importance of 'personalisation' (see Chapter 2), he presents learning as "taking place in different ways for different people." At the same time, he recognises the need to 'juggle' the priorities of a standardised curriculum. This necessitates 'mediation', such as the time when the staff came together to discuss their concerns about new national tests for literacy and numeracy. Beyond 'product' orientations, discussions revealed the staff's support for a learning 'process' that facilitates, over time, "deep thinking, interactive group work and dialogue." There was another occasion when staff came together to discuss standard monthly reports that detail what items of the curriculum have been 'covered and learned' by the children.[26] They resolved to mediate these reports to acknowledge the teacher's wider use of a range of learning methods, different types of assessment, more individualised pupil profiling and critical spaces for reflection. And there was the time when teachers came together to discuss some children's drift towards speaking English in-between classes. They decided that it would be undesirable to punish pupils for not speaking Irish as this could create negative associations.[27] Instead, they would persevere with praise and encouragement and the 'carta buí' system of reward. These incidences indicate two things. First, a significant degree of collegiality is evident in decision-making and school planning. This form of 'distributed leadership' (Harris and Spillane, 2008) is perhaps best captured by TJ's constant use of 'we', in place of 'I'. Second, they demonstrate the material power of a pedagogical assembly, specifically its capacity to create (or constrain) certain learning possibilities (McGee and Fraser, 2001). Learner identity, it seems, is significantly shaped by this power base.

Power also shapes pupils' behaviour in the school. There is a regulatory system of conduct to be learned by children and teachers are ultimately charged with its supervision. For TJ this is necessary for all to "feel safe, welcome and comfortable in a school environment." In classical psychology, behaviour is regulated either 'extrinsically' (from without) or 'intrinsically' (from within). More often than not, 'discipline' is associated with the former, as typified by long lists of school rules outlined in 'codes of behaviour'. This connection can fail to make important *learning* links (e.g. the cultivation of 'self-discipline'), which is ironic considering that the original meaning of 'discipline' has more to do with learning than it has to do with behaviour (*disco* in Latin means 'I learn'). In reality, a wide regulatory scale exists in schooling, with one limit designating rule-based compliance and another pointing in the direction of learner self-discipline. A school's stance on discipline, weighed against its relative position along this scale, can significantly shape learner identity.[28] TJ indicates his own school's attempts at 'balancing the scale'. At the start of every academic year, each class draws up a school contract. There are rules to be complied with, such as those guided by health and safety conventions and core school principles. But attempts are also made to engage pupils in some degree of co-authorship. This appears to value the dispositional and motivational qualities of behaviour and promotes discipline as something that is voluntarily and

Figure 1.2 Seats of learning

independently engaged. Moreover, it represents some even-handed alignment of power relationships. It is significant in this regard that teachers are known by their first name in this school. This is indicative of the school's navigation along the scale and its steady efforts to balance teachers' power identity.

In my two months visiting Gaelscoil an Ghoirt Álainn, I can now reflect on TJ's role in shaping the school's identity. While no one person can ever be described as an 'identity maker', it is clear that the head teacher has a special identity purpose for, and with, others.[29] TJ's professional vision is to contribute to a school that is "as interactive, democratic and child-centred as possible." And while there is much evidence of this being 'lived', a "review of culture" is constantly foreseen. There is personal interest in this pursuit. As someone who is "in a very different, non-traditional, family make-up", TJ instinctively seeks to name and celebrate diversity. These complementary qualities of identity, namely the personal and professional, may elucidate why he is *vocationally* dedicated.[30]

Learning identity in the classroom

I am surrounded by 22 5 year olds in the *naíonáin bheaga* (junior infants) classroom. Squeezed into a chair among a group of boys and girls, one child turns to me and obligingly whispers, "we speak Irish here." I guess he must have spotted that I don't quite fit in. Soon the whole class is noisily calling out, not always in unison:

Chonaic mé Mamaí agus Daidí ('I saw mammy and daddy').

Bhí tú ag rith leis an liathróid ('You were running with the ball').

Tá cóta deas orm ('I have a nice coat').

An bhfuil do hata ag Daidí ('Does daddy have your hat?').

The apparent randomness of these statements is amusing but this is a grammar class and there's serious work to be done. These fledglings are being initiated into an Irish language community. They are also being schooled for the first time. Both rites of passage present their challenges. A number of children impulsively mix Irish with English. Some restlessly shuffle on their seats. They find it difficult to sit neatly at tables and raise their hands to question or answer. One little girl asks a lot of questions, seeking affirmation it seems at every turn. The teacher's probes are greeted with a straining chorus and a frantic wave of wagging fingers. Enthusiasm is palpable. Still it doesn't last long as concentration levels inevitably wane. The teacher draws the children back in. *"Lámha ar do cheann"* ('hands on your head') she exhorts, as all are reminded of the importance of disciplinary focus. As group work is assigned, the children are now tutored in the ways of cooperative learning. This variety brings with it renewed efforts, though soon after 2 boys are admonished for being disruptive, while 2 girls are praised for tidy work. Over break-time, I reflect on how gender identity is cast and learned at such an early age.[31] As I do so, I notice masculine attires interspersed with the decoratively pretty uniforms of the girls. I sit alongside one boy eating happily with some female peers. His best friends, he tells me, are Brian, Sean and Luke.

In the other *naíonáin bheaga* classroom, the children are getting ready for a mathematics lesson. One little girl notices her neighbour still eating. "Will I help you pack?" she enquires in a kind bid to assist her classmate and, at the same time, cooperate with class rules. Later a pupil murmurs the correct answer to a classmate, echoing similar intent. Another intercedes on behalf of her peer who has yet to get a turn to answer. Such incidences indicate children's agency, as they act out their own learner identity *as pupils*. Glowing in the light of the teacher's approval, they are affirmed in this deed. "*Ar fheabhas ar fad*" ("absolutely fantastic") is met with animated delight and all the children hanker after those coveted stickers when gifted. The class is put to work on a common problem. They are given 5 cubes and asked to write down all the pairings that can be placed in 2 sets. The teacher tells the pupils that this question is "*an-deacair*" ("very difficult"). It seems to adversely affect some pupils. Others are praised for being "*an-tapaidh*" ("very fast") with their answers. While they appear neutral, such remarks internalise the idea of hierarchised ability among peers. This separating out of ability stands in contrast to the unifying sight of the class cheerily counting in song. As they recite different numbers of chicks hatching in their nests, I notice the teacher caring for one little girl who has wet herself. It is a tender image that reminds of the educator's nurturing role. Scanning around, the children appear happy in this space. It is their class and pictures of their family and loved ones adorn its borders. Learning too, of the creative kind, is nurtured in this space, with visual art, musical CDs, toys, puppet screens, hanging shapes, ICT screens and books setting a colourful and vibrant scene. It's hard to imagine how a dull dreary exterior could conceal such an incandescent inner core.

The 2 naíonáin mhóra (senior infants) classes have had time to settle in school. And it shows. Pupils in one group are diligently focused on independent work. A countdown is later summoned, which finally discharges group song and dance. The pupils respond fluently to this shift in learning methodology. Now they are chanting and grooving to the formation of English sentences, with no syntactic labels in sight:

When I watch a tennis game, my head goes back and forth.

We are clinky castanets, clink, clink, clink.

I like to hop, hop up and down like a bunny.

English lesson later gives way to mathematics but not before an Irish verse is recited to ease another code-switch in language. Now they are suitably tuned into working in pairs. One girl, perhaps mistaking me for an inspector, whispers "are we the best class?" The notion of 'a good learner' appears well established at this early age. This is positively sculpted by a competitive culture of schooling. In this class, pupils seated at various tables are designated colour codes. "We get sweets", says one boy at *bord buí* ('the yellow table'), "if we put things back tidy and work good." The teacher reveals the latest table (literally) of merit. *Bord gorm* ('the blue table') leads. Its members are discernibly proud, if not modestly boastful. Now, somewhat ironically, and without the slightest reference to tables of merit, the teacher explores the mathematical concept of 'rank order', that is, first, second, last, etc. For the purposes of demonstration, she calls for volunteers. One boy in the final line-up feigns a soldier's salute. This humorous gesture displays keen intelligence and pleads for peer approval. It seems to work, judging from the roars of laughter.

Afterwards, I stealthily enter the room where *rang 1* (1st class) is undergoing a major maths test.[32] These 6 year olds are being inculcated in the ways of summative assessment.[33] Desks are arranged in single rows and bags are placed on table tops facing left. The physical environment mirrors the individualised form of assessment on show. I have time to reflect on this distorted scene. Assessment derives its original meaning from Latin's 'assidere' – 'to sit beside' (the learner). However, I can't see any evidence of collaborative work here. The teacher calls out the questions in English and Irish (all maths tests are written in English). In retort, pupils' heads are busily buried in worksheets. They learn that early test questions tend to be 'easy'. The teacher cautiously adjudicates, "*tabhair aire le do thoil*" ("please pay attention"). Her care ethic is now focused on academic success. This test demands high levels of literacy, something that is not usually associated with mathematics.[34] I notice that questions are very 'wordy' with some phrases not easily occupying the lexicon of 6 year olds:

- There are 5 bars in each box. How many bars are there in 6 boxes?
- Mark had 6 sweets and Tom had 8 sweets. Each boy ate half of his sweets. How many sweets did the 2 boys eat between them?
- An apple costs 15 cent and a banana costs 20 cent. How much do 2 apples and 2 bananas cost?[35]

As the test proceeds, challenges follow. Pupils learn that later test questions tend to be 'hard'. Some have convinced themselves that these are not for them. Most are test-weary by the time they get there. That's because there are *lots* of questions – 60 questions for 6 year olds. This is as much a test of attentiveness and stamina as it is a cognitive workout. The teacher announces that it is now finished. Suddenly, sluggish bodies resuscitate and a loud chorus of 'yes!' rings out. I am surprised by the forcefulness of these young children's reaction. Perhaps it's indicative, as Maria Montessori might suggest, of their delight at being 'free'. But maybe it's also an instinctive *pupil* reaction, an expected and learned response. After all, this ritual of relief appears to endure throughout the schooling years. In empathy, the teacher's care ethic is now focused on pupils' respite. She reads extracts from Roald Dahl's *Matilda*. One passage describes 2 young girls chatting about a teacher's assessment of the 'bottom class': "If you survive your first year you may just manage to live through the rest of your time here."

When the questions are completed and scripts are collected, the tests relocate to another arena. One of the learning support teachers is collating test data and preparing neatly curved graphs. She does this for every class in the school for mathematics and English. Predictably, the bell curve appears for all age groups. This can often be explained away by an alleged 'natural order' of ability. But such ill-informed explanations rarely focus on *the test's* capacity to reproduce this 'order'. A cursory glance at graphs fails to get the full picture, namely that these are instruments of performative judgement that validate superior and inferior learner categories (as depicted by the outer areas of the bell curve). Moreover, these identity tags are verified against the purported and, in my view, inconceivable[36] concept of the 'average' pupil (as illustrated by the swelled area). Beyond imagery, tests demonstrate a proclivity to produce and authenticate ability identifiers. Teachers too may discern their ability being tested. This reflects present politico-ideological values of teacher accountability and performativity (O'Brien, 2013). Certainly, as the learning support teacher indicates, staff are keenly aware of parents' (particularly middle-class parents') and pupils' renewed interest in test scores. A few teachers, she tells me, feel under pressure to prepare for fashionable tests. Many are uncertain about the role test results may yet play in shaping school culture.[37] Virtually all are of the view that these tests "hold a lot of weight." Perhaps, I reflect later, the greatest authority of these tests resides in their 'scientific' claim to learning success. All the more important, as Pierre Bourdieu might remind, to question the 'science of science' (Bourdieu, 2004).

The learning support teacher shows me a few case studies where there's a 'dip' in pupils' performances from the previous standardised tests. A positive 'diagnosis' here suggests that learning support can be 'accelerated' for those children should further consultations with the class teacher affirm this need.[38] This appears reasonable, though further discussions problematise this judgement. High levels of personalisation (see Chapter 2) are demanded by the children who work alongside the learning support team. Peer and teacher-pupil relationships shape a highly collaborative and discursive climate. Away from the hidden corners of mainstream classrooms where active passivity resides, pupils inhabit a more open, error tolerant space. Nevertheless, new challenges surface that "can be overwhelming at times." Pupils' needs are exceptionally diverse and their development takes much time and support. But progress is evident. There is the girl whose language skills are expanding and the boy who is developing more confidence and self-esteem. Other successes are manifest in improved personal and social skills and specific physical and intellectual advances. All of which does *not* appear in the graphs that are designed to collate groups along comparative cognitive 'norms'. Here, the individual is literally positioned and his/her development viewed as a constant[39] trajectory of exam scores. Validated against others' outcomes, the successful learner 'becomes'. By stark contrast, the marginalised learner has discrete cognitive, affective and spiritual (see Chapter 2) needs. Development takes an uneven trajectory and success is measured against oneself. Such incongruity is not lost on the learning support teacher as she divides herself between scaffolding children and constructing graphs. But for all of this confusion, there are identity lessons to be learned:

> I have definitely changed. Before I would have been guilty as a class teacher of probably teaching to the masses and to differentiate would have been very hard. I would try harder now with the lower ability kids, use group work, help them on the computer [using assistive learning technology]. I think every teacher should have a stint in learning support. It completely opens your mind.

How important learning support is to all teachers. And how important it is to all pupils. I expressly recall that child who tries so hard in class, is supported and praised by the teacher and delights in personal accomplishments. How long will it be before the smooth trajectory of graphs imagines a marginal identity?

The clustering of children around 'standards' reflects a general 'group think' in schools concerning age and ability. Uniquely, I find myself in a classroom setting where 3rd and 4th classes are amalgamated.[40] As one half quietly and diligently sets to work on an English text, the other half is keenly debating more complex ideas with the teacher. I notice a few from the former group eavesdropping and wonder how much learning occurs in advance of one's years and one's self. Learning materialises after all as a consequence of development with others,[41] such as when children perform as understudy in the knowledge acts of parents, teachers or older peers. This appears to me vividly as I recall that (rare) summer scene where sixth class pupils and junior infants sat and read together on dry downy grass. Now on the walls of the classroom, the work charts another map of cognitive intervals. It reads as distinctly formal with grammar, vocabulary and arithmetic casting a *schooling* journey. Fittingly, the two halves come together in mathematics. The teacher directs flash card questions to different pupils in the different age divisions. The boy who has just arrived in 4th class from an English-speaking school needs help in translating his answer. The girl who avails of learning support has her problem scaffolded. All the pupils are included in problem solving. This adept use of differentiation[42] demonstrates the teacher's craft. It prompts me to later question why schools at large see age as children's primary common identifier. Experience shows that, even *within* a particular age group, there is not one way to teach or learn. Varied interests, motivations, abilities and developmental needs all present a (literally) *different* reality. Yet for all of this evidence, why is it that 'mainstream' representations endure?

The hidden hand of identity touches each class I visit. Direct connections appear between the school's ethos and teachers' methodological positions. In one teacher's efforts to democratise the curriculum, pupils are encouraged to have their say and listen to each other's points of view. This comes with a shared responsibility for community values. When book titles are being catalogued for the library, she challenges and engages the class:

Boy A:	That belongs to the girls' section.
Teacher:	Why do you say that?
Boy A:	Because it's about dresses and stuff.
Teacher:	Maybe there's another way of saying this?
Girl A:	It's a story about princesses.
Boy A:	So it can go in the fairy-tales section.
Teacher:	I agree. Do you all agree with Sean's [a pseudonym] choice? Here's another title. What kinds of people live in North America?
Girl B:	Indians.
Teacher:	Maybe native Americans and Inuit people, not just Americans or Canadians?
Boy B:	We can put that in the special interest section.
Teacher:	Do you know what it's like if somebody loses their temper and is not nice to someone? Or if teasing happens?
Boy C:	That's bullying!
Girl C:	We can put that in the self-help section.[43]
Teacher:	What about this book by Janaki Sastry? Where will we put this?
Girl D:	In folk tales from the world.
Teacher:	Good idea Lucy [a pseudonym].
Girl E (later):	Where is India anyway?

In another class, pupils are learning about various countries on a Google map of Europe. The teacher periodically summons pupils to identify a country and point out some interesting facts about it. I notice one boy alongside me whispering to his friend and gesturing towards a peer who cannot find Ukraine on the screen. He appears to deride his efforts and is ably assisted in this satirical show. When subjects shift from geography to mathematics, I get a chance to speak with the pupils. Both scorners appear to be high achievers that come from middle and lower middle class backgrounds. Their sardonic target is a low achiever with a working class profile. Throughout the lesson he regularly slouches and shields his face inward. He couldn't make himself any smaller. I ask him if he needs help with his maths. After a while he tells me that they're not his answers, while his nearby classmate looks guilty. He openly tells me that he has problems with school. I reflect, this time from a social class perspective, on how children act out their own and others' identity. Personal and social forms of identity cannot be removed from children's *material realities*. Despite recent politico-ideological attempts to obviate its status,[44] it is important to remind that *social class* remains the dominant determinant of educational achievement.[45] While I can't be certain that the incident I witness is nothing more than two boys belittling another's ability, I find it troubling to overlook contingent class judgements (Bourdieu, 1986). This is because children not only internalise their relative class status and the possibilities that this may/may not present, they also act this out with others and themselves (Bourdieu, 1989;

Skeggs, 2010). Beyond identity categories, then, class remains *performative* since it brings into effect that which it names (Butler, 1999).

'Who we are': The identity acts of parents and pupils

I decide to put Lisa's theory to the test. The call goes out and, sure enough within a very short period, I have a parents' focus group arranged for later that week. All eight, a theoretical magic number for such events (Parvanta *et al.*, 2011), meet me in the upstairs prefab for a coffee and chat. One parent endorses my own experience: "I think you don't get to know the school until you walk in." Unlike me however, parents come to know at a much deeper level the school's "dynamism", its "sense of community." After all, they routinely escort their children along affective, social and learning journeys. Crucially, they are privy to their child's growth in character. The school plays its part here since, as one parent asserts, "it promotes equality and justice and teaches our kids to think for themselves." "I see this in my own family", says another, highlighting how her son's identity is so much different to his older sister's (the latter having attended a different school environment, at a different time). Somewhat mischievously, I read aloud some views on Gaelscoil parents. But they do not rise to David McWilliams' (2006) typification bait. One parent elucidates that this Gaelscoil "offers a particular window to the world", albeit one that appears tainted by "misrepresentation." Another more emotively asserts:

> It can be a bit annoying because we're sort of outside the mainstream. Well there's a perception that we are and that will start to influence our identity. This all gives a kind of siege mentality[46] in some respects. Now I actually like the prefabs because I think there's a nice vibe to it all and, in a way, it's getting away from the institutionalised-type buildings that we were used to and that we all suffered in, perhaps.

Another parent pitches in:

> The Gaelscoil breaks the mould. That is, it's different. And then the conservative elements of our society and our community resist change. And this is the fundamental problem.

Like TJ, parents wish to properly communicate the school's identity. "Perception" says one parent, mindful maybe of the impact of image in postmodernity, "is nine-tenths of the law" and must be "fielded." This is noteworthy because it indicates that identity perception (what one is *not*, perhaps) affects authentic identity (what one *is*, or claims to be). Certainly, perception appears to have real effects. One parent speaks of walking his child to school and encountering neighbours "who will not salute me on the street." "I get that as well", says another, "the level of animosity can be huge." I reflect later on John

B. Keane's play *The Field* (1965) which, based on a true story, tells how a land dispute divides a community. As the narrative unfolds, terrestrial spots in the Irish psyche are skilfully unearthed. Alongside religion, as Rosa González (1992, 83) retells, "land has been one of the most potent symbols of unity and conflict in the history of Ireland." Though ultimately for these parents, the tank field dispute has a unifying effect. "We are interested in our children and what they are about in school", says one parent, echoing another perception that Gaelscoil parents tend to be more involved in matters of school organisation and management (MacGiolla Phádraig, 2003).[47] Certainly, these parents substantiate their children's sense of school identity. "This is not being elitist", says one, "but we do put an extra bit of effort into homework with the language." "And we almost choose to be interested in the type of school for our kids", adds another. Even the political challenge is presented as a scaffold to learner identity:

> There is a feeling of injustice creeping into our identity, and I think the children's identity, and it may be a good thing down the road. If you want something, it's important and you mustn't let what people think or say affect you negatively. You listen to them, take on board their views and then you strike your compromise and go on. I think there may be great learning in it.

Another parent comments:

> When I drive up my hill, I have four signs ['Save Our Tank Field'] presented to me. It's not nice to live in an area like that. But I still know that I must respect their opinions and that's what I teach my son.

How experience shapes identity.[48] And how views of childhood shape experience.[49] Is it possible (even desirable) to see children as social actors, as "competent commentators on their own lives" (Prout, 2002, 68)? It is clear that parents and children act together, but can children 'do' identity to themselves? Operating as they do within systems of relations, not least familial, class, gender, ethnicity and so on, can children "speak for themselves and in their own way"? (Prout, 2002, 75). These parents tell me that they can and they do. Routinely, children culturally negotiate (at cognitive and affective levels) the different systems of relations (Long and O'Brien, 2012). For example, school, peer and home lives may correspond but they may also conflict. It is the child who primarily negotiates such tensions. And children who "question knowledge and authority" in some relational spaces can be viewed as "opinionated" or sometimes "unruly" in others. Indeed, parents indicated to me that the latter is sometimes observed in their own homes! Perhaps all of this demonstrates children's use of critical literacy as they learn to 'read [and re-read] the world' (Freire and Macedo, 1987). And most of the parents I speak to would not have it any other way, if the choice was theirs to make. Attitudes to religion are interesting in this regard. While most children are Catholic and follow church rituals,[50] they are respectful and supportive of the school's multi-faith position. Parents want their children, as one puts it, to "see that there is a [religious] choice", unlike other schools "where it is a given." Commenting on voluntary support for after-school instruction, another parent wants the Catholic Church to more fully acknowledge families' "support for *it* as a particular choice" (my emphasis). Certainly, whatever choice is made, parents emerge as active social agents in their children's religious identity. Though ultimately, it is the child who negotiates relational spaces; it is the child who does the identity work.

Parents are very mindful of the increased demands and pressures on teachers. One suggests that, in tandem with teachers, parents could support lunchtime supervision and anti-bullying practices; another speaks of parental involvement in a proposed homework club; while the rest debate the logistics and legalities of such schemes. I ask all how much value they place in formal tests. "I'd hold huge value in them", says one parent, "because they're highly valued outside, for work and life opportunities." However, she qualifies this value by stating that she wouldn't like to see any child being "stereotyped as a poor learner." "I notice", says another, "that kids judge themselves" against tests and get "very anxious." Tests appear useful for highlighting learning needs, one parent indicates, but what happens when "it becomes an animal in itself?" Pursuing his own line of thought, he warns of "mainstream preparation for tests", which "is not what this place is supposed to be about." While the rest appear to agree, I sense thornier efforts at resolution. Notwithstanding their proclaimed separation from pedagogical decisions, an unsettling chasm appears when school tests ("the only game in town") are set alongside school identity ("keeping our ethos to the forefront"). But time is against us and this tension is suspended for now. Though, I push for one more (related) question: What are your views on the perfect school? Parents don't take long to deliberate; their children are best placed to respond:

> I suppose the perfect school for me would be when your child wakes in the morning and wants to go to school. You know, wanting to be on time, wanting to abide by the rules, wanting to participate in learning.

Another parent describes what the perfect school is *not* before settling for a most positive ideal. I am struck by this enlightened exchange of childhood and school identity:

> It isn't one where they don't feel safe, where the teacher isn't nice to them. [It's a place] where they're getting really creative learning. A place where they're being honoured really.

It is two years since Maarten passed away and the pupils and staff are honouring his memory. Today, a cake sale is raising funds for cancer research, and this year's school walk (*Siúlóid Maarten*) is in aid of the children's charity Barnardos. Those

Figure 1.3 Maarten's chair

too young to have met Maarten know of him. It is to his chair they go for comfort when they bruise themselves in the schoolyard. This peaceful place is lovingly preserved at the school's façade and symbolically preserved in pupils' portrayals of 'who we are' (see Figure 1.3). Maarten's classmates are now in their final summer at Gaelscoil an Ghoirt Álainn. Most have spent 8 years of their lives here and I want to acknowledge *their* identity expressions. I am conscious too of sensitivities; these young people are about to leave childhood bonds to traverse a new growth threshold (Smyth *et al.*, 2004).

The 2 sixth classes (12 year olds) generously accept my invitation to participate in an identity project. Imagine, I posit, someone who knows little or nothing about you and this school. And suppose you have to select photographic images that best illustrate 'who we are' to this person. What images would you choose to capture? To help you decide, I add, you may work in small groups of 4 to share the use of a camera (comprising 24 photos). Each group may settle on the top 4 photos (from a total of 16 available for collaborative work). Also, each individual in the group may take 2 personal shots (expending the remaining 8 photos). These are the project's only guidelines. The aim here is to empower pupils to capture and articulate their own, as well as peer group, configurations of identity.[51] Equipped with the requisite disposable cameras, pupils set out to craft their chosen images. I return a week later to participate in the project's finale. Here, I witness pupils' illustrations and reports of 'who we are'.

Art is frequently seen as a reflection of identity, but identity is also reflected in the art we create. The images that I review are largely pre-formed; but, evidently, children *performed* them too. As I read these images, children's innermost thoughts and emotions become externalised (Igoa, 1995). And as the children enlighten my reading, the images appear more profound. Children's strong sense of belonging is now on display. One might expect sixth-class pupils to exhibit special bonds at this most sensitive of schooling periods. But there are plenty of images too where young and old are creatively captured (see Figure 1.2). Here, I am struck by the care and attention shown to younger peers, as well as to those who will always be with them (see Figure 1.3). And I am taken by children's strong draw towards this (seemingly) uninviting location (see Figure 1.1). Of course images of the physical environment attract deeper meaning, with notions of 'belonging' and 'pride of place' presenting as metaphysical spectacles. A photo of austere railings shows the school being held back from the tank field's expanse. It is (surprisingly) a positive image. Its creators are proud of the building's sideline setting. They have spent long periods of their life here and (I am reminded that) they have never given up on the campaign for a new site. There are photos too of children tidying their classrooms and creating school art. And there are photos of rooms that once housed their youth, with teachers' names inscribed on doors and pupils' memoirs.

There are plenty of school scenes that celebrate camaraderie. Children make careful efforts to gather and arrange in-group photos. Some individual photos exhibit comic character. There's the boy with knuckles pressed to lips, as if to model Auguste Rodin's 'Le Penseur' (1902).[52] And there's another boy gazing at the heavens, as if to audition for Captain Boyle in Sean O'Casey's play *Juno and the Paycock* (1924).[53] Both perform the role of student for the camera. Others play this role too, though perhaps less wryly. There are creative displays of textbooks across the age spectrum. Other photos show pupils busy at work, while some focus on the packed contents of schoolbags. Yet more photos, including one family picture, illustrate younger and older pupils working on different cognitive tasks. All appear as participants in a common intellectual journey, with *age* paving the (only) discerning path. Diversity is more roundly captured in photos of the school mural, with its illustrations of global religious symbols and different pupil portraits. And boys and girls compete in inclusive images of sport, while the silver-lined trophy cabinet features their shared efforts.

There are stark images too of the concrete playground. Some children refer to it as "our place" and they appreciate their play time there. But it is inimical to full-bodied sport or aesthetic respite. Badminton nets are erected on site, only to disappear again. Hurling and football matches are improvised before they are interrupted by streams of spectators. And all players are wary of care appointments to Maarten's chair. A girl photos the small cheerful shrubs that grow besides the steely fence. She tells me that she goes there sometimes to draw and sketch, that it is her "quiet place." I reflect on the importance of environment in nurturing creativity and an aesthetic sense of self (Penuel and Wertsch, 1995). And I recall that day when a child handed broken glass to the supervising teacher. "That happens a lot [be]cause" says one boy, "there's a pub at the corner of the yard" (referring to the GAA's pavilion). I can't help thinking of this improper intrusion on childhood space but I come to accept that the children may not see it like I do. For all its bleakness, this is still a *play* ground where childhood relations and imaginations thrive.

I search for signs of originality in pupils' photos. Portraits are undoubtedly creative and there are strong signs that the children have inserted themselves into the visual text. A girl stands proudly clasping the camogie[54] cup; she had played no small part in the school's victory and sees herself as an accomplished athlete. A boy is pictured practising his guitar; he is proud of his musical ability and the opportunity to share this with others. Another is captured helping his younger sibling with homework; he likes sharing what he knows and might even be a teacher one day. Most children present some personal insights into 'who they are' in these photos. But as I ponder this notion of originality, I remind myself that these photos are largely snapped on a school site that produces its own semiotics. Even in their school *uniforms* children wear a particular public image of self. While this public image is never singular, equally it is never fully expressive of who one is "deep down" (Ward, 1997, 123). Personal identity (who one becomes) is shaped by the mediation of sociocultural factors (that perform upon us) and individual factors (that we perform upon ourselves). In this way, individuality is not in opposition to group identity. Rather, it connects with the social,[55] finding its tracks at different times and contexts.[56]

Schools undoubtedly have an important role to play in identity formation (Oakes, 2005; Reay, 2010). But more critical attention needs to be focused on their *preparation* of children and young people. In his book *What's the point of school?* Guy Claxton sets out his position:

> The purpose of education is to prepare young people for the future. Schools should be helping young people to develop the capacities they will need to thrive.
>
> (Claxton, 2008, Preface)

Such a ('psychological') view tends to present the common educational task as "producing a particular kind of individual [. . .] with a particular set of moral qualities and dispositions" (Biesta, 2010, 558). 'Preparation' is depicted as somewhat distant, projected in time. In his 'My Pedagogic Creed', John Dewey challenges these assumptions:

> I believe that education [. . .] is a process of living and not a preparation for future living. I believe that the school must represent present life [. . .]
>
> (Dewey, 1897, Article Two. What the school is)

Hannah Arendt adds moral weight to this critique. She believes that schools cannot simply prepare children for the (adult political) world *unless* children are ready to fully understand such a world and make informed decisions concerning its maintenance and transformation (Arendt, 1993). What is strongly understood in Arendt's work is that morality is not sufficient for making (political) identity possible; rather it is the latter, particularly children's *thinking* acceptance and renewal of 'our world', that makes morality possible (Arendt, 1998).[57] So the function of school is to "teach children what the world is like" in order to "prepare them in advance for the task of renewing a common world" (Arendt, 1993, 192, 193). 'Preparation' here is seen as continuous and changeable. And children's identity is viewed as "not finished but in a state of becoming" (Arendt, 1993, 185).

These ideas enhance my reading of the photos with the children. I accept that I can only witness a small part of their identity story. And I can only witness part of this school's gradual introduction of children to the world (Arendt, 1993). As I finally reflect upon this journey, a photo stands out on my desk. It is of a young girl pictured at the top of stairs, her eyes fixed on the camera below. The caption beneath her photo reads: 'I make this school by being myself'. I unearth records of our conversations together. "I feel good in this school", she tells me, and "I can be myself [here]." "I enjoy being with my friends", she follows, and "I'm confident [and] lucky for my family's and teachers' support." At which point, I am now better placed to re-view this solo picture. I begin to conjure up silhouette figures to develop the photo's background. And a fuller picture of learning identity gradually appears.

Figure 1.4 An scoil nua ['The new school' site]

It is over 2 years since I visited Gaelscoil an Ghoirt Álainn and some things do not appear to have changed. The new school has not materialised (see Figure 1.4), there are still disputes[58] and identity work continues. But much *has* changed in effect. A new Principal is in situ (Deaglán Ó Deargáin), teacher-pupil, peer and 'self' relations are in flux, 2 naíonáin bheaga classes have since passed their schooling induction and 2 sixth-class groups have completed the early years of secondary school. As I finally review classroom observation notes and student photographs, I am reminded of the 'precious opportunity'[59] they present. While time has passed, records still shape us. And however slow time appears, there's dynamism in its advance.

I have learned from this research that learning identity is constantly formed and re-formed. There is perhaps no better illustration of this than seeing a child gradually become his/her 'own' person, develop his/her capabilities and relate well to peers and adults. These learning experiences are central to the educational goals of 'identity and belonging' and 'well-being' (as promoted in *Aistear*, the Early Childhood Curriculum Framework in Ireland).[60] Of course societal, cultural and political changes[61] present new challenges and possibilities (none of which are straightforward) in meeting these educational goals. On the one hand, children are no longer compelled to behave and conform; rather, they are encouraged to think for themselves, to question who they are, where they are situated in the world.[62] At the same time, children still depend on others' support in negotiating their identity journeys. Teachers have a meaningful role to play here. They can facilitate students to gradually build on who they are and what they can do. And teachers can shape how identity is practised in the school and classroom. Specifically, teachers can influence others by how *they* speak and act, how *they* engage knowledge, and how *they* relate with others. And in self-presenting ('who am I, where am I personally/professionally situated'), teachers can take a lead in learning identity.

Guiding research (notes)

1 Officially, Irish (Gaeilge) is the 'first' language of the Republic of Ireland. Suppressed by powerful colonial practices, the (re)establishment of the language became a corner stone of independence in 1921 and was given constitutional primacy in 1937 (O'Byrne, 2007). Official state documents and street signs appear in both Irish and English (in that order); Irish is (compulsorily) learned in school up to the age of eighteen and can be studied in every university in the country (ibid.). Yet for all this, "the language is not pre-eminent" (ibid., 308). Moreover, it is the first language of less than 5 per cent of the population and the second language of less than 30 per cent (ibid.). Even special geographical areas dedicated to preserving the language (Gaeltacht regions) illustrate subordinate trends. Ó hÉallaithe (2012) observes from the Census data of 2006 that of the 95,000 people living within the official Gaeltacht, approximately 17,000 belonged to Category A (areas in which Irish was the 'predominant community and family language'); 10,000 to Category B ('weaker areas of transition'); 17,000 to Category C (language used 'in some social networks, by a minority of families and within education'); with approximately 50,000 people not meeting the minimum criteria. More positive evidence of Irish as a 'living' language may be seen, however, in the state roll out of

media communication (e.g. dedicated radio programmes and a new television channel – TG4), as well as the advancement of Gaelscoileanna (Irish-speaking schools).

2 As the first mixed-gendered, multi-denominational, Irish immersion school, Gaelscoil an Ghoirt Álainn has unique status on the island of Ireland. The school officially opened its doors on 1 September 1993. At that time, there were 33 pupils and 2 teachers. The school has grown considerably since – in 2013, there were 16 teachers, 2 Special Needs Assistants (SNAs) and 306 pupils. The school is affiliated to both the Educate Together (ET) movement, an umbrella organisation for all multi-denominational schools in the country (see Note 19), and the Gaelscoileanna movement, umbrella organisation for all Irish-speaking schools.

3 The Gaelic Athletic Association (GAA) is an all-island sporting and cultural organisation that promotes Gaelic games, such as hurling and football (these team activities are unique to Ireland). As a celebrated amateur association, the GAA has a sports club network that extends throughout virtually every village, town and city in Ireland. In 2012, the Association had a 2,300 plus sports club membership (www.gaa.ie/about-the-gaa/).

4 The term 'apartheid' (regrettably) appears again in one of the most popular *Irish Times* articles of 2012. The article in question is written by an anonymous parent (Flynn, 2012).

5 'Bonus' here refers to the additional points scheme at Leaving Certificate (final post-primary examination), which is aimed at encouraging pupils to take all chosen subjects through Irish. In reality, the 10 per cent figure is somewhat misleading. This bonus percentage is only given to students who fully complete exams in the Irish language and who receive 75 percentage marks or less. Bonus percentage points may total 5 or 3 per cent (or none at all), depending on the student's final exam result. Thus, the bonus reduces along a scale for scores that lie above 75 per cent.

6 Most Gaelscoileanna are established by parental pressure groups who can demonstrate a need for a Gaelscoil in their area. If they can evidence that there are at least 17 children interested in being Gaelscoil members and provide arguments for a suitable school site (among other conditions), the state will fund the creation of a new Gaelscoil.

7 These figures illustrate the number of Irish-medium schools in all of Ireland (32 counties) and exclude those Irish-speaking schools in the Gaeltacht regions (i.e. those special geographical areas dedicated to preserving the Irish language; see Note 1 above). There are approximately 43,133 pupils receiving education through the medium of Irish outside the Gaeltacht (2012 figures accessed from the website www.gaelscoileanna.ie/about/statistics/?lang=en).

8 This economic period in Irish history became known as the 'The Celtic Tiger' years. The spirit of the age was marked by corporate profits and optimism, government budget surpluses, high consumer spending (and credit), low unemployment and net immigration. This zeitgeist is encapsulated in the opening sentence of McWilliams's book – *Ireland has arrived* (McWilliams, 2006, 3).

9 "The kids are playing football in the yard, speaking in Irish to each other. The parents are arriving now. Yummy [from the disparaging term 'yummy mummy'] has parked half way up Charleston Road [an affluent area of South Dublin] so as to be able to partake in the walk to school initiative. She grabs Sorcha and the twins (the tell-tale sign of mid-thirties IVF [In Vitro Fertilisation]) and rounds the corner into Oakley Road [. . .] Bizarrely, Irish is not heard. Not one parent speaks a full sentence to their child in Irish at the gate, but there are lots of gratuitous sláns [goodbyes], Dia duits [hellos] and the like", etc., etc. (McWilliams, 2006, 238–9).

10 The phrase 'extracurricular' is somewhat misleading, if not undesirable. It implies that such activities as field trips, sporting events, musical and language supports are some-how 'separate' from the formal curriculum. These activities may be planned 'outside' formal school timetables/hours, but they are nevertheless central to a pupil's guided learning programme. This centrality may be lost in a phrase that assumes such activities as 'add-ons'.

11 With government funding to schools (via Capitation grants) reduced in recent budgets, parents in Ireland are increasingly asked to make a 'voluntary contribution' to cover such costs as reading materials, music resources and equipment, ICT systems, test manuals, and classroom supplies. A recent National Parents Council (Primary) survey indicated that over 40 per cent of parents who responded said that they felt under pressure to pay it (see www.npc.ie/npc/page.aspx?pageid=565). In its 2011 School Costs Survey, the children's charity Barnardos revealed that the *average* cost of sending a child to junior infants (5 years) was 350 euros, rising to 805 euros for a student starting post-primary school (12 years). The average 'voluntary contribution' element of total school costs is between 70 and 100 euros (see www.irishtimes.com/newspaper/breaking/2011/0802/breaking30.html).

12 Gaelscoil an Ghoirt Álainn is a small community with some 330 pupils registered in 2012. Lisa registers families for the school records and can profile in accordance with parental profession(s) and residential address(es). She has informal knowledge of parents' employment status. In work conducted for this study, Lisa kindly estimated the broad socio-economic group distributions presented.

13 A cautionary note is provided here. The *most* disadvantaged social groups are relatively (and often acutely) affected by recession. Lisa estimates that a small percentage (approximately 4–5%) of the student population come from families in depressed socio-economic circumstances.

14 The school is officially set within a disadvantaged area of the city and is surrounded by primary and post-primary schools that have DEIS status. DEIS (Delivering Equality of Opportunity in Schools) is a designated disadvantage-status scheme for schools that identifies and regularly reviews levels of disadvantage and provides an integrated School Support Programme (SSP). It enables such additional resources as free school meals, reduced class sizes, additional learning supports and a books grant scheme (see www.education.ie/en/). Gaelscoil an Ghoirt Álainn is not a designated disadvantaged school and has never formally applied for DEIS status. Therefore, the impression could be that, by exception, it is an 'advantaged' school. However, as Lisa's conversation indicates, this impression appears too simplistic. Conversations with the principal also reveal his initial 'bewilderment' as to why the school had not attained DEIS status. He subsequently made enquiries with the Department of Education and Skills (DES) and the National Educational Welfare Board (NEWB) but all parties have yet to formalise any application.

15 Foucault's (1970, 1972) early work outlines that, within any particular historical setting, an epistemic structure (or 'archaeology') provides 'conditions of possibility' for thought, for example, a society's attitude towards mental illness or sex. For Foucault, powerful social forces 'behind'/'aligned to' particular knowledge claims ultimately shape individuals' thoughts and control their behavioural (including 'bodily') actions (Foucault, 1977). These Foucauldian insights reveal that individual/institutional change depends (to a significant degree) on *societal* identifications that are (re)constructed and legitimated in time and context. A school's 'ethos', therefore, is never of its own making.

16 By way of illustration, a Forum on Patronage and Pluralism in the Primary Sector was established in 2011. At the time, 96 per cent of primary schools in Ireland were under denominational patronage (the vast majority being Catholic). A key brief of the Forum was to investigate how a transfer/divesting of this totality could be advanced to ensure that demands for diversity of patronage (including from an Irish language perspective) could be identified and met (see www.education.ie/en/ for the *Report of the Forum's Advisory Group*, April 2012).

17 There are a number of bicultural, mixed-nationality families in the school (5 in 2012). There is also anecdotal evidence of the increased presence of returned Irish emigrant families.

18 Crucially, a school that *has* a sibling policy – that is, a policy that affords school entry to a brother/sister of a present/past pupil – can sometimes confer unfair advantage to settled,

local families at the expense of transient (e.g. Travellers/Roma) and new migrant (often non-Irish national) family groups.

19 Gaelscoil an Ghoirt Álainn is officially an 'Educate Together' school. Educate Together is the patron body of schools in Ireland that operate in accordance with the Educate Together Charter. This Charter, specific to a cluster of state-funded schools, supports an ethos that is multi-denominational, co-educational, child-centred and democratic. Educate Together is an independent non-governmental organisation (NGO) that seeks to guarantee equality of access and esteem to children irrespective of their social, cultural or religious background. In 2012, Educate Together operated 65 multi-denominational primary schools around the country, with plans for the first Educate Together post-primary schools to operate in 2014 (for further information, see www.educatetogether.ie/). In 2014, 77 Educate Together schools were in operation in Ireland, with one other operating in the UK (Redfield Educate Together Primary Academy in Bristol, England).

20 The reader is invited to critically review this formal curriculum programme and its suggested resources (Kelleher *et al.*, 2004).

21 Sociocultural learning theory forges a direct connection between language and conceptual development (Vygotsky, 1978). It is contended that meaningful access to words/terms/symbols has the power to liberate more developed forms of thinking. Sociocultural learning theory also stresses the 'culturally situated' (Lave and Wenger, 1991) nature of knowledge where social groups make sense of their experiences together and classify, codify and communicate these experiences symbolically. Here, meaningful access to words/terms/symbols has the corresponding power to liberate influential networks of social relations.

22 'Code-switching' refers to pupils' concurrent use of 2 or more languages and/or symbolic forms. The term acknowledges bilingual learners' adaptive capacity to read, listen, write, speak and think in 2 or more languages for different purposes, in different contexts, with different people (Moschkovich and Nelson-Barber, 2009, 122).

23 This is a moot point. Code-switching between languages does not appear to affect the quality of conceptual thinking (Cumming, 1990). It may be beneficial, allowing learners to problem pose and solve in different ways and in different contexts (a type of additive bilingualism?). Or code-switching may be a hindrance, such as when a pupil does not fully understand a mathematics word problem written in his/her second language (a type of restrictive bilingualism?). Simple conclusions, then, cannot be drawn about a pupil's thinking on the basis of his/her code-switching actions (Moschkovich and Nelson-Barber, 2009).

24 Jim Cummins's work is highly instructive here. Cummins (1994) suggests that students working in 'additive bilingual' educational settings have higher levels of success than those whose first language and culture are institutionally and societally devalued.

25 The Italian language is offered to fifth (11 year olds) and sixth (12 year olds) class pupils in the school. It was originally provided as a subject following the 'pilot' establishment of the Modern Languages in Primary Schools Initiative (MLPSI). MLPSI has since been disbanded post Budget (December 2011) and the money (2.5 million euro) for this scheme divested towards the national implementation of the literacy and numeracy strategy (costing 19 million). Many have decried the loss of modern languages in the primary school curriculum, including the Royal Irish Academy. Opposition voices have highlighted how this decision counteracts the recommendations made by the Expert Group on Future Skills Needs (2005) and the Council of Europe Policy Profile (2008). Gaelscoil an Ghoirt Álainn supports the curricular provision of modern languages and, with the help of parents' contributions, continues to offer Italian to fifth and sixth classes. For many of these pupils, Italian serves as a 'third' language.

26 Monthly reports that detail what items of the curriculum have been 'covered and learned' by the children appear to make sense. Not least, they are likely to be supported by those that call for greater (managerialist forms of) teacher accountability (see Chapter 3).

However, from an educational perspective, the reports necessitate closer scrutiny and, at the very least, mediation. In curriculum theory, for example, Kelly (1999) refers to the difference between the 'planned' and 'received' curriculum. Here, the official or 'planned' curriculum refers to what is laid down in syllabi, whereas the actual or 'received' curriculum is the reality of the pupils' experience. Gaps between prescription and reception are always likely to occur. Hence, the need for questions not only about *what* is 'covered and learned' (content), but *how* this is to be achieved (methodology) and *why* (rationale and assessment). These other questions are raised in the interest of regular *educational* intervention.

27 History offers up some valuable lessons here. The great irony is that the Irish language was repudiated in the past not just by colonial practices (which are well-documented) but by the actions of native speakers (which are less so). In the years before Independence (1921), many parents wishing to promote the use of English (mainly due to its 'economic' value) punished their children for speaking Irish; children were encouraged to report one another to adults; and teachers would physically abuse children for their use of Gaeilge in school (O'Byrne, 2007). It would be most ironic, not to mention harmful, if a modern Gaelscoil decided to commonly punish children (however 'soft' e.g. use of detention, 'lines', etc.) for *not* speaking Irish. Here, I am reminded of George Santayana's (1905, 284) cautionary words: "those who cannot remember the past are condemned to repeat it."

28 A school's stance on discipline is influential in positioning learners along this scale, though there will be students who will invariably occupy different locations at different times. We might think here of the case of the child who needs clear rules of conduct in order to advance (over time) a more self-disciplinary position. However, we might also think of the child who remains relatively static on this scale, due perhaps to his/her inability (for varying reasons) to 'comply' with school rules. Here, I am mindful of those children who find themselves all-too frequently positioned outside the head teacher's office. Such children are likely to experience even greater rule-based intervention that serves to locate them separately, and statically, within a school's disciplinary code.

29 A head teacher is officially tasked with inspiring all partners to subscribe to, and act upon, a common educational purpose. I questioned earlier if this exceptional task is reasonable. In response to my own question, I believe that it may be unreasonable to expect one person to solely fulfil this task. And it may be unreasonable to expect that person to *directly* motivate, since all he/she can really do is *influence*.

30 Is it possible to be vocationally dedicated to teaching if one is not, to some significant degree, *personally* engaged? I pose this question to you, the reader.

31 See Bronwyn Davies's (1989) insightful article on the discursive production of the male/female dualism in school settings. Francis and Skelton (2003) claim that the strongest period of 'gender role maintenance' takes place at 4–5 years, where young children are anxious to act out their 'correct' gender functions. These functions are firmly internalised by older age groups who make sexuality connections. Thus, as the Irish dance teacher in the school informed me, "older boys don't like holding hands."

32 The test in question is the 'Drumcondra Primary Mathematics Test' which is devised by The Educational Research Centre (St Patrick's College, Dublin) and is annually administered (alongside literacy tests) to each year group in the school. The main work of the Educational Research Centre is the development of standardised, diagnostic and profile test systems in Ireland. To illustrate, the Centre analyses the results of state examinations; monitors the 'outcomes' of education in areas of literacy and mathematics, 'connecting' with international tests such as PISA (Programme for International Student Assessment), PIRLS (Progress in International Reading Literacy Survey) and TIMMS (Trends in International Mathematics and Science Study); and develops new assessment instruments (such as those pertaining to the recent National Literacy and Numeracy Strategy, 2012).

33 Summative assessment refers to an attempt to measure learning at a particular time, following a period of work. A test is typically administered with a view to (literally)

summarising learning up to this point and comparing this 'outcome' to some set of standards or benchmarks.

34 Literacy, in both linguistic and symbolic forms, is ever-present in mathematics. And a strong cultural dimension to mathematics literacy also exists, though this is seldom acknowledged (O'Brien and Long, 2012).

35 These questions produce some language challenges. For example, in relation to the first question, one little girl asked the teacher if 'each' box meant 'one' box. In relation to the second question, one boy later confided in me that Mark and Tom had no sweets left to share – after all, how could they share half-eaten sweets! And, in relation to the last question, a little boy asked the teacher if he was required to write down the cost of 2 apples and the cost of 2 bananas separately. These are all intelligible responses that illustrate pupils' discord with academic language codes. This is more pronounced over time for children from disadvantaged backgrounds (e.g. Bernstein, 1975). Hence, the need for a broader discussion on standardised tests that takes into account well-established patterns of class inequality (e.g. MacRuairc, 2009).

36 The purported 'average' pupil is an inconceivable identifier. Using mathematical logic, an average score is the mark that every child in the class would get if all the marks in that class were totalled and then divided out equally. In effect, this means (if you pardon the pun!) that pupils are judged against an imaginary peer who scores an imaginary mark. *In reality* though, the average score does have material significance, since it enables judgements to be made on pupils' ability along a sliding scale ('at', 'below' or 'above' average). The question begs: If tests judge in accordance with an 'average', should we be surprised if the bell curve constantly reproduces itself and 'others'?

37 At the time of writing, teacher allocation to next year's classes was being considered. Decisions were to be based on a combination of factors such as a personal wish list, a desire for teacher rotation, a teacher's particular affinity with age groups and, crucially, the outcomes of recent test results. The latter's cultural function was never fully explicated (nor indeed made knowable) but its very consideration is itself significant.

38 I deliberately use the terms 'diagnosis' and 'acceleration' here. Great care needs to be taken with language use and meanings. As Roger Slee (1998) reminds, the field of special educational needs is replete with medicalised discourse. Learning support systems can borrow heavily from this glossary, commonly utilising (either formally or informally) such terms as 'diagnosis', 'remediation' (in line with 'norms'), 'recovery' (as in the 'reading recovery programme'), 'prognosis' (as appearing in IEPs – Individual Educational Plans), 'acceleration' (as in 'study' or 'after-school' clubs), etc. Marginalised groups (such as special educational needs pupils, 'below average' learners, those with 'disciplinary problems', second language learners, etc.) are often identified with this language and are therefore susceptible to deficit learning assumptions and supports.

39 The term 'constant' is deliberately used here to indicate that a *regular* series of tests is likely to produce *persistent* patterns of 'success'. Many will find that this 'success' bunches around the 'average' standard (as illustrated by the swelled area of the bell curve). It seems incredible that so many pupils will identify with this average middle ground for so long in their schooling years. Is this proclivity towards stability a sign of *learning development*?

40 This class was amalgamated due to an original surplus of numbers at junior infants' stage.

41 In sociocultural theory, learning leads development, that is, learning occurs as a consequence of development. Vygotsky's Zone of Proximal Development (ZPD) highlights this relationship well (Vygotsky, 1978). Here, an individual's learning is measured by the distance between his/her 'actual' developmental level (determined by independent problem solving) and his/her 'potential' developmental level (determined by problem solving under adult or 'more capable' peer guidance). Of course, older 'more developed' children can also learn from younger, 'less developed' peers; for example, peer reading schemes may nurture pedagogical relationships, with younger *and* older children benefitting from such care provision.

42 Differentiation in learning represents the variety of ways in which to engage 'difference', such as via subject knowledge (e.g. choice of materials, varying 'entry points' (Gardner, 1991)); the learning process (e.g. methodological approaches that reflect diverse learning styles, strengths, interests and needs); and assessment (e.g. use of diverse methods and measures).

43 Bullying is an endemic problem in schools. The 'Irish Health Behaviour in School-aged Children' report (HBSC, 2010) notes that the percentage of 3rd and 4th class children (ages 8–10) who report ever being bullied stands at 37 per cent. In 2011, the Irish Society for the Prevention of Cruelty to Children (ISPCC) received over 11,000 calls from children who directly experienced bullying. The significance of self-care work in schools cannot be underestimated, therefore, as this seeks to promote a positive sense of self-identity among children. A stark and sad reminder of this function surfaced at the time of writing when 2 Irish teenagers took their own lives as a result of separate cyber bullying incidents. They are remembered here: Ciara Pugsley (15 years old) from Leitrim and Erin Gallagher (13 years old) from Donegal. In a tragic development, just 6 weeks after her sister's (Erin's) death, Shannon Gallagher (15 years old) took her own life. At her funeral mass, Fr. Duffy told mourners that "society has failed 2 children, 2 sisters within 2 months . . ."

44 Recent politico-ideological interest in *teacher quality* has focused on the quality of teachers being the most important (school-based) factor affecting achievement (OECD, 2004; 2005). The danger of this focus resides in its proclivity to obscure the wider, and *more dominant*, effects of social class (including parental levels of education). Moreover, teacher quality is very difficult to measure. One needs to consider, inter alia: Teachers' identity (who they are); their professional context (e.g. where they work); their levels of experience; their qualifications; their salaries and Continuing Professional Development (CPD) engagement; their openness to change and creativity; their methodological qualities; their educational achievements, etc. Evaluating teacher quality in terms of limited 'outcomes' (such as 'exam scores') may make measurement 'simpler', but it may be no less achievable.

45 Indeed, Smyth and McCoy (2009, 8, 9) highlight how school performance (as measured by state exam grades, reading and mathematics scores and retention rates) is "strongly patterned across social class lines." To illustrate, in the case of Ireland: "While 58 per cent of students from higher professional backgrounds achieve four or more 'honours' grades in the Leaving Certificate [the final State Examination], this is the case for just 16 per cent of those from semi- and unskilled manual backgrounds." Further, around 75 per cent of higher professional groups progress to higher education as compared with two-thirds of those from farming and lower professional groups and just 38 per cent of those from semi- and unskilled manual groups.

46 I am reminded of one teacher's reaction to the visible presence of the 'Save Our Tank Field' campaign: "When I drive into school each day and I see those signs, they tell me that I'm not welcome here." For this teacher, and others within the school community, a form of 'siege mentality' is strongly felt.

47 It is important to note that such a perception may partly emerge because of a) the initial (and explicit) involvement of parents in the establishment of Gaelscoileanna and b) the fact that these schools are relatively new (MacGiolla Phádraig, 2003, 78). In the case of Gaelscoil an Ghoirt Álainn, the political campaign for a new school building appears to engage high levels of parental involvement. But besides this engagement, it is very evident from this research study that parents actively contribute to the school's mission, policy and practice.

48 Paulo Freire is reputed to have said that "no one is born fully-formed: It is through self-experience in the world that we become what we are" (no reference available).

49 At the time of writing, the 'Children's Referendum' was being voted upon in Ireland (10 November 2012). In support of Constitutional amendment, advocates argued that children would have greater protection under State systems, children's interests would be of paramount concern in all judicial cases involving their care and children's views

would have to be listened to and given due attention in law. Moreover, against the terrible legacy of child abuse, supporters believed that a Yes vote would positively endorse how Irish society values children. In the end, these arguments won out, with the majority of the Irish people voting in favour of the Constitutional amendment. History will now be the judge of its delivery and success.

50 Many school families are regular church goers and fully participate in First Holy Communion and Confirmation ceremonies. Catholic (and other religious) instruction occurs outside school hours, with parents on site to supervise and pay for this 'service'.

51 The research method used is *visual*, defined by Jon Prosser (2007, 13) as "the production, organization and interpretation of imagery." It is a particularly useful method to ascertain the symbolic meanings attaching to environments, such as schools (ibid.). Care must be taken, however, in how texts (including visual) are read, as there are likely to be multiple interpretations/assumptions made (ibid.). Care must also be taken in how texts (including visual) are perceived to be written/crafted, since the writer/illustrator may exhibit 'several indiscernible voices' (Barthes, 1967). In an attempt to address these 'author' (Barthes, 1967) and 'reader' effects, this project facilitated pupils in not only crafting their images, but also in *reporting* on them.

52 As an iconic representation of philosophy, *Le Penseur* (The Thinker) depicts a naked man in contemplative inquiry. The original sculpture is located in Le Musée Rodin, Paris.

53 Sean O'Casey's *Juno and the Paycock* (1924) is set in the Dublin tenements during the Irish Civil War years of 1922 and 1923 and tells of the comic (and ultimately tragic) story of the Boyle family. The father, Captain Jack Boyle (a retired merchant seaman), famously ponders in Act 1: "I often looked up at the sky an' assed meself the question – what is the moon, what is the stars?"

54 'Camogie' is hurling (a national sport that employs a stick/'hurley' and a ball/'sliotar') played by sportswomen (see also Note 3 above).

55 Fiachra Long (2013, 3) argues that "the individuality of children is derivative and a function of a set of relations impacting on the child."

56 Whether individuality is 'authentic' and/or 'possible' is for further postmodern analysis (Lacan, 1977; Baudrillard, 1994).

57 As Gert Biesta (2010, 565) helpfully adds: "Arendt had good reasons for taking this stance, since she had convincingly shown 'that under Nazi rule those who could think and judge for themselves were more likely to resist the regime than those who possessed a moral code'" (Quoting Hansen, 2005, 6).

58 Teachers in the school were recently prohibited (by threat of fine) from parking on the grass alongside the road that leads up to the gated entrance. As a result of having to park within the school/GAA grounds, one length of the 'playground' became significantly restricted for the pupils.

59 This phrase is borrowed from Damon Albarn's song 'Photographs (You are Taking Now)'. My own thoughts on the school's photographs were triggered by listening to this song from his creative album *Everyday Robots*.

60 I am grateful to my colleagues Rosaleen Murphy and Maura Cuneen for their insightful knowledge on *Aistear*'s principles and practices (see www.ncca.biz/Aistear/).

61 Of particular relevance to this chapter is the advent of Educate Together schools (see Note 19). In Cork, the Republic of Ireland's second largest city, it is noteworthy that (as of 2014) there were only 4 primary Educate Together schools and no secondary school option (indeed in the city centre there was no mixed-gender secondary school option). Most recently, however, Educate Together has been confirmed as patron of 5 (out of 9) new secondary schools planned for 2015/2016 in Cork, Cavan, Dublin and North Wicklow. The state (through parental expressions of 'preference' and in the interest of 'plurality') takes an active role in the provision of greater school 'choice' (see Chapter 3). Its 'demand-led' change 'encourages' the Catholic Church (with the Archbishop of Dublin, Diarmuid Martin, as strategic partner) to divest its patronage status from a number of primary schools. In 2013, 23 primary schools were set to lose their Catholic Church

patronage (see www.newstalk.ie/reader/47.301.341/7564/0/) but, as of July 2014, only 2 of the state's 3,169 primary schools (one Protestant school and 1 Catholic school) have changed patronage status (see www.irishtimes.com/news/education/ruairi-quinn-report-card-b-for-pluralism-but-d-for-higher-education-reform-1.1852926). Despite slow progress, Education Minister Ruairi Quinn always showed keen interest in engaging the 'plurality' question. But he has since announced his resignation from cabinet (2 July 2014).

62 Of course children too face challenges in being 'caught up' in postmodernity (Long, 2013).

References

Arendt, H. (1993). The crisis in education. In H. Arendt, ed. (173–96). *Between past and future: Eight exercises in political thought*. New York. The Viking Press.

Arendt, H. (1998). *The human condition*. 2nd edn. Chicago. Chicago University Press.

Ball, S. J. (2003). The teacher's soul and the terrors of performativity. *Journal of Education Policy*, 18, no. 2, 215–28.

Barthes, R. (1967). The death of the author. *Aspen*, 5–6.

Baudrillard, J. (1994). *Simulacra and simulation*. Translated by Sheila Faria Glaser. Michigan. University of Michigan Press.

Bernstein, B. (1975). *Class and pedagogies: Visible and invisible*. London. Organisation for Economic Cooperation and Development.

Biesta, G. (2010). How to exist politically and learn from it: Hannah Arendt and the problem of democratic education. *Teachers College Record*, 112, no. 2, 558–77.

Bourdieu, P. (1986). *Distinction: A social critique of the judgement of taste*. London. Routledge.

Bourdieu, P. (1989). Social space and symbolic power. *Sociological Theory*, 7, no. 1, 14–25.

Bourdieu, P. (2004). *Science of science and reflexivity*. Translated by Richard Nice. Cambridge. Polity Press.

Butler, J. (1999). Performativity's social magic. In R. Shusterman, ed. (113–29). *Bourdieu: A critical reader*. Oxford. Blackwell Publishers.

Carey, S. (2008). Gaelscoil parents want to have their cake and eat it. Article written in *The Irish Times*, December 24. Retrieved from www.irishtimes.com/opinion/gaelscoil-parents-want-to-have-their-cake-and-eat-it-1.1275738

Claxton, G. (2008). *What's the point of school? Rediscovering the heart of education*. Oxford. Oneworld Publications.

Cumming, A. (1990). Meta-linguistic and ideational thinking in second language composing. *Written Communication*, 7, 482–511. Cited in Moschkovich, J. and Nelson-Barber, S. (2009, 123). What mathematics teachers need to know about culture and language. In B. Greer, S. Mukhopadhyay, A. B. Powell and S. Nelson-Barber, eds (111–36). *Culturally responsive mathematics education*. New York. Routledge.

Cummings, D. (2008). Ireland's 'Gaelscoileanna' creating educational divide. Article dated November 03. Retrieved from www.findingdulcinea.com/news/education/october-08/Ireland-s-Gaelscoileanna

Cummins, J. (1994). The acquisition of English as a Second Language. In K. Spangenberg-Urbschat and R. Pritchard, eds *Reading instruction for ESL students*. Delaware. International Reading Association.

Davies, B. (1989). The discursive production of the male/female dualism in school settings. *Oxford Review of Education*, 15, no. 3, Gender and education: Current issues, 229–41.

Dewey, J. (1897). My pedagogic creed. *School Journal*, 54, 77–80.

Flynn, S. (2012). To see real educational apartheid, look no farther than your local Gaelscoil. Anonymous parent article to the *Irish Times*, October 23. Retrieved from www.irishtimes.com/news/education/to-see-real-educational-apartheid-look-no-farther-than-your-local-gaelscoil-1.556604

Foucault, M. (1970). *The order of things.* Translated by Alan Sheridan. New York. Vintage.

Foucault, M. (1972). *The archaeology of knowledge.* Translated by Alan Sheridan. New York. Vintage.

Foucault, M. (1977). *Discipline and punish.* Translated by Alan Sheridan. New York. Vintage.

Francis, B. and Skelton, C. (2003). *Boys and girls in the primary classroom.* Buckingham. Open University Press.

Freire, P. and Macedo, D. (1987). *Literacy: Reading the word and the world.* London. Routledge and Kegan Paul.

Gardner, H. (1991). *The unschooled mind: How children think and how schools should teach.* New York. Basic Books.

Giddens, A. (1991). *Modernity and self-identity: Self and society in the late modern age.* Cambridge. Polity Press.

González, R. (1992). The unappeasable hunger for land in John B. Keane's *The Field. Revista Alicantina de Estudios Ingleses,* 5, 83–90.

Hansen, P. (2005). Hannah Arendt and bearing with strangers. *Contemporary Political Theory,* 3, 3–22. Quoted in Biesta, G. (2010, 565). How to exist politically and learn from it: Hannah Arendt and the problem of democratic education. *Teachers College Record,* 112, no. 2, 558–77.

Harris, A. and Spillane, J. (2008). Distributed leadership through the looking glass. *British Educational Leadership, Management and Administration Society,* 22, no. 1, 31–4.

Holden, L. (2007). The rise of the Gaelscoil – is this the new playground of the elite? Article written in *The Irish Times,* 17 April. Retrieved from www.irishtimes.com/news/educa tion/the-rise-of-the-gaelscoil-is-this-the-new-playground-of-the-elite-1.1202171

Holmquist, K. (2008). Language of educational apartheid. Article written in *The Irish Times,* December 09. Retrieved from www.irishtimes.com/search/index.html?rm=listresults& keywords=blackrock&rows=100&start=5670

Igoa, C. (1995). *The inner world of the immigrant child.* New Jersey. Lawrence Erlbaum Associates.

Kelleher, M., McGovern, F., Mulcahy, C. and Murphy, P. (2004). *Learn together: An ethical education curriculum for educate together schools.* Dublin. Educate Together Publication.

Kelly, A. V. (1999). *The curriculum: Theory and practice.* 4th edn. London. Paul Chapman Publishing.

Lacan, J. (1977). *Écrits: A selection.* Translated by Alan Sheridan. New York. W. W. Norton & Co.

Lave, J. and Wenger, E. (1991). *Situated learning: Legitimate peripheral participation.* New York. Cambridge University Press.

Long, F. (2013). *Educating the postmodern child: The struggle for learning in a world of virtual realities.* London. Bloomsbury.

MacRuairc, G. (2009). 'Dip, dip, sky blue, who's it? NOT YOU': Children's experiences of standardised testing: A socio-cultural analysis. *Irish Educational Studies,* 28, no. 1, 47–66.

MacGiolla Phádraig, B. (2003). A study of parents' perceptions of their involvement in Gaelscoileanna. *The Irish Journal of Education,* xxiv, 70–9.

McGee, C. and Fraser, D., eds. (2001). *The professional practice of teaching: Second edition.* Palmerston North. Dunmore Press.

McWilliams, D. (2006). *The Pope's children: Ireland's new elite.* Dublin. Gill and Macmillan.

Moschkovich, J. and Nelson-Barber, S. (2009). What mathematics teachers need to know about culture and language. In B. Greer, S. Mukhopadhyay, A. B. Powell and S. Nelson-Barber, eds (111–36). *Culturally responsive mathematics education.* New York. Routledge.

Oakes, J. (2005). *Keeping track: How schools structure inequality.* 2nd edn. New Haven. Yale University Press.

O'Brien, S. (2013). Re-representing education's image and status: In the 'interest' of pedagogical innovation. In G. K. Zarifis and M. N. Gravani, eds (TBC) *Challenging the 'European Area of lifelong learning': A critical response.* London. Springer Publication.

O'Brien, S. and Long, F. (2012). Mathematics as (multi)cultural practice: Irish lessons from the Polish weekend school. *Journal of Urban Mathematics Education,* 5, no. 2, 133–56.

O'Byrne, A. (2007). Learning a strange native language. *Social Identities,* 13, no. 3, 307–23.

OECD. (2004). *The quality of the teaching workforce.* Paris. OECD Publishing.

OECD. (2005). *Teachers matter: Attracting, developing and retaining effective teachers.* Paris. OECD Publishing.

Ó hÉallaithe, D. (2012). Flawed Gaeltacht bill in need of brave revision. Article written in *The Irish Times,* July 03. Retrieved from www.irishtimes.com/newspaper/opinion/2012/ 0703/1224319264356_pf.html

O'Sullivan, D. (2005). *Cultural politics and Irish education since the 1950s: Policy paradigms and power.* Dublin. Institute of Public Administration Publication.

Parvanta, C., Nelson, D. E., Parvanta, S. A. and Harner, R. N. (2011). *Essentials of public health communication.* London. Jones and Bartlett Learning International.

Penuel, W. R. and Wertsch, J. V. (1995). Vygotsky and identity formation: A sociocultural approach. *Educational Psychologist,* 30, no. 2, 83–92.

Prout, A. (2002). Researching children as social actors: An introduction to the children 5–16 programme. *Children and Society,* 16, 67–76.

Reay, D. (2010). Identity making in schools and classrooms. In M. Wetherell and C. T. Mohanty, eds (277–294). *The Sage handbook of identities.* London. Sage Publication.

Santayana, G. (1905). Reason in common sense. In G. Santayana, ed. (284). *Life of reason.* New York. Charles Scribner's Sons Publication.

Skeggs, B. (2010). Class, culture and morality: Legacies and logics in the space for identification. In M. Wetherell and C. T. Mohanty, eds (339–59). *The Sage handbook of identities.* London. Sage Publication.

Slee, R. (1998). Politics of theorising special education. In C. Clark, A. Dyson and A. Millward, eds (126–36) *Theorising special education.* London. Routledge.

Smyth, E., McCoy, S. and Darmody, M. (2004). *Moving up: The experiences of first-year students in post-primary education.* Dublin. Liffey Press.

Smyth, E. and McCoy, S. (2009). *Investing in education: Combating educational disadvantage.* Dublin. ESRI Publication.

Vygotsky, L. (1978). *Mind in society: The development of higher psychological processes.* In M. Cole, V. John-Steiner, S. Scribner and E. Souberman, eds Cambridge, MA. Harvard University Press.

Ward, G. (1997). *Postmodernism: The teach yourself series.* London. Hodder Headline Plc.

2
PERSONAL LEARNING

The year is 1959 and the setting is Waterford on the south east coast of Ireland.[1] A young 17-year-old girl presents herself as a postulant at the gates of the Ursuline convent. She is wistful, trusting and enthusiastic, still fated to her destiny. From an early age she always wanted to be a teacher, and "teachers [then] were nuns and nuns were teachers." Her longing is stirred by warm personal experiences of teacher nuns – it was they who filled her secondary schooldays with "civility, decorum, hockey, tennis and steaming cups of Bovril at 11; an Enid Blyton world where the idea of hitting a child would have been unthinkable." Now inside secret corridors, her experience of "normal living" is shaken to the core. It begins when she is forbidden to speak with those same teacher nuns. It ferments with the continual insistence on an unquestioning obedience to 'the rule'.

In many ways, the woman who writes about this girl is unaltered. But over the course of life experience, she is also enriched. She now provides a stronger, sagacious presence alongside her younger self. Nascent misgivings over organised religion have matured into profound convictions. She promptly identifies and questions the "dehumanizing process of monastic spirituality." Why is it, she asks, that the most virtuous achieve their "sanctity through suffering" and why does this 'virtue' replicate forbidding institutional practices?[2] Why too is it that the mother of Jesus is known as the Blessed Virgin or the Virgin Mary? Nobody, she remarks, refers to the Virgin Jesus or to the Virgin Benedict 16th (the previous pope). It can only indicate a "warped perception of the female" which "deems the young virgin more fully feminine than the ample granny whose face is lined with love, with arms open to the child." And though Jesus founded his church on married men, why is it that the established (Catholic) Church still chooses "a completely celibate religious caste?" Questions, burgeoning questions that eventually unveil a broken spirituality. After 7 years, she leaves the convent.

Later she meets and falls in love with JJ. Soon they are married and, having changed her name for a second time, she becomes *Nuala Jackson*. Over time, they are blessed with 4 children (Finola, Eoin, Michelle and Clodagh). They and their grandchildren (presently Kevin and Rosaleen) mean the world to her. In kinship with her Irish forebears, Nuala perseveres with her faith. But her faith is in a Christianity that: Respects the heritage of Celtic spirituality; loves and serves one another; celebrates marriage and sexual union; and has as its nerve centre the home, not the Church. It is a faith that honours "the spirituality of motherhood" and sees all of us as "made for something cosmic." I pause to think about this. I really need to grapple with its profundity. My search for further enlightenment leads me to her poetry work. There I unearth one piece, 'Reflections of Eternity'. It tells of a mother's joy watching her daughter at play:

> The lark who trilled through the tumble of my childhood was still filling the world with the song of a bird
> The same tall cow-parsley swayed its usual graceful salutation, as if my long years a growing had never occurred
> The shining brown seaweed glistened and bobbed lazy as ever in the gentle green swell
> The craggy barnacled rocks dismissed time as had the ever unchanging, changing tide and the salty sea smell
> In this eternal sameness, a young girl splashes squealing into the sea
> I am suffused with joy, not of memories of past moments but with the sense of a present eternity
> That young girl is me.

This philosophical idea of an infinite time and space where finite bodies (perpetually) exist resonates with Friedrich Nietzsche's (1883) concept of the 'eternal recurrence of the same'.[3] Throughout numerous verses I find a woman whose life is so habitually examined, Socrates would surely approve.[4] In various stanzas, she marvels at the wonder of children, all living creatures and nature; each and together offering a "taste of eternity" in the present. Here, Transcendence isn't something remote, such as the promise of salvation in another life. Thus, in 'The Prayer':

> We belong to each other
> We celebrate each other
> We enfold each other
> And if there is no God, then you and I have created God together
> And God is love.

How often she would return to this – her – view of Transcendence: *I in you, you in me, both one with a larger cosmos.* Throughout her life it would shape the essence of her humanity.

One may be forgiven for assuming that someone so candidly contemplative could not but be of solemn temperament. But an obvious, different reality emerges when I turn to her published diary in 2011, the title of which is *Whoopee!! I'm going to die!* Irreverently juxtaposed with Dylan Thomas' (1951) poem 'Do not go Gentle into that Good Night',[5] it is a title that celebrates the humour, humility and honesty of ordinary family life.[6] Set in 1986, it tells the story of the Jacksons and their real-life struggles with constant bills and unexpected costs; camaraderie and relationships; birthday gatherings, community celebrations, harvest work, family outings and discos; and care-free moments in the hills, countryside and beaches of County Waterford. Ultimately, it is a mother's story of contented family life. But one diary entry regularly appears as an irksome disruption to this tranquillity – the children's *schooling*. At the time, Nuala had been working in an all-boys' school (where she would remain for 30 years). Here she becomes well-versed in school culture, busily establishing her own pedagogical repertoire. But it isn't a conflict of pedagogical principles with other teachers in other schools that produces familial disorder, at least not immediately. Rather, it is her children's unhappy accounts of school that first germinate this disharmonious force. It begins with the youngest, Clodagh (6 years of age), traipsing off to school with her 'magic cloak'.

This 'magic cloak' turns out to be nothing more than "an old knitted cot-blanket tied around her shoulders" (Jackson, 2011, 13). But it is sure to make her invisible and therefore exempt from producing her homework or being tormented by bullies in the playground. By the end of the school day, however, the cover has lost all its powers. As would later pleadings from her mother to allow Clodagh cross the playground to be with her bigger sister (Michelle), away from harm's reach. There was the time too when Michelle (8 years of age) was tasked with writing out a whole blackboard full of verse. She had told the teacher that she couldn't do this – the ache in her hand and stomach was too much. The teacher concluded that she couldn't because she wouldn't. And Nuala wondered if "perhaps she couldn't and wouldn't because she shouldn't" (Jackson, 2011, 18). Repressing her own instincts, however, she listens to the authoritative voice. It bellows more 'inadequacies', most notably Michelle's poor spelling. And it informs of parental duties, pointedly announcing that Nuala is "the kind of parent who only wants to hear good things about her child" (Jackson, 2011, 19). Perhaps there is only so much appetite for disapproval; perhaps there is too much passivity in heeding counsel. But now a rare moment of clarity surges from Nuala's reply to the teacher:

> You are absolutely right. I am such a mother. So if you have anything to celebrate about my child, even if it is only the pretty colour of her hair, I will never tire of hearing it. But if you have nothing good to say, don't say anything at all.
>
> (Jackson, 2011, 20)

At once, a deeper affinity *with the child* is aroused. In private reflection, Nuala pens 'Michelling and Spelling':

My pretty, my gentle, my shy Michelle
Your loveliness won't wilt if you can't spell
In the symphony of creation your special part
Is the sweetness of your singing and the pleasure of your Art.

So let your wonder sparkle through life's meandering course
When the cascade of creation tumbles to the vastness of its source
And you confess, "I tried and I tried but I couldn't spell"
He'll laugh; "You never needed to my sweet silly Michelle."[7]

She and JJ become "more and more at odds with the school" (Jackson, 2011, 43). On the 10th of March 1986, Nuala makes an appointment with the principal of another institute to discuss a possible transfer for her "school-scarred kids" (ibid., 47). The ensuing move brings "a healing moment of humanity" (ibid., 61). Michelle is praised for the spellings she actually gets right. And Clodagh bursts with excitement in preparing for the new school play. But no matter "how much nicer" their teachers become, the system maintains a dispiriting course (ibid., 237). Homework is a case in point, as it dictates numerous hours of unethical pupil commitment. Other features of the "bleak spiritual environment" are sketched in Nuala's private letters. Here she outlines how schools habitually cultivate motivation through fear of failure, coercive sanctions, a dearth of affection and an apartheid points' race. Now, as if drawn back to an earlier challenge to an unquestioning obedience to the 'rule', she renews her pedagogical vision. And what emerges from this 'spiritual exercise' (Hadot, 1995)[8] is the exaltation of the child as *a spiritual being*. She resolves that the child needs and desires physical, mental and *soulful* care,[9] and the educator is obliged to value the individual and *act upon* well-being deficiencies in the system.[10]

Over time, Nuala engages in national debates on youth disaffection, writes newspaper articles in support of young people's happiness in school and speaks on their behalf in public forums and on television and radio programmes. In her personal correspondence, she notes:

> We are never going to hear our children if we do not pay attention to what they are saying. If we don't hear them, we will not know what concerns they have; what is important to them; what they fear; what hurts them; what is ethical to them. It is our ignorance of their spiritual journey which leads to adult bafflement at the behaviour of young people which appears immoral by societal standards.[11]

She connects with social activists, such as Harry Bohan,[12] Peter McVerry[13] and Scott Boldt.[14] They share a liberal theological worldview where 'human capital' perspectives are seen as educationally and spiritually bankrupt (see Chapter 3). They also share a desire to engage with lives, seek meaning and purpose in experiences (however adverse) and, ultimately, validate people's existence (Frankl, 1984; 2011). And they view education as necessarily humanistic, with the "duet between the person of the teacher and the person of the student" taking centre stage (Hederman,[15] 2013, 2). For humanists, education not only reflects society; it shapes it. For Nuala, in particular, education demonstrates how well we "look after our young, worry about them and nurture them." Education, to her mind, is about *being* not *having*. This presents as a hopeful message since what has gone before in young people's lives cannot dictate the future (Freire and Freire, 1994); they are trusted to walk their own path (Horton and Freire, 1990); and their 'self-actualization' (Maslow, 1943) or potentiality (Rogers, 1961) has yet to be written. It is a message that opens up avenues for positive change.[16]

One such avenue now presents itself to Nuala. Her strident criticisms of 'the murder machine' of schooling (Pearse, 1959) are momentarily tamed, then fused with a new sense of purpose. She decides to set up her own school.[17] In the still and tranquil setting of Brownstown Head, she pens its pedagogical manifesto.

Figure 2.1 Brownstown Head, County Waterford

The XLC Project

> The first thing I plead for [. . .] is freedom: Freedom for each school to shape its own programme in conformity with the circumstances of the school as to place, size, personnel, and so on; freedom again for the individual teacher to impart something of his [sic] own personality to his [sic] work, to bring his [sic] own peculiar gifts to the services of his [sic] pupils, to be, in short, a teacher, a master [sic], one having an intimate and permanent relationship with his [sic] pupils, and not a mere part of the educational machine, a mere cog in the wheel; freedom finally for the individual pupil and scope for his [sic] development within the school and within the system.
>
> (Pearse, *The Murder Machine*, 1959, 35–36)

Nuala sets out 10 key principles for her new school. These are practically informed by experiences of working with and learning from disaffected students. They are also borne out of a pragmatic desire to enable them to attain an educational qualification:

1 Motivation through excellence *not* fear of failure (we all thrive when we *excel*, such as in the *Leaving Certificate*, so the new school will be known as The XLC Project).
2 Teachers must like teaching and children.
3 Homework, if necessary, should be negotiated and produced within a thirty-hour week.
4 Learning should be fun; it thrives on cooperation, not competition.
5 The same respect must be accorded to students as is expected from students.
6 Good enough is good enough – comparisons and grades are irrelevant.
7 Streaming is discrimination and must be outlawed.
8 Everybody should blossom and dance at their own pace.
9 Evaluation should celebrate our successes.
10 Students should be proud to be identified with their school. If this means wearing a uniform, students should be consulted.

In 1998, Nuala rents a room and with the help of her son, Eoin, establishes this as a tuition centre for over 20 students at Junior Certificate and Leaving Certificate levels.[18] In the mornings the school caters for the younger students, while in the afternoons Leaving Certificate students attend. After school (from 7 pm in the evenings) and throughout the holidays, Nuala does outreach work with others who have left (or have been forced to leave) the school system. In the first year the project is largely self-funded, with part finance secured from the Waterford Area Partnership. Funding presents a constant challenge. Fifteen years on, XLC has not received mainstream funding from the Department of Education and Science (DES). It has survived due to interim funding from the Department of Social and Family Affairs (DSFA), the Back to Education Initiative (BTEI) scheme, the Irish Youth Foundation (IYF), the Waterford Area Partnership (WAP) and unpaid voluntary work. Donations are regularly sought, with staff and students once making a music single 'XLC: Against most odds' and Eoin publicising his attempts to sit 30 different Leaving Certificate subjects in the same year.[19] Catering for some 60 Leaving Certificate students and 10 Junior Certificate students, XLC operates on a budget of just over 80,000 euro in 2013. This budget comprises full administration costs, a salary of 18,000 euro for Eoin and 12,000 euro for Finola, both of whom work full-time. Nuala, who has always worked full-time, has never drawn down a salary. For policymakers this represents real 'value for money' (to use market parlance); for educationalists, it characterises a vocational summit! The volume of students who have been part of the XLC story, and have experienced exam success, is likewise impressive. From 1999–2012, over 700 students have sat their Leaving Certificate with an average of 85 per cent of the cohort passing 5 subjects or more.[20]

Over the same period, some 200 students have sat their Junior Certificate with an average of 95 per cent of the cohort passing this exam. These figures exclude many other students who continue to utilise XLC facilities and resources.[21]

The work of XLC it seems is always in demand. At times, this can be overwhelming. In 2004, the 3 core teaching staff (Nuala, Eoin and Finola) and a handful of volunteers felt overstretched and were compelled to abandon a 'night group' and discourage correspondence students. Since 2010, they work mainly with a full-time group of Junior and Leaving Certificate students, and a part-time group (of mainly older learners) who attend on Friday only. It is remarkable to think that a small staff assembly can facilitate such a broad-based curriculum (18 subject disciplines were enabled in 2012). Delivery varies, however, since formal teaching periods are prioritised for 'core' curricular subjects (e.g. English, Irish, Mathematics, Religion, History), while others are alternatively supported (e.g. via individual/ group work, practical workshops, online resource access). Similarly, the school caters for a diverse student population. It does not discriminate against any potential participant and various non-traditional students are supported, including single parents, older learners who left school without academic qualifications, asylum seekers, refugees and Travellers. A large number (some 40 per cent) of XLC's students have been expelled or indefinitely suspended from school. The vast majority of these come from areas of socio-economic disadvantage within the city. Approximately 25 per cent of the student cohort is classified as 'mature', comprising mainly of young single mothers and unemployed men in their twenties. A further 20 per cent (approximately) constitutes those who have recently moved house/ school and/or are unhappy in school for one reason or another; while the remaining 15 per cent (approximately) have been bullied in school or suffers from some form of social phobia. In 2012, one third of the Leaving Certificate cohort and less than half of the Junior Certificate cohort had some specific learning difficulty (e.g. Dyslexia, Attention Deficit Hyperactivity Disorder, Dyspraxia, etc.).

Students are constantly referred to XLC. Under the auspices of the Waterford and South Tipperary Community Youth Services (WSTCYS), XLC maintains effective working relationships with all referring agencies, including the Probation and Welfare Service, the Gardaí (Police) via its Juvenile Liaison Officers, local youth projects, the Health Service Executive (HSE) and the Schools Completion Service. There are also a number of self-referrals to XLC, as well as referrals by parents/ guardians. Nuala prefers students to be the ultimate authority here, since XLC seeks to counterbalance *compulsory* facets of schooling. Notwithstanding obligatory rules and some relative improvement in school retention,[22] a significant number of students still leave school every year before their Leaving Certificate. The ESRI's (Economic and Social Research Institute) report *No Way Back* (Byrne and Smyth, 2010) shows this total to be 9,000, equivalent to one in six students dropping out of school before the age of 18. Much higher levels are found among young people from working–class and unemployed households (ibid.). Lower stream classes are also much more likely to leave school early owing to their particular experience of low expectations and negative student-teacher interactions (ibid.). Worryingly, a recent Department of Education and Science report (Tickner, 2013) shows that in the 2009–10 school year, 4,300 students left school between first (12 years of age) and fourth year (16 years of age). While a number of these students may have emigrated or migrated to their birth countries or transferred to certain Youthreach/FÁS/SOLAS (employment-training) programmes, it still indicates how early students are quitting the system and how some continue to 'slip through the net'.

All of this points to the significance of projects such as XLC. Yet I can't help thinking about its real perception value. Does this project depict a hidden, inconvenient story? Does it suggest a malaise rather than a milieu, with those inside marked as curiosities? Nuala is cognisant of negative portrayals. In her private letters, she composes the acerbically apt 'An Apologia for Scumbags'. Teenagers, she writes, are frequently depicted "as moody, irresponsible, untrustworthy, rebellious, disliking their parents, into drugs and sex, a source of conflict . . ." If one were to say the same thing about 'the Irish', 'the blacks', 'working class people', 'Travellers', "there would be outrage." We ought to have moved from imposing conformity via the authority of power and status to "the authority of authenticity and truth [where] there is respect for the sacredness and diversity of the individual." The only way to nurture trustworthy young people, she writes, is to "trust them." A system so ethically informed is likely to "build up community, protect community, support community, strengthen community." And in 'belonging', one can internalise a sense of self-worth and, crucially, happiness:

> At the heart of community is the charter for happiness. Community cherishes you for being, not for doing.

However, within a competitive education system and marketised society 'belonging' is progressively contingent on the opposite. What of those that don't 'succeed' – those without the correct qualifications, those who don't attain high status? They are likely, Nuala writes, to find admiration, respect and affection among their peers (with positive and negative effects I might add). And "the respectable pillars of society" are likely to "fulminate against their behaviour." This same paradigm, she claims, locates the problem of the early school leaver with the child which, in turn, "informs the latest research and the failure of so many 'initiatives' to tackle the problem." Echoing Paulo Freire's political work (Freire, 1996), she dismisses an associative 'charity sentiment' that often sets up a *Them* and *Us* duality, in which *Us* 'saves' *Them* by inculcating *Us* values. This form of external oppression has its most potent and enduring sway over those who faithfully (even *fatefully*) internalise such values (ibid.).[23]

Nuala's writing points critically to the education *system*. She questions its class-based foundations (e.g. middle-class curriculum), its materialistic philosophy (e.g. points race), its inequitable structures (e.g. streaming), its authoritarian culture (e.g. discipline), its deficit policies (e.g. early school leaver initiatives) and its distorted spirituality (e.g. negative teacher-student relations). To what extent, I reflect, is *the system* perceived as a significant source of the problem of early school leavers?[24] I have to hand two research studies that may enlighten. Both of these employed XLC as a case study. The first examines the link between early school leavers and school culture (Greene, 2005), and the second looks at early school leavers' experience of teacher-student bullying and aggression (Meaney, 2011). Both highlight how student-teacher relationships play a key role in students' schooling experience.

Greene's study (2005, 8) cites Lynch and Lodge (2002) who stress the importance of giving students respect and a degree of responsibility in the running of a school. She finds that these experiences were afforded to students in the XLC project alongside efforts to sustain high (though realistic) levels of academic expectations that celebrate achievement[25] and circumvent de-motivation and disaffection. Inherent in Greene's (2005) study is a critique of streaming, even 'main-streaming', practices in schools. This is mirrored in Meaney's (2011) study. The latter (Meaney, 2011, 14) cites the first Irish longitudinal study into early school-leaving – the aforementioned ESRI study by Byrne and Smyth (2010) – which followed a cohort of approximately 1,000 students from first year to their completion of post-primary education. The research shows how a punitive school culture (e.g. suspension) not only alienates students but can actually trigger school departure, particularly among certain groups, for example, working-class males (Byrne and Smyth, 2010, 172, 180). Meaney's (2011) study also demonstrates how the widespread presence of school bullying can adversely affect *all* students (O'Moore *et al.*, 1997). Here, the author does not shy away from the perhaps least reported aspect of school bullying, namely that which may (in some cases) derive from teacher-student bullying and aggression.[26] In her focus group research with 11 XLC students, she demonstrates how the vast majority had positive relations with at least one teacher in their previous school. However, most of the students had experienced disrespect (e.g. 'being talked down to'), sarcasm (e.g. 'being made a show of'), anger (e.g. 'being shouted at'), and disregard (e.g. 'being ignored', as well as 'ignoring bullying by others').

I want to speak with the students myself; to meet Nuala, Eoin and Finola; to see XLC in action. Evoking childhood family trips, I make the familiar journey from Cork to Waterford. As I cross county borders, I stop for breakfast to indulge in an obligatory 'rasher blaa'[27] (or 'bacon bun'). Arriving at Dungarvan and with time to spare, I take the gentler 'copper coast' drive. So-named because of the tradition of copper mining in the area, this guides me through the pretty coastal villages of Stradbally, Bunmahon, Boatstrand, Annestown and Fenor. On a cold sunlit morning, the sea at Tramore still looks inviting. But I steer my way inland towards the conurbation of Waterford. There I discover the XLC Project, nestled inside old city walls that provide some shelter from the crisp January winds.

The elevator advances to the second floor of the Youth and Community Centre. There a long narrow corridor earmarks various chambers. I make my way towards the smaller of these and arrive at the administrative hub of XLC. Christine

Figure 2.2 The XLC Project, Edmund Rice Youth and Community Centre, Manor Street, Waterford

(an intern from the FÁS/SOLAS training and employment programme) is on the computer, tucked away in the corner. Dick (a volunteer and past pupil) is working on the attendance register. Books fill the side shelves and overflow on to the office desk where Eoin procures some space. He is finalising the list of students' subject choices for the Leaving Cert exam. Finola and a number of students drop in to supplement the gathering. The atmosphere is casual, familiar and relaxed.

In quieter moments, I talk to Eoin and Finola about their work. I ask them what distinguishes XLC from other schools. Eoin refers to their mother's pedagogical creed – "too much focus is put in schools on teaching and not enough on learning and how people learn best." They have long held in XLC that knowledge is more freely available than ever and can be more deeply engaged by learners by means of individual and/or cooperative approaches. Using the latest jargon, this *methodology* resembles 'flip teaching' where a type of reverse instruction cultivates the so-called 'flipped classroom'.[28] The other big difference is *discipline*. At the start of the school year, says Eoin, students are prone to doing "stupid school things" – "you know, they mess around, throw things, take the piss out of the teacher [. . .] it's a learned behaviour" (see Chapter 1). Finola pitches in. The two siblings and colleagues could finish each other's sentences if they had to. They sometimes think they're coming into "a really rough place and are soon surprised to find how friendly and nice and welcoming everyone is – the atmosphere is totally different." And, she states, "there are no stupid rules", just "those rules that are against the laws of Ireland are against the laws of the school." Like using drugs, she includes, or "murdering someone." "That's a good rule", Eoin adds playfully. There is of course a 'red line' that cannot be crossed, not least to protect from financial "vulnerability" and "poor image." Students too are consulted about regulations[29] and their sense of independence and autonomy is honoured. While the Junior Certificate students (14–15 years old) may need "more minding and structure", the intention is to create a more mature, responsible environment. Finola affirms:

> If they want to smoke, they can smoke as long as it's outside because that's what the law says. What frustrate our young people in school are things like: You can't have ear piercing;[30] you can't have tattoos; you can't wear this colour sock. Those rules at 14 and 15 really piss them off, whereas the important rules don't matter so much and are diluted by all of this.

The presence of older learners helps too. Since the recession, mature students in their twenties – many of whom had been in the building trade – are returning to secure educational qualifications. They make up a large part of the Friday group but there are a few in the main Leaving Cert cohort too. In my two months visiting XLC, I observe their positive influence on younger learners. They openly tell me that they have been given a 'second chance' and I witness how discerning they are about their own educational paths. I am struck too by how all the students appear comfortable with each other. Their differences appear to unite them. Some are older, into music, dress differently, have learning and health challenges, have varying academic expectations, are gay, have been bullies or were bullied, are from fractured homes, are 'who they are'. All seem happy to have found this school. When I ask Finola why this is so, she offers a little anecdote. "We had this student once", she recalls, "he was very moody when we interviewed him with his mother and mum [Nuala] just asked him, 'look do you want to come here?'" And it appeared that he didn't because he had "some fixed ideas about the place." Nevertheless, he took up the invitation to try out XLC for two days. After this trial, his mother rang to say that he now wanted to stay. When pressed for a reason she replied, "he was treated as a person." "Funny that", retorted Finola, "we thought he was a person."

It is not until my second visit that I get to meet Nuala. With characteristic warmth and candour, she regales me with numerous stories and events throughout her life as a teacher. I am struck by her generosity of time (two-and-a-half hours!), her knowledge of past pupils and her cultured reflections on her own learning trajectory. We talk about XLC's take on discipline. "It's important", she tells me, "to ignore what's going wrong and reward what's going right." This doesn't mean that bad behaviour is always neglected. She can, as I witnessed, admonish students for being discourteous or for talking to others when the teacher is addressing them. "That's just common-sense and good manners", she would say. But it is also indicative of her values as a mother and a traditional teacher. Complementing these values, for they need not conflict, is a more progressive disposition that aims to have students "on our side." Students can openly and respectfully question Nuala's views and actions. This is something they learn in XLC, she adds, since schools do not allow for this greater equalisation of power relations. She acknowledges that schools may have some student disciplinary problems, such as those famously highlighted in a Teachers Union of Ireland report (TUI, 2006). But she objects to the fact that not one child who left school or one parent of such a child was consulted in this report's preparation. Nor was there any reference to teacher bullying in its substance. I posit that there are many features of XLC that set it aside from 'mainstream' schools and permit greater student association. "Yes, we play pool here", she states, "students don't have homework, they don't have uniforms and they don't have sanctions or reports." "We talk to the child about coming here", she adds, and attendance is regular,[31] without being 'officially' compulsory. All of which suggests a radical schooling departure. But Nuala insists that there are many invaluable lessons that mainstream schools could take on board from XLC. Echoing Finola's earlier position, she believes that the real reason for students' connection is their *personal* treatment. In an oblique reference to Procrustes,[32] she exhorts greater emphasis on *the system fitting the individual*, rather than the (obligatory) individual fitting the system:

> I have always said that the reason they're leaving schools is because they don't like school and instead of trying to change them, you know fit them into the bed, you need to look at the school. Ask the child what it is they don't like about school [. . .] make schools work for them.

I see fifth year (17 years old) students in voluntary attendance. They choose to remain post Junior Certificate, despite the fact that XLC cannot cater for them. Instead of returning to their previous schools, they prefer to help out here, socialise and initiate their own Leaving Certificate study. I am struck by this strong sense of belonging. Nuala reminds me that this is a community where "we expect all to help one another, if they so need." In opposition to "materialist schools", XLC's ethos is imbued with a Christianity that "has nothing to do with going to mass [church] but with helping one another." Pedagogical relations are thus shaped. "We often say to the students", Nuala explains, to "go and teach the others." Analogous to Rousseau's[33] philosophy, there is a belief in the child and his/her ability to identify learning needs – "whatever you tell me, we believe you." But there remains a spiritual role for adults to model cooperative, mentor-type relations. This ethic of reciprocity appears to me to reflect the Christian dictum 'do to others as you would have them do to you' (Matthew 7:12; Luke 6:31). It is also a practical matter, owing to teacher-pupil ratio and broad-based curriculum concerns. Moreover, Nuala alludes to features of Celtic spirituality that shape pedagogical relations in XLC.[34] I reflect again on how the person of the teacher is never too far from the person of the learner.

Throughout my time in XLC, I observe these pedagogical relations both inside and outside the classroom. But the exacting focus on *exams* has me wrestling with my own educational principles. I understand Eoin when he tells me that XLC is about getting the exam for "anyone who doesn't like school." It is of course a real-life concern for those students[35] and there is a strong care ethic involved in providing such practical opportunities. Undoubtedly, if kept in check, exams may offer students their own degree of motivation and achievement. And if there's a greater suite of subject choice (as there is in XLC), then students may sit an exam that is actually of personal interest to them. But there are some real (and 'unreal') practices that trouble, even rankle, educational sensibilities. One such practice involves the ritual of predicting exam questions. Eoin tells me that he keeps a map of "nearly every topic in every subject that has come up over the years." While predictions are not always reliable, they serve as an aid to students' exam preparation and they are well received. The rhythm of time too is commanded by exams, with intense periods of instruction being planned before deadlines. "The last 3 weeks", Eoin tells me, "will make or break you." And this is the time to even consider, incredibly, *new* subjects. This is strategically designed to help certain students who may be in danger of not 'crossing the line'. Indeed, subjects are sometimes chosen on the grounds that they are more likely to be 'passed'. In music class, I talk to two students who (unlike some of their peers) have no musical background and are not particularly interested in the subject. When asked why it is they chose the subject, one replied "it's school isn't it, we have to do something." While such exam practices trouble me as an educationalist, I do not wish, nor is it my place, to judge. I recognise that there is huge commitment involved in supporting these marginalised students within a concise school year. And XLC doesn't exist in a bubble, since an 'outcomes-based' system envelops all schools' practices and is widely culturally accepted (O'Brien, 2013).

To what extent, then, is XLC just another 'grind school' – that is, a school that grinds/distils[36] the curriculum to harvest best results? Nuala, Eoin and Finola do not contest the title. "Aren't all schools grind schools?", asks Nuala. "For a doctor's son or daughter", she continues, "exams matter"; "and for our students, exams help them on to the next stage of life." I suspect that there's more going on than just grinding out results. Eoin alludes to the context once more, stating that "the Leaving Cert is like a bottleneck, a measure of respectability in some ways."[37] One may not need the exam to perform in life and work but it appears as an appraisal of what society expects of you. One senses a need to 'use the system in order to fight the system'. It's clear in XLC that students are empowered to build up their knowledge slowly, to experience success. As far as possible, Nuala uses 'their' language to access 'official' curricular forms. And there is a genuine desire to develop students' self-concept. Yet the Leaving Cert, she openly evaluates, "will have no part in your life again." What will remain, she insists, are "the friendships you have, the sort of person you are." Students are reminded of these higher measures of 'success'. Before class each day, Nuala inscribes them on the board:

> Make a good home
> Do something you like as a job
> Raise tranquil children.

They are admirable parameters of success. But they are also vulnerable. For all their wisdom they can so easily become subjugated by a default 'exams' position. Such a position oversees the import of subject content and grade criteria that can, ultimately, desensitise the personal nature of learning.

There is a strong appreciation that not all learners learn at the same rate, at the same time or in the same way(s). This sets XLC in opposition to mainstream, stand-ardised practices. I imagine that ideal scenario where students personally choose their subjects – ones they are actually interested in. In adult education, this would be upheld as sound methodological practice (see Chapter 4). Is this the same for schools? I witness during class time a focus on both independent work and peer support in XLC. Teachers do whatever they can to help learners and desist, in the words of Eoin, from "giving out all the time and chasing students for work." In assessing their efforts, teachers focus on positive aspects, while highlighting areas in need of further development. Students too are encouraged to self-assess. This appears to mirror an *Assessment for Learning* (AfL) approach, as championed by the National Council for Curriculum and Assessment (NCCA). But while they may instinctively (and faithfully) practise this approach, neither Nuala, Eoin nor Finola are aware of its 'official' endorsement. This highlights their distance from 'official' support structures (and vice versa), which prompts me to wonder how much XLC would gain, *as well as lose*, from greater systemic cooperation. What *is* clear is that there is strong personal commitment to one's work in XLC. Teachers' personalities are pervasive and they are especially sensitive to the needs of their non-traditional student cohort. Further, a strong self-awareness is evident that goes *beyond* the parameters of a 'professional code'. Finola demonstrates this well when referring to teacher-student relations:

> Sometimes it can be the teacher who has the issue, not the student. If so, that teacher needs to 'cop the fuck on'. I know myself[38] that I can be very harsh but at the same time if I'm out of step, I'll come back and apologise.

Strength of character follows through to one's teaching. Resources are personally crafted, lessons are directed to challenge students' viewpoints, and the teachers are keen to present themselves as culturally relevant (e.g. use of Facebook, contem-porary and interactive materials).

Nuala concurs that "we all have different teaching styles." And that she is quite traditional, since she makes frequent use of rote learning and repetition.[39] I witness students responding well to this in class and wonder why they may not have done so in their previous school. It is most curious. It must, I conclude, point to the power of student-teacher relations which may be a more compelling force than methodology. Of course the latter is complementary, for example, small class sizes, literacy and peer supports, error-tolerant classrooms, no streaming or 'ghettos', etc. But it is the very person of the teacher that significantly matters. I recall John McGahern's (1934–2006) reflections on his own important relations in life. In his *Memoir* (McGahern, 2006), the eminent writer recounts the positive influence of his mother, who was his educator and spiritual guide; a thoughtful schoolteacher who visited his home and advocated for his pursuit of higher study; and a kindly eccentric neighbour who offered full access to a library's treasures. Each was instrumental in breaking down learning boundaries, normally fixed at the school's gates. Each presented as role models and understood the value young people place upon their adult relations. Each understood the power of curiosity and the desire to know for and about oneself. A good teacher, I reflect, enables such relations. And a good teacher is good to students. "Students nearly won't learn for someone they don't like", adds Nuala. It's as though they instinctively know if you are 'fighting their corner' and "want them to reach their potential." It helps too to present as "human", to show students that "we don't have a clue sometimes" and to encourage *them* to "have a go." While "we don't agree with [the notion of] stupidity", says Nuala, we tell them that "your ignorance is ultimately your responsibility." Crucially, one doesn't rely on the teacher for one to know. Too often, she remarks, school students "think it's the teacher's job for you to know." How learning dependent is this arrangement, I consider. And how limiting is its conception of student-teacher relations.

Throughout my time in XLC, I witness the informal curriculum at work. I often hang around the pool room where the students go to socialise at break times.

Figure 2.3 The Pool Room

There, I learn of the importance of Eoin's pool competition. Everyone in the school is obliged to 'give it a go' and there are 'doubles' events that attempt to balance ability levels. Eoin, a quiet, gentle man, becomes mischievously animated by the competitive spirit that these games induce. There are other opportunities for students to engage in informal learning, such as the occasional visit to the theatre and the National Heritage Park. Resources are limited though and students are asked to save some money well in advance. Each year the staff, with the help of Michelle and Clodagh, organise choir events for the students. At lunchtimes, it not unusual for most members of the Jackson family ('The Jackson 5') to meet in the staffroom. Such occasions are filled with news about school events. And there is plenty of time devoted to students' personal stories. Conversations are easy and relaxed and allow teachers to openly share their feelings. Sometimes they offer an opportunity to 'let off steam', garner group guidance and take the time to laugh. But they are also occasions to learn more about individuals, their issues, concerns and interests. And ultimately they provide a nurturing space for both student and teacher.

The impact of XLC

Becoming a teenager may not be all about 'storm and stress', as first typecast by Granville Stanley Hall[40] in 1904. But it is a time of significant psycho-social and identity development (Erikson, 1968). At this stage young people seek to become more independent in their thoughts and actions. At the same time, they feel a strong need to 'fit in', with family and (increasingly) friends forming strong bonds of affiliation. While many can be incubated from full adulthood, some are thrust into mature roles early, particularly by conditions of insecurity, for example, bereavement, parental separation, bullying, addiction, migration, peer pressure, etc. This causes them to seriously question their own sense of morality and identity. Progressively, and naturally, young people seek judgements about their own actions ('what do I want to do?') in opposition to others' opinions ('do what you are told'). And these judgements are made in the context of an everyday culture that is no longer 'norms-regulated', but 'preference-related' – that is, within a culture that is "oriented towards personal preferences and sensitivity" (Ziehe, 2009, 187). This brings with it both "an increase in liberation" and "a more demanding strain on orientation" (ibid.). While teenagers cope with such (post)modern tensions, their choices are *not* of their own making. Rather than viewing teenagers as mere individuals or conscious subjects, Michel Foucault reminds that we are all at least partially *subjected*, that is, we are subject, via social and power relations, to productive conditions of possibilities and constraints (Foucault, 1977; 1991). To illustrate, Fran Abrams (2010) writes about those who 'learn to fail' in school and demonstrates 'how society lets [them] down'. Specifically, she exemplifies how one's geographical location, socio-economic status, class/racial/gender profile, health and employment opportunities and relational milieus will inevitably (and differentially) affect one's educational aspirations and prospects (ibid.).

It is troubling to acknowledge these uneven educational chances (Bourdieu, 1977; 1988). It is troubling to identify strong links between poverty, low educational attainment and early school leaving (Byrne and Smyth, 2010). And it is troubling to observe numerous reports' findings that demonstrate how wider societal concerns continue to negatively affect children's education; for example, a significant minority of Irish primary school children lack sleep and basic nutrition (Eivers and Clerkin, 2013), a record number of families are now seeking help from charity organisations (Boland, 2013) and bullying is increasing in Irish schools (UNICEF, 2013). Schools alone cannot solve these problems, though they are frequently treated as 'the wastebasket of society' (Halsey *et al.*, 1980). Yet they can and do make a difference – *if* supported to do so. Crucial supports include sufficient state investment[41] and professional provision.[42] Both have a direct impact on children's educational potential. At the same time, there is responsibility on the part of schools and teachers to stay culturally connected with young people. And there are resources there to help: for example, the *Growing up in Ireland report;*[43] *State of the nation's children* (2008),[44] *The Irish health behaviour in school-aged children* (2010),[45] and *Dealing with bullying in schools* (2012).[46] Academics have also contributed to a better understanding of 'well-being' (O'Brien, 2008; O'Moore and Stevens, 2013), including children's understandings of this concept (Nic Gabhainn and Sixsmith, 2005). And they have instituted centres for supporting school children in their personal and emotional development (e.g. Anti-Bullying Centre at Trinity College Dublin). The Irish government has responded by producing school guidelines for mental health promotion and suicide prevention (2013) and an action plan on bullying (2013).[47] The positive message from these and other more popular texts (Bazelon, 2013) is that children's well-being matters and must be sustained.

While this message is encouraging, I wonder about its true impact. Well-being is not deeply understood and is often referred to in conceptual, abstract terms. There is also a sense that one has to experience well-being and/or be strongly empathetic in order to appreciate its essence. So when reports are presented that speak of others' well-being, how much of this is really sensed/felt by the reader? And what does it mean to those whose well-being is the focus of these reports? What does it mean to be statistically significant? To be spoken about in aggregates? Likewise, policy-oriented approaches to well-being can, paradoxically, desensitise 'the personal'. Besides, if there are no complementary efforts to truly transform school culture, then perhaps 'the media is [ultimately] the message' (Baudrillard,[48] 1994). I feel the need to resuscitate the *person*. So I conclude my visits by talking to some parents and students, both past and present. I specifically ask them about their experiences of XLC.

Linda (a pseudonym[49]) is the mother of Joy, a Junior Certificate student (15 years old) who recently joined the school. Joy was diagnosed with dyspraxia and she also has speech and language difficulties. Over the years, her mother has been served up a smörgåsbord of professional advice from psychiatrists, psychologists, neurologists, occupational therapists and educational psychologists. Deep down, she and her husband always believed that Joy could attend a mainstream school.

They garnered hope from positive signs. Joy responded well to her primary school SNA (Special Needs Assistant) who understood that she "wasn't good at auditory processing", that she was a 'doer', someone who liked visual and sensory learning. But anxiety and challenge were never far away. Not all teachers personalised the learning experience. Linda too observed her daughter growing up with others. While Joy was certainly liked – she has a sweet smile and a kind heart – she always found it tough to socially integrate. Touchingly, Linda tells of her "heartbreak as a mother" to observe how hard it is for her daughter to become "long-term friends" with someone, to witness school outings where she would be that child who sits alone on the bus. She simply had to help her more, both socially and educationally. Her enrolment on a SNA course would not only inaugurate new relations with her daughter, it would mark the start of *her own* personal learning.

The first lesson was the realisation that special needs demand a "special role for a special kind of person." Linda could see that some were more suited than others. She wanted to know more about their qualities. So she decides to enrol on extra courses that engage brain coordination and integrated energy therapies. And she finds herself changing. She acknowledges Joy as the architect and catalyst for this change:

> I used to be pragmatic, much more 'black and white' and 'it either works or it doesn't', you know. I just wouldn't have looked at the 'grey area'. I suppose I learned that the world is different. I learned a lot about Eastern culture and how they look at things and I learned about the education system and how it works from the inside. I was learning about learning . . .

This newfound knowledge leads her to volunteering, and eventually working part-time, in adult literacy. In the meantime, her commitment to Joy's learning is spurred on by her increased competency. She feels more in control, that is, until one day (during Joy's final year of her Junior Certificate) she is summoned to the principal's office. She is told that the school can no longer cater for Joy's learning needs and that alternative arrangements should be explored. The news is sudden and startling. Shock soon gives way to anxiety. Joy has been bullied for some time. This is relayed to Linda by a parent whose daughter receives a text from Joy. It reads: 'I'm scared to go back to school'. A mother now confides in her child:

> Joy, you'll never put that uniform on you again. So you need not ever worry. Nothing will ever harm you. That's it.

Beyond embitterment,[50] the primary emotion is relief. But what next?

They hear of the work of XLC and Linda decides to ring Nuala. She is nervous; after all, her daughter's schooling is at stake.[51] Nuala listens while Linda asks if she could be sent some XLC manuals. "What manuals?", dismisses Nuala. Linda then asks if Nuala wants to see any psychological reports on Joy. "I don't want to see any of those reports" is the rejoinder. "Look, you come down here on Monday morning, you and your daughter – what's your daughter's name?" Linda still likes the fact that Nuala was never interested in her own forename. And she recalls with some attachment how the conversation ended – "we'll help you." Up to that point, she poignantly adds, "nobody had said they'd help me." In her eyes, Nuala is a "non-conformist", a "saint offering hope." And Joy is a beneficiary of this hope. She has friends that now accept her; and she is happy:

> She's walking taller. You know this kind of shoulder thing – I didn't notice it until it was gone. I didn't notice that she was caught in the shoulders until I saw her walking more upright in the world. It's as if she's saying 'I have a place I belong to now and I'm happy' . . .

Even though XLC was full to capacity, Joy was welcomed. She attends twice a week – Monday and Thursday. Linda comes along for one of those days and is accepted as a tutor. She too has integrated well into the school community. And XLC is happy to facilitate Joy's personal learning plan, both in and out of school (she has home-school tuition for the other days of the week). This contrasts sharply with her former school's position. Linda recalls the words of the school principal upon that final meeting:

> You know we did talk before about the option of a special school. I don't feel that Joy will be able to achieve her Junior Cert.

Linda had thought to herself then, "no she can achieve her Junior Cert." And she thinks now, "what's the worst thing that could happen anyway?" In reply, she echoes Nuala's stock phrase: "All you can do is fail." However, when the Junior Certificate results are finally announced, Joy attains worthy honours in all her subjects. And Linda contemplates sending the proof to all those who helped Joy, as well as to a sceptical principal.

I speak with another parent Margaret whose daughter Claire had previously attended XLC.[52] Margaret has a longstanding public role in Waterford city that qualifies her to comment on the project's civic impact. She had been involved in the Waterford Area Partnership that part-funded XLC in its foundational year. She knows how Nuala has "run the place for so long on so little." And she has always identified XLC's primary role as "getting kids over a big hump in their lives." Little did she know that, one day, she would personally petition the school to fulfil this primary role. Claire had been attending an all-girls' Catholic school. She was always studious and "never got so much as a detention." Then on the night of her seventeenth birthday she became pregnant. When she eventually told her mother, she was very upset – "she was roaring crying and couldn't stop hugging me." There and then they resolved to work through it together, to support one another. "At face value", Margaret recalls, "the school was good." But, in hindsight, good wasn't good enough since "they [really] needed to be proactive." A parent, she explains, has an instinct for these things and "they just weren't authentic."

Teachers "never really went the extra mile", she adds, and some "could not hide their disdain for a pregnant 17 year old." At the very best, the situation was dealt with insensitively, as exemplified by the words of the deputy principal to Claire: "Are you ready for all this – up all night with sore boobs?" Mother and daughter soon observed the school rules coming "thick and fast." The head of year pointed out problems with Claire's uniform as the bump appeared more prominently. Homework was more and more demanded. And 'the last straw' came when Claire's phone was confiscated (she being a mother at this stage). The *rigidity* of the institution was clearly exposed:

> One of the issues with mainstream schooling is that it doesn't cater for the individual. Schools can't do that and they won't do that. They cannot bend and teachers cannot have real relationships with the students.

Its *care*-lessness too was revealed. After five-and-a-half years in the same school, Claire is told that she cannot go to her Debs.[53] The reason for refusal is given: You "didn't finish out the year."

Claire's final schooldays are spent in XLC. Margaret recalls how "everything seemed to ease up for her at this time." There was no uniform, no homework, "no stupid rules about make-up and phones." And Claire was "treated like the adult that she had to become." Margaret describes Nuala as "fearless", "a round peg that can't fit into a square hole." This has its advantages as XLC "enables relationships" to take primary root.[54] But, Margaret concedes, Nuala can be "her own worst enemy" since she is "unbending" to a system that doesn't *really* share the same values. While all schools "have the policy" around care, she adds, this doesn't mean that they themselves 'care'. To what extent, I ask, is this critique of mainstream schooling widely recognised? Her response is both spirited and measured:

> I don't think the critique of mainstream is mainstream! Here is Nuala fighting her corner, but who interacts with Nuala day-to-day? Nuala's problem is that what she does is difficult to measure; she doesn't fit the Department of Education's categorisation.

The resoluteness of early school leavers is also not widely recognised. Margaret pays tribute to the students of XLC, many of whom "are brave to leave the system." But she is keen to stress that this is a journey that cannot be undertaken alone. In Claire's case, "she didn't know she could leave school until Nuala told her she could." XLC also enabled Claire to become more "personally empowered", "confident" and "academically prepared for third level [education]." She is now in university and enjoys her chosen discipline. While her newfound roles as student and mother are not without their challenges, Claire remains steadfast. She works 8–9 hours a day each weekend as a waitress and hopes to soon find a place of her own. And she is moving on from older school experiences – glad that she didn't finish out that year.

I speak with John, another past pupil of XLC.[55] At 16, he was suspended from Nuala's old school. Nuala had been one of his teachers then and he describes her as "pro-students", not one of those who would always be "dogging [aggravating] you." She gave the "bones of a year" of her own time to support him while he was planning his exit from the system. And when she set up her own school, he was encouraged to join the maiden class of '98. He fondly recalls Nuala's use of song and rhyme in history, geography and religion and how if there was any disagreement, "five minutes later it was all forgotten about." He speaks candidly of Nuala's personal influence – "if it wasn't for her, I wouldn't have my own business now." It was she, he elaborates, who made him recognise his strengths. It was she who enabled him to reclassify past 'failures' and ascribe these to his undiagnosed dyslexia and to a system that insisted that he learn in a particular way (e.g. "I hated having to read in class"). And it was Nuala who showed him how to be "positive, ambitious and happy." "I needed that alright", he reveals in his own diffident manner. I meet another student whose story somewhat resonates. After leaving school early (at 14 years), Liam returned to XLC as a mature Leaving Certificate student (at 21 years). While the leave-taking was not of his making (he was expelled), there is no resentment shown to his old school:

> You see I had ADHD (Attention Deficit Hyperactivity Disorder) but I didn't know it. I think I was too hard for them to handle up there. I was in trouble a lot. I was 'hyper' in the classroom, in the corridors, the whole lot . . .

In truth, Liam had already encountered changeable, unstable events in his young life. His parents separated when he was 9 years of age. For the following three years, he lived with his mother and siblings before moving in with his father and partner. He recalls how his dad always tried to help him with homework, even when he was expelled from school. Subsequently, Liam stayed at home for two years. It was, he confides, a "hard time" in his life:

> I wanted to go back to school because I didn't want to be sitting around doing nothing, waiting for everyone else.

At 16, he moved back to his mother's house and enrolled on a FETAC (Further Education and Training Awards Council) level 3 course. This enabled him to achieve the equivalent of a Junior Certificate qualification. He evokes the crafts' subjects, in particular stained glass production, as the highlight of the course. A blend of vocational and academic subjects seemed to suit him and he wanted to stay on and do a higher level course. However, under the FETAC 2-year maximum attendance rule, he was obliged to leave school for a second time. At this point, he resolves to find work and so enrols on a number of FÁS/SOLAS (training and employment) programmes, including welding, core employment skills (such as carpentry, brick paving, etc.), advanced welding and general engineering. During this time the economy, particularly the construction industry, collapses. Despite recessionary conditions, he moves into his own apartment (aged 19 years). The move appears to be as much a class-based decision as an independent turn, since he "didn't want to be a burden on his mother and brothers and sisters." After "a lonely start" he learns "how to shop" for himself and "stand on [his] own feet." When he eventually finds out about XLC, he saves up all his money "in case [he has] to pay for it."

This is Liam's 'third chance' of receiving a more complete education. His resolve in surmounting barriers to participation is inspiring. Undoubtedly, this springs from Liam's character – who *he* is as a person. But there are others there who elevate him. There's his girlfriend who "gave him the encouragement to come back to school." She's studying childcare in university and is clearly a positive influence in his life. Liam expects to join her there and study electrical engineering. Failing that he has a plan B: Construction technology. A mature approach to his educational path has a lot to do with personal experience. But it also owes itself to progressive relations in XLC. It is a system of education that suits Liam and enables him to 'fit in'. He tells me that "you can be yourself here" and that "time flies when there's a bit of fun in learning." He doesn't miss a day of school. I witness him on one occasion admonishing his younger peers for not paying more attention in class. They listen to him. He speaks fondly of Nuala, Eoin and Finola and emphasises how helpful they are whenever he feels "confused" or needs them to "explain things properly." And they are willing to talk through his future with him and give him "personal time." Liam is mindful that those closest to him – he names his girlfriend, mum, Nuala, Eoin and Finola – will all be delighted if he succeeds. And he's out too to "prove that I can do something." He even highlights the impact of this success on his prospective children. Certainly, he would "advise them to stay in school." But he would prefer "a softer approach" to schooling for his kids, with encouragement not "force" to the fore. And he wants them to "follow their interests." It isn't hard to see Nuala's words of 'success' spiritually inscribed:

> Make a good home
> Do something you like as a job
> Raise tranquil children.

I'm nearing the end of my research journey when I meet Grace. The softly spoken 16 year old approaches me and asks if I might tell her story. Her experiences, she explains, might help other kids who read the book, since "no one understands what bullying is and it's good to talk about it." Touched by her kind-hearted spirit, I agree on one condition – it is told in her own words.[56] They don't make for easy reading:

> It happened really at the start of first year, two months in. It was horrible. I had books stolen from me; my PE (Physical Education) gear was stolen; my runners; calculators and they're 15 euro each you know. We didn't have money to be buying more books. It was 400 euro alone to get books and

they were stolen from me. It started with name calling and it didn't really hurt me at first because I was 'look I'm bigger than this, I can get through this.' Then I remember one day mum came into me and said 'c'mon up for school' and I just turned over. I said 'I'm not going to school' and then I remember going on the bus but I didn't go to school. I just stayed on the bus for ages until I got off at a different stop. Like I was so unhappy with myself and unhappy with life and unhappy with the world, you know. I was mad with everything. As soon as I went home I was abused on MSN and Facebook and I couldn't even go to the bus stop without getting 'a dig'. One time I actually went to the bus stop and a girl came down and I knew that she was going to do something. I said 'what do I do here'? Do I cross the road or do I just stay where I am? Do I, you know, 'man up' here and just, you know? But she spat her sweets at me. She had them in her mouth and she just spat them all over me and they were caught in my hair and that really did it for me then. [After two-and-a-half years] I was forced to leave that school, you know, because the bullying got so bad and the bullies are always protected. Nothing ever happens to them. It's always the victim like. I had to go. I was forced to go. I don't mind, like I wanted to get a good education but I'm not going to stay somewhere where I'm not happy and you know, I got so down. I got so skinny. I didn't eat and I thought my life was so bad that I overdosed and I was in hospital for a week. I remember that day. I just got 50 tablets and I went up to my room with a pint of water and I downed every single one of them.

I had to go to the hospital. It was that bad that I just didn't think that any one liked me. Like, I'd no friends. I had no one to talk to. There was no one. It was hard to talk to mum as well because she was an alcoholic and I don't . . . like me and my dad we're like a light switch with our relationship. It was a cry for help. But when I was getting the tablets I was like 'seriously I want to go.' I just wanted to die. I have no one in my life. I had no friends and I come home and mum was drinking and I get given out to for everything and dad didn't care about me. I just came home every day and I just cried myself to sleep and I didn't eat. I got so [pause], I'm sorry it's so horrible . . .

We stop and let the tears out. When I read these words again I can still picture and feel Grace's hurt that day. But she lives with it constantly.

In reflective mood, I return to Milan Kundera's (1979) masterwork *The Book of Laughter and Forgetting*. The novel centres on the concepts of memory and forgetfulness. It begins with the tale of two Czech communist leaders, Klement Gottwald and Vlado Clementis. From the balcony of a baroque palace in Prague's Old Town Square, the former addresses a rally and is flanked by the latter. It is a bitterly cold day and Clementis thoughtfully places his fur hat on his comrade's bare head. Thousands of pictures of the balcony scene are produced and distributed on posters, in schoolbooks and museums. Four years later Clementis falls out of favour with the regime and is hanged for treason. Thereafter the balcony scene is re-circulated, this time with no Clementis on view. All that remains of him is the fur hat on Gottwald's head. Kundera's book powerfully reminds how culture, history, even people can be destroyed if memory is removed. Of course, totalitarian regimes have a particular politico-ideological interest in pressing 'forgetfulness', to the point where any resistance necessitates both the preservation and control of one's memory.[57] In extraordinary circumstances, such as surviving the holocaust, memory becomes central to self-identity and self-empowerment. However painful and burdensome, memory is shown here to be fundamental to one's humanity (Frankl, 1984, 2011; Levi, 1987). Even in more ordinary circumstances, it may be attractive to think that one can fully release one's psyche of any disharmony (such as in Freudian analysis). But selfhood is more likely to always be insecure, incomplete and in-transit (Lacan, 1977). In this normal state of flux, memory is both conserved and regulated, not least to censure the present and even guide the future. In such a way, the assemblage of memory presents important lessons for humanity.[58] Failure to learn from these lessons is likely to lead to a failure of social and individual human rights. As if to remind, at the time of writing, a *Prime Time* [television programme] investigation exposed incidences of physical and psychological abuse in a number of Irish crèches (28 May 2013). Close to 1,400 children were abused over a sixteen-year period in Rotherham, England (1997–2013). A well-established Swedish school had been shut down due to bullying (28 August 2013). Thousands of Syrian people were killed in a chemical weapons attack (21 August 2013). And somewhere else spiritual vigilance ceded to *more memory loss*.

In light of the above, it is worth reconsidering the significance of Grace's request to tell her story. It is, I believe, a request to keep alive her memory. In reviving memory, an edifying[59] array of humanist values is revealed. Selflessly, this act fortifies others who may be in danger of being written out of history. And it empowers Grace who could easily be written out of *her own* history. Self-empowerment is not easy though and I witness her *personally* wrestle with preserving and forgetting memory:

- I don't think anyone knows the real meaning of the word bullying because they didn't think they were bullying me, like I'm shaking just thinking about it now [. . .] There are kids up in that school now who are getting bullied and in any school and nothing is being done about it.
- I'm just sick of being down and stressing about things and worrying about everything and I need to stop thinking about the past and the future – just don't think about tomorrow or the next day or next month or next year. Just don't think about it. Just live in the moment and get on with that . . .
- I've been to America and I've always wanted to go to America to live. There it's like blue skies and I think a blue sky is positive, you know, it's lovely and everyone is happier when it's sunny and everyone is so outgoing. They're so chatty and they're so positive . . .

Old and new memories naturally converge in Grace's spiritual journey. It takes strength and resilience of character to control these, while she is helped along the way. I attend to the supportive voice of her counsellor through Grace's words of 'positivity' and her yearning to become a therapist one day. I attend to the warmth of her renewed relations with her mum, with whom she unconditionally shares her life. And I attend to the relational bonds Grace has made in XLC. Here, students and teachers are respectful of Grace's personal history and where she is now on her life journey. In her previous school, she was constantly checking herself ("you never feel good enough"), whereas now she *is* more herself – "isn't life too short to be anybody else?" There is more "confidence" about her which helps her to academically achieve all over again. She "speaks [her] mind" and defends 'de Manor' (as XLC is colloquially known) to all those who ill judge. And while guilt still shadows her, she is resolved to make the most out of life. For now, the blue skies of Florida are replaced by a hazier Waterford. But this is where Nuala, Eoin and Finola "put a smile on my face every time I think of them." And if happiness is taken seriously as a goal of education (Noddings, 2004), then this is not a bad place to be.

The sun sets on Tramore Bay on my final return from XLC. Now and then I reflect on my own personal learning. I realise that I never fully understood the spiritual role of a teacher, mentor or parent. Nor did I fully recognise education as a spiritual activity. I am now, I hope, more aware of the *soulful* needs of the

Figure 2.4 The 'Jackson 5' (from left to right: Michelle, Clodagh, Finola, Eoin and, in front, Nuala)

child and the ways in which these can be sustained by keeping memory alive, being more attentive, acting more justly, enabling potential, fostering curiosity and engendering happiness. Spirituality refers to 'a way of being' that transcends religious and cultural borders (Schoonmaker, 2009). And spirituality transcends rational functions to centre on the person of the teacher and the person of the learner, and their positional role in a more just world. Those who practise care in schools, I suggest, are mindful of such transcendence. And in schools that care, pedagogical relations are shaped by a type of transcendence that cultivates deep awareness of one's self and others.[60] This attentiveness to the person, like philosophy itself, doesn't come easy and demands constant 'spiritual exercise' (Hadot, 1995). Nowhere is this more apparent than in schools where, year-on-year, teachers mature and pupils stay young. Relational work – knowing one's self and others – is always in flux and demands time, energy and character commitment. Yet for all its challenges, relational work enriches. After all, this is where the spirit of personal learning excels.

Guiding research (notes)

1 The biographical descriptions that follow are sourced from this woman's personal writings, where I was afforded free and open access. This opened channels to her inner thoughts, though of course I do not profess to fully know these. In the interest of reciprocity, this woman had free and open access to my analysis (as outlined here).

2 Forbidding institutional practices are highlighted in the extreme by the recent cases of child abuse in industrial schools and religious orders. In Ireland, the Ryan Report (2009) and Murphy Reports (2009, 2010) record the shocking maltreatment of children in Church and State care.

3 What may not resonate is Nietzsche's (1883) belief that 'God is dead' – though Nuala's description of those places responsible for appalling child abuse (she refers to them as 'Godless institutions') points to some (recurring) stages of history where we may have indeed, as Nietzsche famously claimed, 'killed Him' (Nietzsche, 1882).

4 Socrates is recorded as stating that "the unexamined life is not worth living for a human being" (in Plato's Apology, 38a).

5 Dylan Thomas is reputed to have written this poem while his father was dying. It highlights the deep love and grief felt by a son as he implores his father to fight imminent death: "Do not go gentle into that good night; Old age should burn and rave at close of day; Rage, rage against the dying of the light."

6 Of course there may be a deeper message behind the title *Whoopee!! I'm going to die!* Following the Epicureans, the title may convey the view that one ought to live each day as if it were one's last, as if to say 'I have lived!' or 'my life is over!' (Hadot, 1995).

7 The first and third verses of 'Michelling and Spelling' appear here (all 3 verses are available in Jackson, 2011, 42, 43).

8 Pierre Hadot (1995) argues that philosophy is more about spiritual exercises than it is about some devotion to any particular position, that is, philosophy is *practised* over-and-above it being espoused. I am grateful to my colleague Fiachra Long for introducing me to Hadot's work.

9 This strongly mirrors an Aristotelian position. Aristotle believed that the flourishing of an organism was an important end in itself. One's bios (or 'way of life') flourishes in concert with social (and *soulful*) relations (e.g. *Nicomachean Ethics*, Book 8).

10 In her personal writing, Nuala notes: "To be true of itself community should embrace all its members. To the extent that it oppresses or exploits any of its members (e.g. women,

minorities, old, ill, young), it moves from an experience of community to an experience of *system* (my emphasis). The more a community cherishes the individual the more complete an experience of community it is. If the functioning of the community is put before the needs of the individual, it stops being community and becomes *institute* (my emphasis)."

11 I am reminded here of Mary Rose O'Reilly's words: "One can, I think, listen someone into existence, encourage a stronger self to emerge or a new talent to flourish. Good teachers listen this way, as do terrific grandfathers and similar heroes of the spirit. Teaching has much in common with the ancient art of spiritual guidance" (quoted in Miller, 2009, 2705).

12 Father Harry Bohan is Chairperson of the Céifin Centre (named after the Celtic goddess of inspiration, Ceidhfionn), an organisation that encourages rural communities across Ireland to determine their own future. Based on strong community values, the organisation enables young families to stay in their localities while supporting them to access new housing and cheaper credit.

13 Father Peter McVerry works with homeless children and young people in inner city Dublin. He has opened a number of hostels and residential drug care programmes and continues to campaign on their behalf. He believes that the education system is hugely divisive, with marginalised populations disproportionately suffering from its effects.

14 Dr Scott Boldt is director of the Reconciliation Programme in Edgehill Theological College in Belfast. He works directly with ex-combatants, church and community leaders, and people who have been marginalised to create opportunities for relationships and transformation in Northern Ireland.

15 Mark Patrick Hederman is Abbot of Glenstal Abbey, County Limerick, Ireland. In a recent address to the IPPN (Irish Primary Principals' Network) Conference (25 January 2013, 1) he asserts: "Education should be the art of cultivating the emotional, physical, psychological and spiritual dimensions of the developing child. Anything less than this is a betrayal of our trust, their trust in us. Every child is more than a future employee; every person's intelligence and abilities are far more complex than his or her scores on standardized tests."

16 It's important to put 'positive change' in context here. Spiritual forms of learning cannot be simply *applied*, such as the presentation (as in Pattakos, 2010) of prescriptions for how one should live one's life in a 'deeper' 'meaningful' way, or the presentation of learning outcomes detailing what one *should* know/be able to do at the end of a particular learning programme (O'Brien and Brancaleone, 2011; Brancaleone and O'Brien, 2011). Moreover, as spirituality becomes increasingly commercialised (e.g. via the 'care'/'mindfulness' industry and 'scientific' (e.g. via certain positive psychology research), the danger is that sociological causes of well-being become ignored in favour of 'self' responsibility and 'self' transformation. Such capturing of the 'self' does not sit well with a humanistic education process (as described here).

17 The concept of an independent school is not new. James O'Malley's (2011) interesting study charts the revival of the earlier lay tradition of hedge schools in the 18th and 19th centuries to the modern-day (20th century) establishment of Catholic and co-educational lay schools in Ireland. Diverse independent schools are shown to share some characteristics, such as personal leadership styles, a pragmatic outlook on education, some ideal social purpose, a lack of funding and inadequate facilities. Inevitably, not least due to the absence of state support, there was a significant decline of unitary/independent schools (only 3 exist in rural Ireland presently from a height of 57 between the years 1922–1975). In 21st Century Ireland, it appears that lay educational enterprise has now been transmuted into commercial institutes that target students 'competing' for higher points (to gain entry to college/university).

18 The *Junior* Certificate examination is normally taken after 3 years' study in a *secondary school* (at 15 years of age). Typically, a student takes 9 to 12 subjects – including English, Irish and Mathematics – as part of the Junior Cycle. An innovative Junior Cycle will

introduce new subjects and short courses, emphasise literacy, numeracy and key skills, and develop new approaches to assessment and reporting. School leavers in Ireland will typically take the *Leaving Certificate examination* (at 18 years of age) two or three years after completion of the Junior Certificate in order to reach standards for employment, *college* or *university* entrance.

19 During my research visits (January and February 2013), Nuala received word that a local philanthropist bequeathed some money from his estate to all the schools in Waterford City, including the XLC Project. This news was met with some delight.

20 There was a peak of 95 per cent in 2011; a low of 65 per cent in 2002, owing largely to an unprecedented increase in numbers that year; and the highest 'college points' scores were recorded in 2012, a year that coincided with the highest proportion of candidates sitting higher level subjects.

21 These include correspondence students, mainstream school students who access XLC resources online, members of an affiliated women's Traveller group (St. Margaret's in Ballymun, Dublin) who benefit from XLC's methodological support, and 'independent' students who follow their own course of study but utilise the Project's facilities.

22 Up to recently (early-late 1990s), school attrition rates were higher, equivalent to one in five students dropping out of school before age 18. The introduction of the Leaving Certificate Applied (LCA) programme in 1995 has been credited with much of the relative improvement in school retention (now one in six students drop out of school before age 18). The LCA focuses on those who demonstrate less interest and proficiency in traditional academic subjects and who are at particular risk of early school leaving. Despite some positive reactions by students to the programme (particularly in relation to course content, work-based learning and continuous assessment), some students in an ESRI study (Byrne and Smyth, 2010) indicated that they felt 'misdirected' by schools into taking the programme. In addition, they often felt segregated from students in the mainstream Leaving Certificate programme (ibid.). In terms of progression, about 28 per cent of LCA graduates advance to further or higher education, which is less than half the rate of the general population of school-leavers (Donnelly, 2009).

23 My own experience of working with and studying adult learners confirms how, for many, prior schooling continues – many years on – to negatively shape their self-concept and attitudes/behaviour towards learning (O'Brien and Ó Fathaigh, 2007).

24 According to the 2000 Education Welfare Act, an *early school leaver* is 'officially' someone who leaves formal education before 16 years of age or before the completion of three years post-primary education.

25 In a survey of 24 XLC students, Greene (2005, 35) found a vast improvement between their previous self-perceptions and their present self-perceptions. Specifically, 4 per cent of students described their academic ability as being 'very good' in their previous school compared to 29 per cent who described their academic ability as being 'very good' in XLC.

26 Of course, teachers may report (in some cases) student-teacher bullying and aggression (TUI, 2006).

27 The 'rasher' (or bacon strip) is thought to have been invented in Waterford city by Henry Denny who developed innovative production techniques in 1820 that led to the modern bacon curing process. The 'blaa' is a floury bread bun unique to Waterford city. It is credited to the French Huguenots who settled in the city in 1693 (source: www.discoverwaterfordcity.ie/index.php?contentid=traditional-waterford-food).

28 Technically this approach would demand an awful lot of 'recorded lessons' (e.g. using ICT), which was not observed in XLC. Recorded lessons allow learners to begin to engage with the requisite knowledge and then substantiate their own understanding via one-to-one tutoring. The work of Salman Khan (founder of *The Khan Academy*, a non-profit educational website) presents as an exemplar of how 'flip teaching' may operate. As with all educational resources, however, one needs to carefully consider their methodological framing.

29   There was a recent case where a couple of students were caught smoking cannabis outside the school building. The whole school population was summoned and told that a serious breach of rules had occurred. They were then consulted about actions to be taken. While many students called for (what Finola termed) "harsh treatment", it was decided that all would henceforth abide by the rule to be drug free or risk immediate expulsion.

30   I met one Junior Certificate (15 years old) student who recalled an incident in his previous school where he was suspended for wearing an ear ring. A female teacher had "given out" to him for his piercing and he had retorted by highlighting her own "big gold ear rings".

31   Students may also choose one morning in the week where they can arrive late to school.

32   In Greek mythology, Procrustes (son of Poseidon) ran a guest house on the road to Attica. There he lured unsuspecting guests to stay the night with the promise that he had the perfect bed that fitted them. If the guests were too small, he would stretch them to fit. If they proved too tall, he would amputate their legs! A Procrustean reference here implies a specific critique of the system – a system where every individual is made to fit it!

33   Jean-Jacques Rousseau (1712–1778) believed in mankind's (and especially children's) inherent goodness. His novel *Émile, ou De l'éducation* (*Émile, or on Education*) is a treatise on educating the whole person for citizenship. This work later inspired French revolutionary thinking.

34   Nuala specifically refers to *Saint Bead*'s (or the *Venerable Bead*'s) accounts of Irish monks in the Seventh Century. In his book *Historia Ecclesiastica Gentis Anglorum* (the Ecclesiastical *History of the People of England*), Bead (673–735AD) records how Irish monastic schools provided English students (and other nationalities) with free board, food, books and instruction. Nuala had remarked that "if they [the early monks] can do it, we can do it." Consequently XLC aims to "turn nobody away" and it doesn't charge students for any resources or instruction. Moreover, Nuala asserts the importance of a broader *Celtic* cultural value-system in XLC, noting (in her personal writing) such strengths as "attention to human presence", "hospitality", "belonging", and "trust and respect, which answers to the deepest yearnings of the human heart and is more germane to a Celtic people than compulsion, coercion and competition of a market mentality." Beyond idealistic/mystical espousal, such values need to be *practised* for a culture of schooling to be truly viewed as supportive.

35   Numerous studies record how lower socio-economic groups underperform at examination time and how this impacts negatively on future educational involvement (Gillborn and Youdell, 2000). The chances of being convicted of a crime are closely linked to low achievement at school (Beinart *et al.*, 2002) and lifestyle/health choices are more restricted to less advantaged socio-economic groups (Wilkinson and Marmot, 2003). Further, higher employment positions require higher levels of educational qualifications, while lower positions are often characterised by less desirable conditions and pay (Hannan *et al.*, 1995; Equality and Human Rights Commission, 2010). Moreover, early school leavers are three to four times more likely to be unemployed than their more highly educated peers (School Leavers' Surveys, 2007).

36   In *Hard Times* by Charles Dickens, the aptly named headteacher Thomas Gradgrind is concerned with cold facts and figures. In a famous passage (Dickens, 1854, 16–18), he calls on his brightest student (Bitzer) to define a horse: "Quadruped. Graminivorous. Forty teeth, namely twenty-four grinders, four eye-teeth and twelve incisive. Sheds coat in the spring; in marshy countries, sheds hoofs too. Hoofs hard but requiring to be shod with iron. Age known by marks in mouth." In praising this response, Gradgrind (*Grade*grind?) demonstrates his concern not just for facts (*grind*ed content), but for results (*grade*s).

37   Of course the Leaving Cert results are a measure of respectability for XLC too. To demonstrate their 'power', ask yourself how you first felt about XLC upon reading the aforementioned statistic: "From 1999–2012, over 700 students have sat their Leaving Certificate with an average of 85% of the cohort passing 5 subjects or more." Now ask yourself how you would feel about XLC if this figure was significantly lower.

38 This reminds of another Socratic dictum – 'know thyself' – a phrase that has been attributed to Socrates and is inscribed in the forecourt of the Temple of Apollo at Delphi.

39 In contrast to its sterile image, rote learning and repetition can be quite colourful in XLC. In reciting the list of Henry VIII's wives, for example, Nuala makes use of such rhymes as: "Anne of Cleaves is number four, she's too ugly the poor hoore!"

40 Granville Stanley Hall (1844–1924) was an American psychologist and educator. He coined the phrase 'storm and stress' in his ambitiously titled 1904 book, *Adolescence: Its psychology and its relation to physiology, anthropology, sociology, sex, crime and religion*. It is fair to say that Hall's belief in Social Darwinism rendered him a non-humanist (in educational terms).

41 In 2005, *before* the recession, Ireland spent 4.6 per cent of its Gross Domestic Product (GDP) on education, compared with 5.5 per cent spent in the EU nineteen countries (OECD, 2008). Between 1995 and 2005, Ireland's percentage investment decreased from 5.5 per cent to 4.6 per cent.

42 In addition to lower state investment in education (see Note 41 above), there have been serious cutbacks (2008-present) to guidance service, special educational needs and Traveller supports in Irish schools. This runs contrary to governmental plans to tackle bullying and mental health problems (including suicide) among young people (see later discussions in the main text).

43 *Growing up in Ireland* is the first national longitudinal study that follows the progress of some 20,000 children across Ireland. It is designed to help improve understanding of all aspects of children and their development (see www.growingup.ie/). Included in the report is children's attitudes towards schooling, their relations with teachers and parents, and their peer relationships, feelings and behaviours.

44 *State of the nation's children* (2008), from the Office of the Minister for Children and Youth Affairs, reports, inter alia, on children's views on being bullied at school, school attendance, social class outcomes in education, intellectual disability figures, alcohol and drug use, self-reported levels of happiness, attitudes to 'place' and leisurely pursuits.

45 Supported by the Health Promotion Policy Unit of the Department of Health and Children, the Health Promotion Research Centre (at National University of Ireland, Galway) has produced this report that, inter alia, engages such subject areas as drug and alcohol use, dieting and food habits, smoking, bullying, exercise, emotional well-being, and perceptions of school.

46 Produced by the Ombudsman for Children's Office (2012), this report consults with 300 children and young people (aged 10–17 years) and seeks their views on bullying prevention and intervention strategies.

47 While the Education Welfare Act (2000) states that Irish schools must provide a code of behaviour to clarify duty of care and policy (regarding indiscipline, bullying and violence), there are still *no legal requirements* in place.

48 From Brancaleone and O'Brien (2011, 513): "It may be argued that all representations can, in the words of Baudrillard, 'neutralize the meaning and energy of events' (1994, 53). Going further, however, he claims that while there may be more representations and more information in the world, this actually produces less and less meaning (Baudrillard 1994, 79). This is because while appearances seduce, they simultaneously deflect from reality and meaning. This speaks to a more serious problem of representation, demonstrating that the sign can construct the real as simulation. Moreover, Baudrillard claims that the greater the circulation of the sign, the greater its domination – to the point of replacing the real. What we end up with is more real than the real. With this endless dislocation from the referent, the very concept of meaning is at stake." For the purpose of this study, then, one must ask how concepts of *personal* learning and *well-being* are really captured and understood. Is the 'message' more real than the concepts themselves? Do we practise the 'message' and not the concepts in schools?

49 Henceforth, all students' and parents' names are pseudonyms.

50 Linda respectfully pays tribute to those teachers in Joy's previous school that enabled her to achieve so much.

51 Joy is also legally obliged to attend school.

52 I learn of Margaret's and Claire's story in passing from Nuala and ask to get contact details for them. The telephone interview with Margaret took place on 13 March 2013 and lasted one hour. I learn of Linda's and Joy's story from meeting them in XLC. My personal interview with Linda took place on 21 February 2013 and also lasted one hour.

53 Modelled on the 'Prom' in North American schools, the 'Debs' is a formal ball for female students in their final year of post-primary school in Ireland.

54 During my visits, I witnessed a discussion between a young woman and Finola in the office. The former explained that she couldn't attend the Friday group for some time since she had nobody to look after her young child. She was very worried that she would fail her Leaving Cert exam. Finola assured her of two things: 1) she would get her exams and 2) somebody somehow would be available to look after her child in school. I was immediately struck by how student-teacher relations (as demonstrated here) contrasted so much with those formerly experienced by Claire.

55 John is a small business owner and past pupil of XLC. He sponsors XLC's advertising activities in the local community. I interviewed John by telephone on 20 March 2013 for approximately forty minutes. The later (personal) interview with Liam took place on 28 February 2013 and also lasted forty minutes.

56 What follows are extracts from our personal interviews on 2 February 2013 and 28 February 2013. Each interview lasted thirty minutes.

57 Kundera refers to Gustav Husak, imposed by the Russians as President of Czechoslovakia in 1969, as 'the President of forgetting'. One of Husak's first acts was the expulsion of some 145 Czech historians from research institutes and universities. For Kundera, this epitomises a state of 'infantocracy', where 'new' generations (especially children) become unburdened by memory. Parallels are to be found in 1975 Cambodia under Pol Pot's 'year zero' regime, where artists, teachers and intellectuals were brutally murdered in the interest of a 'forgetting' society. In 2013, Kim Jong Un's uncle (then considered to be the second most powerful figure in North Korea) fell out of favour, was edited out of a 2013 propaganda documentary and was then executed for treason. In a repeat of history, another regime would attempt to erase memory.

58 Kellie Greene's photographic exhibition of 'Ireland's architecture of containment' (engaging images of industrial schools and Magdalene laundries) is a good example of keeping memory 'alive' in the interest of societal advancement.

59 I find it useful to associate the terms 'edify' and 'education'. The former stresses a type of *enlightenment* in education, where *lessons for humanity* (over-and-above knowledge store) can be identified and practised.

60 I am reminded here of Voltaire's (1759) closing words in *Candide, ou l'Optimisme* (*Candide, or All for the Best*): "Il faut cultiver notre jardin" ("We must tend to our garden"). Taken as a commentary on the impossibility of knowing the universal laws of existence, its humility signifies the need to focus on more immediate, doable tasks in life. An *Enlightenment* reading may also indicate that one has to work on one's self as an agentic (i.e. not an immovable) part of the greater scheme of things.

References

Abrams, F. (2010). *Learning to fail: How society lets young people down*. London and New York. Routledge.

Baudrillard, J. (1994). *Simulacra and simulation*. Translated by Sheila Faria Glaser. Ann Arbor, MI. University of Michigan Press.

Bazelon, E. (2013). *Sticks and stones: Defeating the culture of bullying and rediscovering the power of character and empathy*. New York. Random House.

Beinart, S., Anderson, B., Lee, S. (2002). *Youth at risk? A national survey of risk factors, protective factors and problem behaviour among young people in England, Scotland and Wales*. London. Joseph Rowntree Foundation.

Boland, R. (2013). Record calls to St Vincent de Paul. Article written in *The Irish Times*, 30 January. Retrieved from www.irishtimes.com/newspaper/breaking/2013/0130/ breaking19_pf.html

Bourdieu, P. (1977). Cultural reproduction and social reproduction. In J. Karabel and A. Halsey, eds (487–511). *Power and ideology in education*. New York. Oxford University Press.

Bourdieu, P. (1988). *Homo academicus*. Translated by Peter Colier. Cambridge. Polity Press in association with Blackwell.

Brancaleone, D. and O'Brien, S. (2011). Educational commodification and the (economic) sign value of learning outcomes. *British Journal of Sociology of Education*, 32, no. 4, 501–19.

Byrne, D. and Smyth, E. (2010). *No way back? The dynamics of early school leaving*. Dublin. The Liffey Press in association with the ESRI, NCCA and DES.

Donnelly, K. (2009). 'Practical' exam fails to open up job options. Article written in *The Independent*, December 14. Retrieved from www.independent.ie/lifestyle/education/ practical-exam-fails-to-open-up-job-options-26591190.html

Eivers, E. and Clerkin, A., eds. (2013). *National schools, international contexts: Beyond the PIRLS and TIMSS test results*. Dublin. Educational Research Centre.

Equality and Human Rights Commission. (2010). *How fair is Britain?* July 9. Retrieved from www.equalityhumanrights.com/uploaded_files/triennial_review/tr_execsumm.pdf

Erikson, E. (1968). *Identity: Youth and crisis*. New York. W. W. Norton.

Foucault, M. (1977). *Discipline and punish*. Translated by Alan Sheridan. New York. Vintage.

Foucault, M. (1991). Governmentality. Lecture at the Collège de France Feb 1, 1978. In G. Burchell, C. Gordon and P. Miller, eds (87–104). *The Foucault effect: Studies in governmentality*. Chicago, Illinois. The University of Chicago Press.

Frankl, V. E. (1984). *Man's search for meaning*. New York. Washington Square Press.

Frankl, V. E. (2011). *Man's search for ultimate meaning*. London. Rider Books.

Freire, P. and Freire, A. M. A. (1994). *Pedagogy of hope: Reliving Pedagogy of the oppressed*. London. Continuum.

Freire, P. (1996). *Pedagogy of the oppressed, Volume 10*. London. Penguin.

Gillborn, D. and Youdell, D. (2000). *Rationing education: Policy, practice, reform and equity*. Buckingham and Philadelphia. Open University Press.

Greene, K. (2005). A case study examining the link between early school leavers and school culture. University of Limerick. Unpublished BSc thesis.

Hadot, P. (1995). *Philosophy as a way of life*, Oxford. Blackwell Publishers.

Halsey, A. H., Heath, A. F. and Ridge, J. M. (1980). *Origins and destinations: Family, class and education in modern Britain*. Oxford. Clarendon Press.

Hannan, D., Hovels, B., van den Berg, S. and White, M. (1995). 'Early Leavers' from education and training in Ireland, the Netherlands and the United Kingdom. *European Journal of Education*, 30, no. 3, 325–46.

Horton, M. and Freire, P. (1990). *We make the road by walking: Conversations on education and social change*. Philadelphia. Temple University Press.

Jackson, N. (2011). *Whoopee!! I'm going to die!* Drogheda. Choice Publishing.

Kundera, M. (1979; this English translation, 1999). *The book of laughter and forgetting*. New York. Harper Perennial Modern Classics.

Lacan, J. (1977, English Edition). *Ecrits: A selection*. New York. W. W. Norton.

Levi, P. (1987). *If this is a man – the truce*. London. Abacus.

Lynch, K. and Lodge, A. (2002). Equality and power in schools: Redistribution, recognition and representation. London and New York. RoutledgeFalmer.

Maslow, A. (1943). A theory of human motivation. *Psychological Review*, 50, no. 4, 370–96.

McGahern, J. (2006). *Memoir*. London. Faber and Faber.

Meaney, S. E. (2011). Dropped out or pushed out? Early school leavers' experience of teacher-student bullying and aggression in Ireland. Trinity College. Unpublished MEd thesis.

Miller, L. (2009). Present to possibility: Spiritual awareness and deep teaching. *Teachers College Record*, 111, no. 12, 2705–12.

Murphy, Y. (2009). Report by Commission of investigation into Catholic Archdiocese of Dublin (Parts 1 and 2). Dublin. Stationery Office.

Murphy, Y. (2010). Report by Commission of investigation into Catholic Diocese of Cloyne. Dublin. Stationery Office.

Nic Gabhainn, S. and Sixsmith, J. (2005). *Children's understandings of well-being*. Dublin. The National Children's Office Publication.

Nietzsche, F. (1882). *The gay science*. Translated, with commentary, by Walter Kaufman. New York. Vintage Books.

Nietzsche, F. (1883–1885). *Thus spake Zarathustra: A book for all and none*. Reproduced in A. Del Caro and R. Pippin, eds (2006) as part of the *Cambridge texts in the history of philosophy*. Cambridge. Cambridge University Press.

Noddings, N. (2004). *Happiness and education*. Cambridge. Cambridge University Press.

O'Brien, M. (2008). *Well-Being and post-primary schooling: A review of the literature and research*. Dublin. National Council for Curriculum and Assessment Publication.

O'Brien, S. and Brancaleone, D. (2011). Evaluating learning outcomes: In search of lost knowledge. *Journal of Irish Educational Studies*, 30, no. 1, 5–21.

O'Brien, S. and Ó Fathaigh, M. (2007). *Key aspects of learning partnerships for social inclusion: Exploring lifelong learning contexts, issues and approaches*. Cork. Oak Tree Press.

O'Brien, S. (2013). Re-representing education's image and status: In the 'interest' of pedagogical innovation. In G. K. Zarifis and M. N. Gravani, eds *Challenging the 'European Area of Lifelong Learning': A critical response*. London. Springer Publication.

O'Malley, J. (2011). The catholic lay secondary schools of rural Ireland 1922–1975. National University of Ireland, Cork. Unpublished PhD thesis.

O'Moore, M. and Stevens, P., eds. (2013). *Bullying in Irish education*. Cork. Cork University Press.

O'Moore, M., Kirkham, C. and Smith, M. (1997). Bullying behaviour in Irish schools: A nationwide study. *Irish Journal of Psychology*, 18, 141–69.

Pearse, P. (1959). *The murder machine*. Retrieved on 09 April 2013 from www.ucc.ie/celt/online/E900007-001/

Rogers, C. (1961). *On becoming a person: A therapist's view of psychotherapy*. Boston. New York. Houghton Mifflin Company.

Ryan, S. (2009). *Commission to inquire into child abuse report*. (Volumes I–V). Dublin. Stationery Office.

Schoonmaker, F. (2009). Only those who see take off their shoes: Seeing the classroom as a spiritual space. *Teachers College Record*, 111, no. 12, 2713–31.

Tickner, N. (2013). Early leavers – what next? Report on early leavers from post-primary schools – pupils enrolled in 2009/2010 and not in 2010/2011. Dublin. DES Publication.

Teachers Union of Ireland (TUI, 2006). *Survey examining teacher perception of student disruption in their schools*. Dublin. TUI Publication.

UNICEF. (2013). Child well-being in rich countries: A comparative overview. *Innocenti Report Card 11*. Florence. UNICEF Office of Research.

Wilkinson, R. and Marmot, M. (2003). *Social determinants of health: The solid facts.* Second edition. Copenhagen. World Health Organisation.

Ziehe, T. (2009). 'Normal learning problems' in youth. In K. Illeris, ed. (184–99). *Contemporary theories of learning: Learning theorists . . . in their own words.* New York. Routledge.

3

LEARNING SUCCESS

It is a land that has carved itself into world literature via the virtuoso writings of Frederick Douglas, Mark Twain, F. Scott Fitzgerald, Ernest Hemingway and John Steinbeck,[1] as well as the cultivated poetry of Walt Whitman, Robert Frost, Elizabeth Bishop, Robert Hayden and Sylvia Plath. Obsessed with diverting ennui, it entertains via the plays of Eugene O'Neill, Tennessee Williams and Arthur Miller, as well as the musical theatre of Cole Porter, Oscar Hammerstein, George Gershwin, Agnes de Mille and Leonard Bernstein. Comedy plays its role in relieving – even mocking – the mundane. Think, for instance, of Bob Newhart, Joan Rivers, Bill Cosby, Larry David and Sarah Silverman, as well as the satire of *Saturday Night Live* and *The Daily Show*. Beyond life's theatre, hyper-reality is entertained in such spaces as Walt Disney World, Las Vegas and the numerous amusement parks dotted along the country's landscape. Hyper-reality too pervades its homes where DVDs, video game consoles and virtual communications abound. This is a land that produces its own cultural images via avant-garde artists like Georgia O'Keefe, Jackson Pollock, Andrew Wyeth, Andy Warhol and Jean-Michel Basquiat. More familiar images owe much to the films of John Ford, Frank Capra, Elia Kazan, John Huston, Woody Allen, Martin Scorsese and Spike Lee. With each new release, new icons are proclaimed – Bogart, Hepburn, Wayne, Brando, Taylor, Freeman, de Niro, Berry, Di Caprio and Portman. While many others appear ephemerally, they all form a lasting legacy.[2] Actors' good looks, off-screen lives and sometimes tragic mortality[3] court wide vicarious interest – if only for a time and under the media's glare.[4] Musicians too attract this interest. In the land that fashioned jazz, R&B, Cajun, country, rock and roll, techno, rap and hip hop, new music idols emerge, while many more are manufactured. 'Reality' shows like *Idol: The Search for a Superstar* and *The X Factor* (where the title implies 'star quality') summon new 'names'. And there is no shortage of candidates. After all, this is America and 'everyone can succeed'.

Many see America through a particular cultural lens – as a medley of blue jeans, Abercrombie and Fitch, shopping malls, beer, speakeasies, national parks, football, baseball, basketball, action movies, westerns, popcorn, hot dogs, French fries and Philly steaks. This is a legitimate, albeit surface level reading. To understand America at a deeper level, one has to see it through its migrants' eyes. From the earliest English colonial settlements in the 17th century to the western advancement of the territories in the mid to late 19th century (the period of 'The West'), one can appreciate the enormity of the United States experiment. Here, migrants' tale is one of conquest (often brutal, particularly against Native American populations), land succession and growth, disputes and accords among diverse peoples and cultures, the establishment of new states and governance structures, and the advancement of market enterprise (such as in the California Gold Rush of 1849 where huge numbers speculatively sought their fortune). While this period was marred by violence, wars, racial conflicts, social inequality and industrial upheaval, the symbol of America as 'the land of opportunity' took root. Then, social commentators like Ralph Waldo Emerson (1841, 1844) were acclaiming the virtues of stoical individuality and (patriarchal) self-reliance. Over time, the 'American Dream', a phrase first coined by James Truslow Adams in 1931, harvested almost mythical status in the minds of prospective Americans. While Adams stressed a transcendent (non-materialistic) vision of social order in his version of the 'American Dream' (Truslow Adams, 1931), individual (material) notions of 'prosperity' and 'success' gradually dominated (Bellah *et al.*, 1985/2007). To achieve the Dream, so it went, you had to work hard and develop your talents; only then could you realise upward social mobility. Success stories soon appeared to sustain this *meritocratic* vision. In the fields of the arts and sport, superstars could elevate themselves from humble (oft migrant,[5] oft poor[6]) beginnings. In science, a bewildering array of inventions, from the mundane to the sophisticated,[7] linked 'innovation' with 'success'. And while inventors, entrepreneurs, investors and marketers formed alliances, a long list of icons emerged: Strauss, Carnegie, Morgan, Rockefeller, Edison, Kellogg, Ford, Merrill, Hilton, Disney, Lauder, Walton, Trump, Winfrey, Jobs, Gates, Dell and Zuckerberg. Each name appeared to verify that 'anyone can succeed'.

To look further into 'the American soul', one must read into its egalitarian ideals.[8] In 1776, Thomas Jefferson pronounced The Declaration of Independence:[9]

> We hold these truths to be self-evident, that all men [sic] are created equal, that they are endowed by their Creator with certain unalienable Rights, that among these are Life, Liberty and the pursuit of Happiness. That to secure these rights, Governments are instituted among Men [sic], deriving their just powers from the consent of the governed.

This declaration represents democracy, appealing as it does to an independent judiciary and a government and military that are responsive to civil power.[10] And it represents human rights,[11] reasoning these to be 'self-evident' among a 'free people' in 'free and independent states'. Such freedom is enshrined in The First Amendment

(1791) to the United States Constitution (1787).[12] While its provisions are constantly subject to scrutiny and Supreme Court challenges, The First Amendment sets forth the principles of free religious choice and exercise (with no favours in law for any religious group), as well as freedom of speech (with implications for a free press, school speech,[13] political critiques, etc.). Ever since, concepts of *nationhood* and 'freedom' have been forged to celebrate America as 'the land of the free'.[14] And freedom's cause has been defended, even to the point of (oft contentious) warfare beyond America's shores. From within too, the defence of 'freedom' has been tragically tested. Twelve years post 9/11, The One World Trade Center (formerly, The Freedom Tower) has just been completed. Its renewal serves as a national and global symbol of America's egalitarian ideals. At the same time, National Security leaks revealed the extent of the US government's electronic surveillance of its (and its allies') population, the National Defence Authorisation Act (2013) made provisions for the 'prolonged detention' of US citizens and Guantánamo Bay remained open. Freedom's cause, it seems, is always under construction in America.

Democracy, human rights and new opportunities are long cherished in America (de Tocqueville 1835, 1840). And while individualism and materialism always threaten (ibid.), there are many that testify to this 'freedom' she bestows.[15] But 'freedom' too is construed by other means. For example, The Second Amendment to the United States Constitution protects the right of the people 'to bear arms'.[16] This particular 'freedom' is highly contested of course.[17] Another 'freedom' attends to the 'pursuit of happiness'. As it appears in the Declaration of Independence, an individual is 'free' to choose his/her own life course direction (including, for example, his/her own path of 'success'). The only proviso is that he/she respects the equal rights of others to do the same. This freedom principle (which derives from classical liberalism) allies subjective values with objective rights. Accordingly, one is 'free' to pursue happiness (such as that which may accrue) in education, health, income, wealth[18] or fame, provided that others have equal rights to those same pursuits. Surely this freedom cannot be contested? There appear, after all, libertarian and constitutional bases for its animation. What's more, economic arguments appear to bolster its cause. Of central influence here is Milton Friedman's (1912–2006) advocacy of a type of economic freedom known as monetarism. As early as 1955, his ideas reflected and later shaped a powerful *neoliberal* agenda.[19] This philosophy originates with the assumption that society "takes freedom of the individual, or more realistically the family, as its ultimate objective", with government's primary role being the preservation of a "free private enterprise exchange economy" (Friedman, 1955, 1). Under this economic system, the 'enterprising' individual is 'free' to prosper and accrue wealth. And in America, where this system excels, (economic) 'success' is routinely prized and culturally celebrated.[20]

This Union of *economic freedom* and 'success' produces unambiguous educational effects. Friedman advocates that parents "meet the cost [of 'training'] directly" and that, as 'consumers', they use school 'vouchers'[21] to 'purchase' educational 'services' (Friedman, 1955, 3). It is envisaged that these services, which "could be rendered by private enterprises operated for profit, or by non-profit institutions", would impose 'minimum standards' (ibid.). The role of government, therefore, "would be limited to assuring [these] standards", in the same way as restaurants are quality inspected (ibid.).[22] Here, education is valued for its 'exchange' or 'gain' measure.[23] It 'makes sense', therefore, to 'invest' in one's 'human capital' in order to reap 'rewards' in the market place.[24] A system that 'denationalises' or 'privatises' education is favoured and is assumed to 'free' up competition and deliver greater investment 'choice'.[25] Accordingly, low trust is attributed to public schooling, high trust to private schooling.[26] Under a private system, it is assumed that competition will enhance 'performativity' – even making "the salaries of school teachers responsive to market forces" (Friedman, 1955, 6).[27] Schools are also deemed to become more 'account-able', though Friedman, *unlike* his successors, does not detail 'benchmark measure-ments'. Perhaps most controversially, Friedman claims that all of this educational 'innovation' makes for a more inclusive society. Here, he affiliates notions of 'competition' and 'incentives' with "eliminating the causes of inequality", and he dismisses the alternative – "outright distribution of income" – as 'impeding com-petition', 'destroying incentive' and "dealing [only] with symptoms"[28] (Friedman, 1955, 14). In making this stark (and as yet untried) political 'choice',[29] Friedman sponsored a specific form of educational 'freedom'. Rooted in a neoliberal agenda, this 'freedom' represents a *politicised* worldview on education, one that speaks to a certain way of being in the world and acting upon it. In Friedman's political vision, the real role of government, and specifically its role in education, is to promote a *workfare* state (one that encourages *individual* 'net contributions' to society via 'human capital' investments and obligations), over-and-above a *welfare* state (one that supports *public* responsibility for education and other facilities and provides assistance therein). While the latter (albeit now, a much diluted version) is generally associated with 'the European project', the former more fully encapsulates 'the American way'.

As policy advisor to Ronald Reagan's administration (1981–1988), Friedman was a powerful influence in the expansive roll-out of a neoliberal agenda. This affected: Reduced taxes, reduced government spend, increased privatisation, and deregulation of the economy and other state activities (the latter was accompanied, paradoxically, by augmented bureaucratic controls). Political right movements in the United States (the Republican Party and, later, its Tea Party affiliation), and in Britain (The Conservative Party), were buoyed by the reign of Reaganomics and Thatcherism.[30] And their merger of *economic freedom* and *political freedom* was evermore instituted.[31] To these, Friedman (1991, 332) proposed a third – *human freedom* – arguing that the market's place lay at its core:

> The essence of human freedom, as of a free private market, is freedom of people to make their own decisions so long as they do not prevent anybody else from doing the same thing.[32] That makes clear, I think, why free private markets are so closely related to human freedom. It is the only mechanism that permits a complex, inter-related society to be organised from the bottom up rather than the top down.

Accordingly, to argue against the 'market' was to argue against human freedom itself. Why can't parents have the freedom to choose their own schools? Why can't they invest in private (and for profit) education? Why can't they evaluate their school's success against others? Why can't they measure their teachers' performances and reward them accordingly? In a bid for such 'freedom', Friedman sought to 'revolutionise' education via "the drive, imagination and energy of competitive free enterprise" (Friedman, 1997, 341). The message was compelling. In a country that nourishes on restless energy and creative ideas, who would argue with this 'innovation'? In a country where nationhood *rights* are durable, who would argue with this 'increased' liberty? And in America where economic success is treasured, who would argue with this newly fashioned 'freedom'?

A new market morality had materialised (Chubb and Moe, 1990). And it was accompanied by an unlikely relation – conservative religious conscience.[33] Ronald Reagan's (1983) speech at the annual convention of the National Association of Evangelicals exemplifies this moral alliance. Written in the context of the cold war, it begins by famously juxtaposing Christianity in American life with the amorality of an "evil empire":[34]

> [The Soviets] must be made to understand we will never compromise our principles and standards. We will never give away our freedom. We will never abandon our belief in God.

And with references to family 'choice', Christian-based literature (C. S. Lewis), Biblical sources (Genesis and Isaiah) and nationhood (the Founding Fathers, Thomas Paine[35]), Reagan concludes:

> . . . the source of our strength in the quest for human freedom is not material, but spiritual. And because it knows no limitation, it must terrify and ultimately triumph over those who would enslave their fellow man.

Margaret Thatcher's (1988) speech to the General Assembly of the Church of Scotland resounds.[36] Here, she presents the moral case for meritocracy and wealth creation:

- We are told we must work and use our talents to create wealth. 'If a man will not work he shall not eat', wrote St Paul to the Thessalonians. Indeed, abundance rather than poverty has a legitimacy which derives from the very nature of Creation.
- You recall that Timothy was warned by St Paul that anyone who neglects to provide for his own house (meaning his own family) has disowned the faith and is 'worse than an infidel'.

In her speech, Thatcher evokes increased 'personal responsibility' and the merits of a 'workfare state'.[37] And, like Reagan, she makes references to Christian-based literature (C. S. Lewis), selective Biblical sources (Thessalonians, Matthew) and nationhood (even citing Abraham Lincoln's Gettysburg address[38]). In both orations, global links are forged between *Judeo-Christian*, *democratic* and *economic* notions of 'freedom'.

It is curious to think how religious and state work has become so enmeshed in America, especially considering First Amendment principles.[39] Reagan's successors (notably Presidents George H. W. Bush and George W. Bush) would continue to forge alliances with conservative religious groups who, in turn, presented as key political lobbyists.[40] And a conservative religious agenda would continue to influence American society, with broad educational support for state school prayer,[41] educational choice (e.g. vouchers, private/religious schools, home-schooling), 'accountability'/'performativity' measures, Creationism (or 'intelligent design') in opposition to evolution teaching, conservative (heterosexual and abstinence-based) sexual education programs, and traditional perspectives on bio-ethics (e.g. anti-abortion, anti-stem cell research). This moral force would not just *effect* education, that is, produce structural and cultural transformations in schooling. It would also *affect* education, that is, petition, persuade and provoke particular sensibility and 'interest' in schooling. Neo-conservatives – an umbrella term used to describe critics of modern liberalism – demonstrate a particular moral 'interest' in education. This 'interest' ranges from endorsing conservative religious agendas (as above), traditional-based pedagogy (e.g. 'core' cultural knowledge), widespread testing (due to an alleged crisis of 'standards'), authoritative systems of professional accountability and nationhood ethics, for example, the focus on STEM[42] subjects (Science, Technology, Engineering and Mathematics) and their role in advancing America's standing in the 'global order'.[43] 'Neocons' would not only support the new corporate reform movement in America, they would rationalise its ethical enterprise.

Somewhat surprisingly, this reform movement enlisted bipartisan political support.[44] Under President Reagan's administration, *A Nation At Risk* (1983) had warned against 'a rising tide of mediocrity' in public schools. And under President George H. W. Bush's administration, *Goals 2000* established a standards framework that focused on outcomes-based measures of education, with attendant student improvement targets.[45] During President Clinton's administration (1993–2001) states were encouraged to set their own standards and test for these under the provisions of *Goals 2000*. And during George W. Bush's Presidency the bipartisan Act of *No Child Left Behind* (2002) required that all schools annually test children in grades 3 (8–9 years) through to 8 (13–14 years old) in mathematics and reading, and all schools produce annual progress reports (based on their quantitative showing that year). Schools that failed to meet (oft unrealistic) 'high stakes' targets were subject to various forms of 'restructuring', for example, staff dismissal, management handover to state or private (*charter school*[46]) control, and/or eventual closure. Presently, under President Obama's administration, *Race to the Top* (RTTT) releases competitive federal funds[47] (close to 4.5 billion dollars) to those states that satisfy performance-based goals, lift caps on charter school numbers, develop new database systems, reduce the number of 'failure' schools and facilitate and extend Common Core State Standards (CCSS[48]). Over the years, then, the corporate reform movement has managed to galvanise a hodgepodge of educational 'interests'. These include private school advocates (Dave Levin/Mike Feinberg, Sarah Usdin), celebrated school leaders (Wendy Kopp, Geoffrey Canada), hard-line educational reformers (Michelle Rhee, Arne Duncan), curriculum crusaders (Eric Donald Hirsch, David Coleman), individual/group consultants (Michael Barber, McKinsey), publishers and testing agencies (Pearson, Harcourt Educational Measurement) and philanthropic authorities (the Bill and Melinda Gates Foundation, Walton Family Foundation). This coalescent[49] may yet prove fragile and flawed.[50] The reformers have their detractors, including a growing number of educationalists (Diane Ravitch, Linda Darling-Hammond), teacher representatives (Randi Weingarten, Denis Van Roekel) and protest movements (*Growing National Movement Against 'High Stakes' Testing, Urban Youth Collaborative, the Dignity in Schools Campaign* and *the Respect for All Coalition*). Still, corporate reformers play *the* leading role in casting education's image and enunciating new ways to 'innovate'. And they appear to verify the very meaning of *learning success*.

There are many who are 'interested' in the 'success' of American education: "Parents, students, teachers, tax payers, private entrepreneurs" (Friedman, 1997, 341), as well as states, politicians, educationalists, unions, moralists, think-tanks, the media, consultants and philanthropists. The more powerful 'partners' present as being apolitical, nationalist, ethical, 'freedom brokers'. Their declaration for education is *Life* (hope, ambition, 'prosperity'), *Liberty* (civil, moral, economic 'rights') and the *pursuit of Happiness* ('inclusion', wealth, 'success'). And while education is bound up with *their* 'freedom', *learning success* is already framed; the scene is set. This is the land of rugged individualism where folks 'pull themselves up by their own bootstraps', where 'a rising tide raises all boats'. This is the land of innovation where old ideas get restored, new ones unveiled. This is America.[51]

'If you can make it there' – New York

I have made it to New York, America's most populous and iconoclastic city. While they share cultural (and enigmatic) qualities, America is not New York and New York is not America. Traditionally a migration city, some 37 per cent of New York's 8 million plus population is born overseas, and its diverse people, cultures and ethnicities sustain its global metropolis status.[52] Its stoic and resilient character is matched by high degrees of broad-mindedness and creativity. This is a city that can't stop inventing, partly out of necessity. Bridges harbour traffic flows, cyclists, joggers *and* pedestrians, while boardwalks stretch out to meet the Hudson's curves. The shimmering skyline shelters up to 30,000 people per square mile, with Manhattan housing twice this figure. And with its population set to grow, New York is rising with it. This is a city that also chooses to invent. From new gadgets and movements to 'hipster' fashion, diets, and ways of speaking and dating, New Yorkers are always moving to the 'next level'. They like to play hard – late night

Figure 3.1 New York – The J Line from Williamsburg, Brooklyn to Jamaica Center, Queens

bars, theatre shows, working out, music concerts, bridge-walking. They like to take it easy – 24-hour convenience stores, laundromats, coffee houses, movie halls, subway 'prewalking'. And they like to work hard, chasing high rewards that are, in reality, not for everyone. New York is home to the world's leading financial centre and has the highest income inequality in America. It has the biggest number of billionaires in the world (Sedghi, 2013), with 1 per cent of its population earning over 45 per cent of total income and the bottom 50 per cent earning just 9 per cent. Its previous Mayor counts as one of the former, select, group. After 3 terms at city hall, Michael Bloomberg survived weather and financial storms and fashioned a number of changes from miles of bike lanes, same sex marriage, and a ban on smoking in restaurants and parks, to sweeping tax breaks, mass (including 'gentrified') developments and a 'stop and frisk' police policy. His successor, Democrat Bill de Blasio, has signalled new change directions from challenging 'a tale of two cities' (about 30 per cent of New Yorkers spend more than half their income on rent[53]) and taxing the rich (in order to support afford-able early years education), to curbing charter school expansion and the 'stop and frisk' policy. His self-styled 'progressive path' may yet guide, and befit, 'the New York way'.

But many obstacles lie ahead. In the way of educational success stands the (biggest) barrier of social class (Reay *et al.*, 2005; Skeggs, 2010). In America this is not always seen:

> Today, the country has gone a long way toward an appearance of classlessness. Americans of all sorts are awash in luxuries that would have dazzled their grandparents. Social diversity has erased many of the old markers [. . .] The contours of class have blurred; some say they have disappeared.
>
> (Scott and Leonhardt, 2005, 1)

In *The New York Times* series on class in America, Scott and Leonhardt (2005, 1) ultimately claim that "class is still a powerful force in American life." And there is much evidence to bear this out. In *Trends in the distribution of household income between 1979 and 2007*, the US Congressional Budget Office (2011) highlights how after-tax income for the highest 1 per cent grew by 275 per cent, while the bottom one fifth of earners had just an 18 per cent increase (Browne, 2012). The thirty-plus years of rising income inequality contrasts strongly with the period of 1947–79 where all income groups in the United States saw gains, with the lowest band seeing the largest increase (Inequality.org, 2011). Current conditions of rising income inequality are attended by growing inequalities in wealth and health[54] (ibid.). And despite narrowing racial gaps in these quality of life parameters, the divide between white and non-white families remains pronounced, even rising in recessionary times[55] (US Census Bureau, 2010). Class and racial inequalities are detrimental to a healthy society (Wilkinson and Pickett, 2010) and a healthy economy (McKinsey, 2009; Stiglitz, 2013). And they do great harm to a nation's education, since "failure in school too closely tracks structures of racial and class inequality" (Hochschild, 2003, 9; Kozol, 1992, 2012). While these facts seem clear, they are often obscured by *class perceptions*. *The New York Times* (2005) nationwide survey[56] exemplifies this point:

> More than ever, Americans cherish the belief that it is possible to become rich. Three-quarters think the chances of moving up to a higher class are the same or greater than 30 years ago.

Perceptions preserve the American Dream and, with this, the promise of social mobility. There is a strong sense that Americans have higher standards of living than previous generations and that a merit system has largely overruled hereditary entitlements. This isn't a new reading. From Horatio Alger's (1832–99) meritocratic stories of 'rags to riches' and the advances of the 'Gilded Age' (late 19th – early 20th century) to the celebration of modern entrepreneurs (Forbes Lists), newfound 'success' has always been cultivated. But there's a more critical script. From F. Scott Fitzgerald's *The Great Gatsby* and Arthur Miller's *Death of a Salesman* to the rise of the Occupy Wall Street movement, 'success' has been unevenly observed. It's not that talent and effort don't matter; they clearly do. It's that 'non-merit' factors like social class, race, heritage and wealth endure to regulate 'success' (McNamee and Miller, 2009). While these macro dynamics produce conditions of *advantage* and *disadvantage*, real social mobility necessitates their realisation and equalisation. And it necessitates an appreciation of, and attentiveness to, 'underdogs', 'misfits' and those skilled in 'the art of battling giants' (Gladwell, 2013). 'The middle class squeeze' now counts itself among this group, as jobs are scarce and household costs are rising in one of the most expensive places to live in America (New York City Council, 2013). And while there is much focus on the need to 'revive the middle class dream' (Center for an Urban Future, 2009), attention must also be given to New Yorkers in the lower and under classes. All of which points to the need for a fairer society – one that reflects, and is reflected by, a just public education system. While such education is key to social mobility, it cannot act alone. Early-education and antipoverty strategies in health, housing, employment and the environs accompany school success. To perceive otherwise is to place unequal faith in schools' success or, more unfairly, to treat schools as 'the wastebasket of society' (Halsey *et al.*, 1980).

In a country where meritocracy and social mobility are cherished and oft presumed, it's not easy to think about, or speak of, class. Besides, class effects/affects are inherently hard to articulate or make visible. I often revert to Pierre Bourdieu for assistance. Bourdieu (1977a, 72) describes a person's *habitus* as "a set of durable, transposable dispositions" that regulates mental and physical actions to the point where individuals are often unaware of its influence. He speaks of a person's attitudes and behaviours as being inculcated from an early age, refined through social and cultural resources (or 'capitals') and often passed on to the next generation (Bourdieu, 1986). In a direct challenge to Friedman's (and others') notion of *rational* 'choice' (e.g. choosing a school), Bourdieu maintains that this is not about individual 'preference', or about performing (necessarily) an 'intentional' act. Instead, 'choice' is more likely to be instinctive (a 'feel for the game'), but still one that's inextricably bound up with an individual's 'lifeworld' (Husserl, 1936/1970). Choosing a particular school, then, is habitually related to one's social position and the school that is eventually chosen is *itself* an act of social positioning. So there are those – most likely in higher social positions – who choose an Ivy League or Russell Group university[57] in the interest of cultural (or educational) *distinction* (Bourdieu, 1979, 1984). And there are many others who choose at uneven educational ranks. Indeed, the notion of 'distinction', as framed within the market model of education, remains undisturbed.[58] Consequently, the promise of (relative) 'success' is advanced that, in turn, provides for the legitimation of social differences. Taste is a (tacit) identifier of these social differences: 'I wish to send my child to this school, not that one'; 'I like that particular college'. And taste, as the UK artist Grayson Perry (2013, 3) reminds, "is an emotional business", with taste decisions oft demonstrating "loyalty to the clan." Thus, as we engage with others with similar social and material histories (what Bourdieu calls 'social capital' networks), we tend to share *class-based* tastes:[59]

> Class is something bred into us like a religious faith. We drink in our aesthetic heritage with our mother's milk, with our mates in the pub, or on the playing fields of Eton [a private school in England]. We learn the texture of our place in the world from the curlicue of a neck tattoo, the clank of a Le Creuset

casserole dish, or the scent of a mouldering hunting print. A childhood spent marinating in the material culture of one's class means taste is soaked right through you.

(Perry, 2013, 2)

Taste standards appear, therefore, under the natural guise of lifestyle (including educational) 'choice'. But they can ultimately serve to legitimate class differences. Working alongside *economic capital* (the ability to afford education[60]) and other *cultural capitals* (learning dispositions, accent, 'official' knowledge forms, cultural membership, linguistic competence[61]), they elevate some, over others, to educational 'success'. Notions of educational 'advantage' and 'disadvantage' are duly produced. And they are habitually *reproduced* by individuals whose personal expectations of 'success' are measured against their objective social conditions. In other words, the possibility of 'success' is measured against likely (or unlikely) outcomes.[62] Yet class, as with talent and hard work, can never *fully* determine 'success'. There will be some individuals who can overcome even the most entrenched barriers of disadvantage. They may exercise strategies that surmount these barriers while, at the same time, playing by the 'same' rules of the game. It is important to recognise, however, that the hurdles are stacked much higher for this group and that those in more advantaged positions have a clearer and shorter run in the 'race to the top'.[63] Those who are disadvantaged also experience the weight of expectations and the necessity of 'success' more cruelly (Bourdieu, 1962/1973, 91). And the 'success' choices they make are always conditional (Bourdieu, 1977a), as 'trade-offs' mean more: Having to work much harder, prove oneself, invest limited time and money, forgo leisurely/creative pursuits, identify with the dominant culture, risk alienation from one's community, be the first to go to college, etc. In transactional terms, it really is 'a big deal'.

New York is the ultimate transactional city. Free market reforms like choice, competition and accountability facilitate the trading of educational 'products'. And managerial authority is secured via direct mayoral control over this 1.1 million student market. Under Mayor Bloomberg's administration, a number of reforms (*Children First*) have been ushered in, including an increase in charters, their co-location, and small schools; new instructional supervisions and tests; a school grading system (from A-F); merit/'success' pay for principals and teachers; and Common Core Standards[64] (Sparks, 2013). Studies of reforms in the United States suggest that gains in student achievements (*which are themselves contested*) haven't been as rapid as hoped (Ravitch, 2011, 2013). And while public schools appear to be working very well for the majority of students, a significant minority has been left behind (ibid.). In New York State, research indicates that the public education system is serving its majority well, for example, graduation rates are improving, more students are earning Regents Diplomas (the 'ticket' to higher education) and college enrolment is up (NYSUT, 2012). However, based on NAEP (National Assessment of Educational Progress), reading and math scores in New York State

(2003–2007), there were no significant gains made, except in fourth-grade mathematics (Ravitch, 2011, 88). Also, over the entire period of this state's reforms, a significant minority has been overlooked (NYSUT, 2012). Despite the evidence, messages of systemic inequality and steady 'success' in public schools are seldom acknowledged by reformers like Joel Klein (ex-chancellor of New York City's schools; now head of *News Corp* Education Division) or Michelle Rhee (ex-chancellor of Washington D. C. schools; now CEO of *StudentsFirst* lobby group).

Instead, recurrent 'reform' messages focus on an educational 'crisis',[65] the hiring and firing of teachers,[66] the expansion of charter schools and the shutdown of some public schools,[67] confrontation with reform 'obstructionists' (such as unions and teacher educators[68]) and praise for the 'private' sector, particularly its authority to *manage* and *replace* 'public' education.[69] The *image* of reform is authoritative, with reformers invested in its authority. Michelle Rhee's appearance on the cover of *Time* magazine (8 December 2008) exemplifies this power, with broom in hand and a resolve 'to fix America's schools'. Her self-proclaimed[70] image as a *radical, fighting to put students first* (Rhee, 2013), serves to *manage* and *replace* authentic meanings of 'radical', 'student-centred' education (see Chapters 2 and 4). 'Success' appears framed by talent, ambition and competitive effort, with no room for non-merit factors. In Rhee's image of 'success', it's a case of *class dismissed!* while she presents as its postmodern proxy. Rhee is not alone in generating *unreal* representations. While she asserts herself as a 'pro-teacher democrat', Joel Klein professes the virtues of democracy and school autonomy. At the same time, Klein helped reorganise the New York education system along corporate, hierarchal lines (Ravitch, 2011). Under his stewardship, schools (and their communities) were held accountable, while overseers (e.g. the PEP: Panel for Educational Policy) appeared elevated and further from view.

The media too plays its unreal part. Here, the reform message is made visible in 'spectacular' ways (Debord, 1967; Baudrillard, 1994). To illustrate, a PBS documentary famously filmed Rhee in the act of firing a school principal. And in 2010, Davis Guggenheim's film *Waiting for Superman* (2010) dramatised the 'failure' of public schools in America. This film is worth seeing for its aesthetic and affective qualities alongside its production values of 'success'. It features the director expressing his 'fear' of sending his kids to a 'failing' school and his good 'fortune' of being able to drive past 3 public schools on his way to their private school of 'choice'. It features Michelle Rhee highlighting how 46,000 kids in Washington D. C. are 'counting on her' and how "most of them are getting a really crappy education right now." And it features young children and their families applying to charter schools. This they do via a lottery system that claims to be 'democratic', but ultimately leaves their enrolment fate to chance.[71] Daisy, a Hispanic girl from East LA, is told by her father to keep her fingers crossed, but her number isn't called (she is one of 135 applicants for 10 spots at *KIPP LA Prep*). Bianca, an African-American girl from New York, also loses out and is consoled by her distressed mother (she is one of 767 children that apply for 35 spots at the *Harlem Success*

Academy). And Anthony – a poor black boy from Washington D. C., whose father died from drugs and whose mother he has never known – is eventually 'successful' in his submission to the *Seed School*. Soon he must leave Gloria, his loving grandmother. She has raised him and doesn't know what she would do without him, or what they would do without each other. But he must pursue his dream. This is how the film ends, with Anthony relocating to new living quarters in a new school. As he lies down on his bunk bed, he tenderly looks at a photo of his cradling dad. It never leaves his side.

Is *Superman*, with his power to save and rescue, really a legitimate image for 'success'? Geoffrey Canada, who inspired the metaphor, features strongly in the film and his 'Promise Academy' (which is part of the HCZ [Harlem Children's Zone] project) is widely endorsed.[72] Paul Tough's (2008) book *Whatever it Takes* had already charted the project's 'success', and President Obama has since funded its replication across twenty 'Promise Neighbourhoods' in the United States. 'Hope' is what's promised. And many hopefuls will (predictably) invest in the schools' privileged, charter status. In the case of the 'Promise Academy', wealthy businesspeople with a clear ideological mission sit on the board of directors and finance the project, alongside philanthropies (e.g. Gates and Walton Foundations), to the tune of tens of millions of dollars each year. This enables a wider social support system that includes a baby college (workshops for parents), an all-day kindergarten, pre-schooler programmes, extended (intensive) school days and SAT prep classes, social services (housing needs and foster care preventions), college assistance (retention supports), health clinics and community centres. These supports validate that the school 'cannot work alone'. But they also endorse the school's 'advantage', even the (oft hidden) influence of wider supports on 'test scores'. This presents as a significant paradox. The Promise Academy officially embraces inclusivity (there are no fees or academic entrance criteria, for example), yet it *is* selective (it has a 'primed' learner population and elevated position vis-à-vis other school providers in the community). Further, there appears to be no critical engagement with class, poverty, race, testing, discipline, school culture, transformative pedagogy, etc. Instead, learners are served up a *conservative cognitive up-skilling agenda*.[73] Can this model really 'flip the script' of educational disadvantage?

Individual 'successes' fill the storylines of the model script. There is no shortage of 'redemptionist' imagery (O'Sullivan, 2008) in Tough's (2008) depictions or in HCZ news items – kids are referred to as being "saved", families and the character of the neighbourhood "transformed." Should we not focus on "what actually works" (President Obama in Tough, 2008) and simply 'get things done'? Is this not about pragmatic change? Do poor, black students have any real choice? Geoffrey Canada puts forward his own conclusion:[74]

> If you want poor kids to be able to compete with their middle-class peers, you need to change everything in their lives – their schools, their neighbourhoods, even the child-rearing practices of their parents.

But is this *a renewal* of educational provision or 'more of the same'? To what extent is this an imposition of others' cultural values that are taken as 'a given', as 'worth having'? I revert to Pierre Bourdieu again. Bourdieu would certainly caution against 'replication'. He reveals how *the imposition* of thoughts and actions on marginalised groups (how one should think about and act upon 'success' in education), and the dominant power behind their construction, often remains hidden (see Chapter 4). Further, denial and 'misrecognition' enable the dominant patterns of power to be perpetuated such that the subjugated[75] often end up co-writing the model script: 'I agree, this is a better school'; 'every child should be able to achieve at this level'; 'we need more tests'; 'performance ought to be measured that way', etc. This he refers to as *symbolic violence*, since 'good choice', 'good taste' and 'good education' are not only self-evident and desirable, they must be (oft unconsciously) replicated. But what is ultimately replicated is the social structure of distinction (Bourdieu, 1977a; 1984; 1996). So for whom is 'success'? I am jolted back to Anthony's story. How, I wonder, does he identify with his 'success'? How are his civil rights being met – explicitly, his right to an education that values *his* family and community associations? Does he, as a poor black student, have any 'choice'?

There are others that critique the model script. One alternative worldview is presented in the Grassroots Education Movement's (2011) film, *The Inconvenient Truth Behind Waiting for Superman*. It defends *public* education and advocates for smaller class sizes and greater professional support for teachers in securing sustainable school 'success'. It questions charter schools' attrition patterns in recruiting teachers and retaining Special Educational Needs (SEN) students, as well as controlling cultures that constantly target 'results'. And it rehearses a different civil rights script that, in the words of Sam Anderson (Black New Yorkers for Educational Excellence and Coalition for Public Education), "enhances black community development" and "the radical tradition" of Harlem and the civil rights movement. Rocky Killion's (2013) film, *Rise Above the Mark*, also defends public education. It highlights the disproportionate influence of politics and corporate 'interests' and the damaging effects of 'high stakes' testing in American education. And it asks some interesting questions, such as: Why are legislators, not educators, 'calling the shots'? Why can't public schools and teachers creatively deliver on 'success'? What if one was to look beyond testing to find other ways of innovating? Linda Darling-Hammond, who features in the film, contends that the "wrong kinds of tests" are being used "in the wrong kinds of ways" (Darling-Hammond, 2010). Diane Ravitch highlights how "absurd" it is for students to be punished, alongside their teacher and school, if they do not always "pick the right answer." And Pasi Sahlberg, a senior advisor to the Ministry of Education in Finland, prompts a reorientation of the 'innovative' capacity in America. Presently, the central problem rests with how 'innovation' is captured by, what he calls, the Global Educational Reform Movement. In keeping with his acronym (GERM), Sahlberg signifies a move away from reforms that have spawned endemic damage to American schooling.

There may be some lessons to learn from Finnish education (Sahlberg, 2012a). And while it's essential not to reify international comparisons,[76] Sahlberg's recommendations may critically signal 'another way':

- Excellence *through* equity e.g. fair funding for education; conjunctural supports like health for all; early educational supports; structures that enable smaller school variations (and *less* 'choice'![77]).
- Smart time management e.g. *less* homework and teaching contact time; no standardised testing (though test samples can be *anonymised* for the purpose of informing pedagogical direction).
- Enhanced teacher professionalism e.g. strong entry requirements that include social and ethical commitments to teaching; methodological responsibility and competence, etc. (Sahlberg, 2012b).

Ultimately, it is for the American people to act. But, as previous discussions highlight, 'freedom' is already cast; *learning success* is framed; the scene is set. Other 'innovations' may not sit well with US *thinking* about 'freedom' and its links to 'success', 'civil liberty' and 'morality'. Going beyond Left-Right and Berlin-Boston divisions, *the science of educational reform* may also diverge. This points to the need, from a scholarship perspective, to 'take a step back', to make an 'epistemological break', as Bourdieu might put it (Bourdieu *et al.*, 1991). Only then can one begin to critique the 'science' of the market model of education (Bourdieu, 2004) and interrogate how it is really 'experienced' by those who work *alongside* it every day (Heidegger, 1927/2008).

I am still grappling with this critique. It's the weekend before my two-week research visit to the Queens School of Inquiry. On Saturday night, an old friend invites me to the New York Athletic Club (NYAC) where he is a private member. Niall's rise in the world of finance is a story in itself and he tells many others about the city's lure of 'success'. Strolling through the opulent Hall of Fame, we are flanked by members' outstanding accomplishments in sport, business and the arts. On the 24th floor of 'the City House', we take in the spectacular views over upper Fifth Avenue and Central Park. Manhattan's prospects, it seems, are always 'bigger and bolder'. A more grounded experience awaits in Williamsburg, Brooklyn; though 'success' is celebrated here too, with musicians and artists aspiring to be invited. Budding entrepreneurs complement the 'hipster' culture by creatively escaping conventions – working from home, dressing down for meetings. Rory is another of our friends who has settled here to develop an innovative business model. He is the perfect host, generously accompanying my discovery of flea markets, second-hand shops, eateries and late night bars. He introduces me to the Hasidic Jewish culture of South Williamsburg, Puerto Rican festivities and Brooklyn sports. I am indebted to Niall and Rory for their 'lived' New York stories. Soon I will script my own short-lived narrative. The J Line will depart from Marcy Avenue, Williamsburg and arrive at Jamaica Center-Parsons/Archer. Thereafter, I must take the Q36 bus to 158–40 76th Rd, Queens. In just over an hour, I'll be in a different world again.

Figure 3.2 The Queens School of Inquiry

The Queens School of Inquiry (QSI)

What makes a 'successful' school? Well, there are a lot of hidden forces: School 'choice' ('the right type'/'in the right place?'); 'meritocracy' ('the right values'); resources ('the right funding'); social class ('the right tastes'); cultural image ('the right appearances'); and 'innovation' ('the right ideas and organisation'). These, in turn, are shaped by 'interested' groups who provide civil, moral and economic rationales for the meaning of 'success'. These hidden forces are rarely considered in response to *what makes a 'successful' school?* Most likely, the 'success' script is read as authored, with readers absorbed in its more 'visible' text – test 'scores' and 'targets', teacher 'performances' and school 'report cards'. But there are hidden forces at work here too. Tests, for example, are strongly correlated with the socio-economic status of learners, and they generate racial, ability and gender demarcations (Hochschild, 2003; Spelke, 2005). Evidence shows that they have not worked, especially in addressing equity-achievement gaps (National Research Council, 2011; Guisbond, Neill and Schaeffer, 2012). Moreover, test effects remain highly problematic and can include:

- Teaching and learning 'to the test'.
- Coaching particular students and 'intensifying supports'.
- Prioritising some subjects and 'narrowing the curriculum'.

- Sublimating 'economic' and 'skills-based' values over-and-above critical, creative, personal and inclusive ones.
- Activating high levels of student 'competition' and 'discipline'.
- Reproducing test preparation materials and better 'test-takers'.
- Shaping student ability, motivation, confidence and, ultimately, 'self-image'.
- Creating unrealistic 'high-stakes' targets that can lead to the lowering of standards, even cheating.[78]
- Conflating test 'scores' with cultural goals, school 'success' and teacher 'quality'.
- 'Gaming' the system to enhance 'performance'.
- Equating 'data' improvement with learning 'growth'.

There are many ethical and scientific reasons, therefore, for resisting a simple reading of 'test scores'.[79] And while tests are tied to 'performance', similar caution needs to be exercised. Tests become 'high-stakes' when they are linked to the shuttering of schools, an escalation in students' and teachers' workload, the hiring and firing of professionals and the roll-out of performance-based pay. Taking the latter, there is increased (economic) 'interest' in rewarding teachers who are adjudged to 'perform'. The New York City Department of Education has already attempted student and school-wide bonuses and is open to developing new measures, while *Race to The Top* encourages all states to evaluate teachers on a sliding scale from 'highly effective' to 'ineffective', with test scores typically commanding 40–50 per cent weighting (Ravitch, 2011, 268–269). To be clear, there is *no* relationship between average student performance in a country and the use of performance-based pay (PISA In Focus, 2012).[80] Despite this reality, performance-related pay is still being supported with less-than-reliable data,[81] while oppositional voices are indicted as being "ideologically motivated."[82] It's clear that teachers can and *do* make a positive difference to students' 'success'.[83] Notwithstanding aforementioned hidden forces, there are factors (beyond remuneration) that can support teachers' competency, from enhancing career status/prospects and trusting practitioners, to valuing 'experience', continuing professional development and teachers' own research capacity. But how productive can it be, I wonder, especially during intense periods of 'innovation', to downgrade 'teacher quality' (despite claims to the contrary)? How is 'success' best served by reforms that overly burden, stress, test and mandate teachers? How well can creative change agents work under such circumstances? The signs of intensification appear obvious. Between 40 and 50 per cent of new teachers do not survive the first five years, while 80 per cent or more from the Teach for America (TFA) programme leave after their third or fourth year (Ravitch, 2011, 177, 190).

Teachers in New York are highly qualified. It is one of only twelve states that requires a Master's Degree certification, while 40 per cent of its teachers earn at least thirty credits beyond this requirement (NYSUT, 2012). Currently, 81 per cent of all New York high school graduates enrol in college, which ranks New York third in the nation in terms of this indicator of student 'success' (ibid.). But there are huge challenges to this progress, not least funding. In 2012–13, the school districts operated with over 1 billion dollars less in state aid, while state support for public higher education (State University of New York [SUNY], City University of New York [CUNY] and community colleges) was reduced by 1.7 billion dollars since 2008–2009 (ibid.). Somewhat absurdly, 'getting in' to college doesn't mean being 'college ready'. To illustrate, 80 per cent of New York public school graduates who enrolled in City of New York *community* colleges in 2012 needed 'remediation' in reading, writing and math (Kamenetz, 2013). Once more, there are hidden forces at play here, as the vast majority are working class, minority students (ibid.). Indeed, after 6 years, just 1 in 4 will have managed to attain any degree (ibid.). Further, of the 'college and career ready' total in 2012 (comprising 35.3 per cent of New York students), 48.5 per cent were White, 15.7 per cent were Hispanic and 12.5 per cent were of Black origin (King, 2013). So school 'success' performs alongside college 'success', with some students excelling (e.g. those from particular socio-economic and racial backgrounds; those who take college-level Advanced Placement exams in high school; those who do well in Regents exams), while others struggle across the divide (e.g. those with less 'advantage'; those on 'remediation' programmes in college).

Besides 'college readiness', *small* schools are officially identified as enabling 'success'. Campaigners in New York (Deborah Meier, Ted Sizer, Ann Cook) advanced not just size and organisation as enabling features but, more significantly, small schools' commitment to democracy, critical inquiry, social justice and personalisation (Meier, 1995/2002). But other (political) 'interests' have since captured and privileged 'school size', endorsing its virtue in delivering upon 'results' and (market-based) 'reforms' (Hantzopoulos and Tyner-Mullings, 2012). And there are other challenges. Limited size can restrict support for English-language learners, broader curriculum programmes and extracurricular (including sports) activities; children may have to transfer out of their neighbourhoods; schools may have to co-locate and share limited space and facilities; and, ultimately, size may have no material impact on student achievement[84] (except perhaps when other 'larger' schools bear the weight of increased numbers of working class, migrant and special needs students). When it comes to classes, though, size does matter. Indeed, small class participation in the early years of schooling has been shown to increase the likelihood of high school graduation (Finn and Gerber, 2005). Despite it being a key factor (among other *inter-related* factors) of 'success', class size appears sidelined by a crude focus on 'teacher quality' (which is *discretely* bordered by bottom-line 'results'). This provokes some searching questions. How can schools discern between varying (oft capricious) 'success' messages? Might they, as Michael Wilshaw (head of the Office for Standards in Education in England and Wales) suggests, prioritise performance-related pay over class size? (Watkin, 2013). Might they, as Brendan Howlin (Minister for Public Expenditure and Reform in Ireland) mimics, apportion 'block grant' resources between teacher, Special Needs Assistant and class size numbers?[85] (Sheahan, 2013). Does this reflect local autonomy or refract from central accountability? Can and should symbiotic 'success' be separated out, ranked and ('freedom') fashioned as the school's responsibility? Who would be a school principal in this 'success' charged climate?

In evaluative times, a 'successful' school exhibits its 'success' statistics. And so the appearance of school 'success' allies to the appearance of 'correct' data such as test 'scores', 'college readiness', teacher 'performance' and school 'stats' (population breakdown, class-sizes, report cards). Data that aims to improve schools, and is "accurate, meaningful, fair, broad and balanced", may be viewed as 'good data' (Hargreaves and Braun, 2013, i). This contrasts with 'data driven accountability' which, in the United States, skews 'narrow metrics' for regulatory purposes (ibid., ii). Reformers may defend such data on the grounds that it can be refined, as if the 'science' itself (which is never in question) can be 'value-added'. Others may caution against a simple reading of data, even those whose work is centred on 'ranking schools' (e.g. www.greatschools.org/; UK Sunday Times League Tables). Nevertheless, problematisation is limited, while more users willingly *surface the data*, (for example, there are 44 million hits on the *Greatschools* website each year). In true postmodern fashion, then, the 'success' message may seem 'unreal', yet it still produces 'real' effects (Baudrillard, 1994). And perceptions, once more, preserve the American Dream, this time through the lens of 'scientific' data.

Mindful of this postmodern puzzle, I turn to the stats of the Queens School of Inquiry (QSI). A surface reading reveals the signs of 'success'. QSI is a small school (in 2012, the student population was 592). The small grade numbers are housed in small classes. Of the 63 students who first graduated in 2012 (out of a possible 65), 84 per cent secured college entry (mostly to CUNY public colleges). This is a remarkably high number, but then again QSI is an Early College Secondary School, from grades 6 (11 years old) through to 12 (17 years old). In 2006, following collaboration between the New York City Department of Education, CUNY, Queens College and the Bill and Melinda Gates Foundation, QSI was founded to prepare high school students for college. 'Disadvantaged' students are officially targeted since they remain heavily under-represented in college. Almost half of all QSI's students come from families that receive some form of public assistance, the majority qualify for the free or reduced-price lunch program and most are first generation college attendees. The school enables these students to earn, in tandem with their high school diploma, up to 64 Queens College credits (this is equivalent to two years free tuition, the duration of an Associate Degree). In his 2015 State of the Union address, President Obama indicated that everybody will soon be entitled to free community college. Up to this point, QSI students have a distinct 'advantage'. Of course they need to work on their prospects. Career and college supports are gradually introduced, with rigorous demands expected in the senior years. Thus, 6th graders visit Queens College on field trips; 7th and 8th graders spend two weeks on campus undertaking non-credit courses with professors; 9th graders take limited college credit courses; while the majority of college coursework is undertaken in the senior years, both in school and on campus. The 11th and 12th graders spend two mornings each week attending Queens College classes. And some of their teachers act as adjunct professors, similarly relocating between learning sites.

Students of varying ability apply to the school via a (highly over-subscribed) *lottery system*. This prioritises 'zone' residents and includes those with special educational needs (12 per cent in 2012), as well as English language learners (less than 3 per cent). The school's rising 8th graders apply through the normal high-schools' admissions process. This affords priority to existing QSI students, while grade 9 'transfers' have to meet certain academic criteria.[86] Attendance rates exceed 94 per cent and community ratings fare well (as judged against *Greatschools* and *Insideschools* websites). Many point positively to the school's diverse profile, which is largely a reflection of its location (Queens is America's most ethnically diverse county). Overall, 40 per cent of QSI's students are Asian, 25 per cent Hispanic, 18 per cent White, 15 per cent Black and 2 per cent Other (Native Pacific Islander or American Indian or Alaskan Native). The school's website can be translated into over 30 languages, home-school material can be printed in parents' native language and a translator may be employed for individual meetings. Official school evaluations are equally positive, with QSI consistently scoring a B grade (e.g. Progress Report 2012–2013), which equates to an overall 'proficient' judgement (Quality Review Report 2010–2011). High 'test scores' reflect years of hard work by those students who first joined (from 6th grade) and those who later transferred (from 9th grade). And they reflect the hard work of teachers and advisors who do much to support their efforts. 'Outcomes', as measured by test scores, signal the school's 'success': 92.2 per cent attain a Regents Diploma; 83.1 per cent attain Math College Readiness Standard' 89.6 per cent attain English College Readiness Standard and 98.7 per cent earn a grade C or higher in a course for college credit (Progress Report 2012–2013). QSI's 'success' is signposted by the parallel 'success' of its college partner; for example, Queens College is listed in the 2014 Princeton Review guide, *America's Best 378 Colleges*.

In QSI, grade-level teams meet daily and subject teacher teams weekly to develop inquiry-based tasks and rubrics. These are aligned to the Common Core State Standards (CCSS) and the additional standards developed by the New York State Department of Education (NYSED). Academic Intervention Services (AIS) are mandatory for grades 6–8 in English Language Arts (ELA) and Math-ematics. In 6th and 7th grades, a full period each day is devoted to students' skill development (4 periods a week are allocated to 8th graders). Students are grouped by ability in the skill areas as identified by the rubric (e.g. 'writing an argument using appropriate and rigorous informational texts'). Smaller group supports are available for the middle grades when 11th and 12th graders are on college campus. And 'intensive' after-school and summer supports are annually provided. Tests form a central part of the school year programme (e.g. QSI Comprehensive Educational Plan, 2011–2012). In October and November, students' pre-assessments are coded. From December to March, smaller interim assessments are given to monitor student progress in each focused skill area. From April to May, students are given a post-assessment, and during the month of June, teachers review data and develop a detailed report of student progress. The school utilises Castle Learning, an online resource that can "create assessments using Common Core aligned questions; deliver pre-tests and post-tests to show growth; and analyse data to differentiate instruction and eliminate surprises" (see https://www.castlelearning.com/corp/). In the upper grades, 6 pupils are reviewed for 'norming' and 'identifying' learning needs. And based on summative and formative feedback, collaborative lessons are designed to meet those needs. In 2011–2012, QSI increased the number of marking periods from 4 to 6 "to provide timelier feedback to students and families of student progress toward credit accumulation" (QSI Comprehensive Educational Plan, 2011–2012, 6). After each of the six report cards, the parent coordinator helps schedule meetings with the parents of students who are struggling to improve, or in Quality Review speak, "are deemed to be progress deficient based on the results from the Progress to Graduation Tracker" (Quality Review Report 2010–2011, 4).

The language and ideas of 'quality' exhort widespread use of assessments and 'scientific' data. In the 2010–2011 Quality Review Report, QSI was encouraged to "expand the practice of measurable, data driven goal setting across all content areas so that teachers concentrate on the academic growth of students through interim benchmarks to accelerate student learning" (Quality Review Report, 2010–2011, 4). This was encouraged "so that student outcomes promote refinements to the curriculum and pedagogy" (ibid., 5). At the same time, the school was obliged to respond to other 'success' messages:

- Instructional resources and decisions do not consistently target the needs of these students who seem to be keeping up but in reality are struggling to do so based on their very competitive environment, a sentiment shared by parents. One student shares that she struggles with reading because she does not like reading and is having a hard time keeping up. A failure to adjust her individual pace and level may contribute to her losing interest, frustration and eventually failure to meet expectations (ibid.).
- Some lessons, although introduced with the school-wide inquiry focus, continue to be traditional teacher-directed lessons, and as such do not provide students with many avenues to engage their peers in asking pertinent and relevant topic-based questions, making rebuttals using text-based reference, or engage in discussion that promotes a higher and deeper level of engagement. A lack of teachers' knowledge about effective or ineffective teaching practices or an explicit school held belief about how students learn best will hinder growth especially at the student level (ibid.).

The school is left to discern between these varying (oft capricious) 'success' messages. On the one hand, the 'Progress to Graduation Tracker' is invoked, along-side 'data-driven goal setting'; while simultaneously, (careful) personalisation is summoned over-and-above (accelerated) 'competition'. A strong faith in data also embraces the belief that curriculum and pedagogy can be refined by 'outcomes', thereby (inadvertently) privileging teacher-directed approaches, for example, teaching and learning 'to the test'. Of course, as a School of *Inquiry*, any 'outcomes' (or *product*) approach presents as a particular paradox.

The school highlights the significant role that parents play in its 'success'. Of the 16 members of the School Leadership Team (SLT), 8 are parents, including the Parents Association President. There's 'an open house' twice a year, and individual and general parent teacher meetings are regularly scheduled. Every December, an International Dinner is prepared (with more than half of all families in attendance). There's also an annual science night, as well as multiple college night events that aim to familiarise parents with admission processes, financial aid packages and transition issues. *Snapgrades* is an online interactive reporting system that enables parents and teachers/advisors to readily track students' progress, from items relating to homework missed, lateness and absence to up-to-the-minute performance tasks. The school has a dedicated parent coordinator whose task it is to correspond on all school matters. There's even a school's 'messenger wake-up call' available for those who find it hard to get out of bed. All of which points to indefatigable efforts to build home-school relations! In conjunction with the SLT, parents are actively involved in supporting key decisions around school 'success'. To illustrate, they helped secure funding for a newly refurbished science laboratory, new literacy coach, and reduced class sizes; direct RTTT Inquiry team money to fund before and after-school help for all grade students 'in the bottom third'; and develop an impressive support team that includes 6 SEN teachers, 2 supplementary teachers in ELA and Mathematics, 2 accommodation paraprofessionals, 2 school psychologists, and 3 guidance counsellors (one of whom offers bilingual support, and another, Queens College faculty member, who closely connects with QSI's Career Institute). In developing such resources, the school benefited from start-up funding from the Bill and Melinda Gates Foundation and other funders, and, as an early college high school, it still supports slightly higher costs than regular schools (5–12 per cent; see www.earlycolleges.org/overview.html).

The Career Institute attends to the 'college and career' priorities of the school. It targets the future – what students will do with their lives. And it focuses the present: How lesson plans, daily activities, tutorial work and college performance tasks can model preparation. The curriculum design combines the senior high school years (grades 11 and 12) and the first two years of college within a single 'coherent' programme of study. Extending the early ('Middle College') work of Janet E. Lieberman, this latest design is coordinated by *Jobs for the Future*, in partnership with The Bill and Melinda Gates Foundation and other funders. Advocates point to benefits that include a smoother transition between school and college, more inclusive college participation, and financial rewards in the shape of reduced tuition fees and enhanced future earnings.[87] Critics may question links between this 'innovation' and a dominant 'careerism' paradigm in education (O'Sullivan, 2005). They may associate this 'innovation' with corporate efforts to buttress education-employment relations (Bowles and Gintis, 1977). And they may emphasise its fit within an emergent 'credit' culture in education, one that steers increased division and exchange of the learning act (Long, 2008). Certainly, economic 'interests' are central to *Jobs for the Future* publications, for example, *The Economic Payoff for Closing College-Readiness and Completion Gaps* (Vargas, 2013). Also, Early College Schools are well placed to leverage from the (economic) value of 'college and career readiness' across *all* schools. Inevitably, as 1 of only 12

Early College public schools in New York, QSI epitomises such value. And the school's 'success' is measured on its college 'merits'. Of the 65 students in the first graduation class of 2012, 22 per cent earned up to 15 college credits, 28 per cent earned between 15 and 30 college credits, while 50 per cent earned between 30–60 college credits.

I'm finally en route to QSI. Outside Jamaica Center-Parsons/Archer metro, I clamber on the Q36 bus with hordes of school children. It's hard not to eavesdrop along the way. New Yorkers, young and old, exude confidence and think little of others' vicarious contact. There are more black people here than in Manhattan and Williamsburg, more diverse ethnicities and nationalities. Jamaica Queens, once an enclave for Irish immigrants, is now home to African Americans, Asians, West Indians and Hispanic groups from Columbia, Peru, Mexico, the Dominican Republic and El Salvador. Along Sutphin Boulevard through to Parson's, I become distracted by fluorescent shop fronts: McDonald's, Dunkin' Donuts, Cookie's Kids Department Stores, VIM Jeans and Sneakers. More esoteric buildings stand out such as Tabernacle of Prayer, Presentation of the Blessed Virgin Mary Catholic Church, and Grace Episcopal Church. The sight of a *rapid school response armoured vehicle* arrests me. Beyond the bustle, kids disembark at their 'chosen' schools. Those

Figure 3.3 Queens College: The *students'* union

who stay do not see the townhouses of Queens, how they frame a charming border. Past neat blocks, I trail their wooden facades, front porches and backyards, marking the sporadic presence of somebody or some fluttering flag. Eventually I arrive outside a block that houses 3 schools. Spanning the second floor, I take in the stretched accommodation of QSI (Figure 3.3). It's not hard to imagine passers-by. The building and its subjects will go largely unnoticed. Much like 'success' itself. Many will be unsighted to the *sources* of 'success' that lie well beyond the school gates, including socio-economic foundations that matter the most (Berliner, 2013). Many will not see beyond a narrow vista of 'teacher quality', nor recognise that there are simultaneous, inter-related 'success' factors at play. And many, whose sights are set on 'outcomes', will not observe *learning success* in rehearsal.

The (cultural) practice of *learning success*

In the entrance hall sit two burly security guards. I exchange pleasantries before they make a prompt, and unexpected, request to see my photo ID. Over the next two weeks,[88] I'll perform the same daily ritual: Show my ID, explain the nature of my visit and sign in. Any budding urge to question this tedium is soon clipped. Later that day (15 April 2013), the Boston bombing sensitises all New Yorkers to high alert. QSI's Principal is summoned to escort me to the second floor. Meredith Inbal is cheerfully warm and welcoming. She speaks fondly of her teacher experiences in the initial school years. As successor to Elizabeth Ophals, the founding Principal, she has come to know this place well. We bump into Suzanne, the college liaison officer who divides her time between school and Queens College. Suzanne, as I witness, is always busy preparing for events. There's the *abroad scheme* that heavily subsidises kids to visit places like London and Paris for language/culture exchange. There are career nights to arrange as early as grade 6 with numerous employers and professionals invited to talk; even now, she anguishes "I can't find a surgeon." And there are a number of students to consult concerning various college choices and scholarship opportunities. I am immediately struck by QSI's 'care ethic', particularly the attention to students' academic progress. Meredith speaks openly about the ubiquity of 'tests' and the practical need to prepare students even for "the language that's used." However, "as an educationalist", she is ever conscious of teachers' anxieties around 'performativity' and the prevalent danger of 'teaching to the test'. On our whistle-stop tour of the H-shaped corridors, I get a glimpse into a high school class at (college) work. Around horseshoe desks, students exchange ideas in groups, make notes for their joint reports and prepare for group presentations. "It's very competitive", remarks Meredith, "which helps them in their prep for how to be a college student."

Having been introduced to various personnel, I make my own way to the staffroom, a cubbyhole that houses two PCs, a photocopier, landline, toilet and a small rectangular table where colleagues congregate during free periods. It's not the most tranquil of spots. One female SEN teacher has just finished speaking on the phone. She confides: "That was a parent who has just consulted her attorney about her son's special needs supports." The parent knows that supports are being "weaned off in the school, so to speak" and "she's concerned about that." I learn that there is early extensive intervention for the first few years; thereafter resources dictate. It transpires that the phone call coincides with 'test day': 13 SEN students are undertaking a 135 minute test in ELA. The SEN teachers are anxious for them to do well. And they are concerned for their well-being (they have snacks and treats for afterwards). The teachers stress that 'success' means something very different for these students with whom they work closely. This, one teacher states, cannot be captured by tests that "judge one child's ability against all the others", or in educational jargon, supports comparative cognitive 'norms' (see Chapter 1). Development, they all agree, takes an uneven trajectory ("progressive and regressive moments"), and a SEN child's 'success' can only be measured against his/her own abilities and needs. In reality, these teachers constantly navigate between emotional (e.g. snacks and treats) and academic (e.g. prep and tests) supports. A humanities teacher joins in: "You have to steer a middle ground; teach how to be 'test savvy' and follow a higher ground of support and inquiry." "I don't claim to get that balance right, especially when it comes to 'exam fever' "; before adding "I'm here a long time now and I'm still stressed out." Relating tests to (un-named) political 'interests', he asserts: "They're trying to make teaching into a clinical science; it's really a subjective, creative art." And on 'teacher performance': "You ask students about the best teachers – they won't say 'standards'."

I'm in a grade 9 US history class. It speaks to modern America. The topic is 'mass consumerism', but the teacher decides to start by discussing the tragic events in Boston. He is an experienced practitioner and knows the value of 'hidden curriculum' work. Kids struggle to understand yesterday's bombing; he empathises, listens and allows them have their say. The flag in the corner is at half-mast. He urges all: "Keep your eyes open and stay safe." Then it's time to refocus students and remind them of impending exams. He sets up the first debate: "Does credit increase everyone's standard of living, or is it a way for businesses to control consumers' lives?" A lively discussion ensues. Some students take notes; others are directed to contribute. References are made to them having to "one day take out loans for college and establish some credit history." Students pitch in: "My brother can't pay back his college loans"; "my cousin is 27 and she's still paying back a lot and hasn't even got a job in her field"; "my brother has a credit score of 500." "Why do we do this?" the teacher exasperates, "we want a lot of things we can't afford." Then the class is taken on a revision slide tour of the New Economy in the 1920s, Ford-line production and the advent of mass media: "FDR [Franklin Delano Roosevelt] was the first President to use the radio regularly"; "Kennedy [John F. Kennedy] used the TV to his major advantage." I overhear a female student next to me: "I love his notes, short and sweet and to the point." A boy comments "I don't remember doing this, when did we do this?" "Do you want my notes?", a girl responds. Then the teacher hands out a worksheet. Another girl asks "is this extra credit?", while the teacher urges "let's see how many you get right." Both effectively manage academic 'performance'. When the students are finished, the teacher collects all the answers. I notice how well prepared he is; all solutions are pre-set on his laptop. Now conscious of other management concerns, the teacher finishes: "Tomorrow we slow it up a bit."

'Success' is clearly on display. The narrow corridors are adorned with the legacy class of 2012. Framed letters of admission to CUNY, SUNY and other prestigious colleges celebrate their achievements. Classroom walls signal the course: 'Regents standards – 3 hours, 1 day, 50 multiple choice questions, 1 thematic essay, 1 DBQ' (Document-Based Question); 'No slacking any time'; 'Good mathematicians can explain their work'. Teachers put faith in *inquiry* as the means to unlock students' potential. I witness them self-present as learners: "I must look that up later"; "I have to read more about attorney delays and judge's judgements around speedy trials." I see them guide good practices: "You should be taking notes here"; "you must research this a little more and come up with your own opinion"; "you'll need to reflect on that problem." And I witness them directly referencing exams: "The teacher grading your regents will give you 3 points for this but if you leave out units, you lose 1 point"; "if you want to be successful in your regents, then you need to come to me after school"; "this question was given in the Regents test a couple of years ago." At times, exams 'drive' teaching which (ironically) diminishes the inquiry focus. Similarly, exams 'drive' *learning* with students successfully knowing 'what' to do but sometimes failing to grasp 'how' or 'why'. Students too make direct references to exams: "Do you get any points for the drawing?"; "do you have notes on this for exam prep?" Students are often consumed by looming tests and 'credit' accumulation. And their teachers are often consumed by aligning curriculum content and skills and tracking grade point averages. Exams appear as a binding force in the student-teacher contract. Teachers' professionalism is bound up with planning, prepping and pinpointing 'success'. They encourage, cajole, remind, advise and check, each time performing a particular (academic) 'care' function. And when teachers are not always at hand, students 'care' for each other via group work, collaborative research, sharing notes, talking out problems and supporting one another's 'success'.

A large open-plan office provides the site for school management. Desks are scattered among various functions – school reception, parents' coordinator, college and career guidance, middle and high school administration. Students are no strangers to this space. A group are at work beside the rudimentary kitchen. Meredith's desk is occupied by one 12th grader. On the phone to his father, he is animated: "It's too much money pop"; "it'll cost 100k by the time I finish." Meredith explains that he has just been accepted into a top culinary arts school in New York and his dad wants him to "follow his dream." I ponder on the sacrifices made for university, particularly by those who can least afford it. It is legitimate to question: 'Is college worth it?' (Bennett and Wilezol, 2013).[89] I ponder on the pressures that young people feel in pursuit of this 'success'. It must be hard to decline Queens College with credit accumulated, money redeemed. None of this burden is now on show in music class. Students' enjoyment surpasses the High School value of 1/2 a credit. "You don't have to follow a strict structure here", a high achieving student tells me, while the serene presence of the teacher adds to a real sense of retreat from the points race.

Curious now to know how students learn off-site, I accompany Suzanne on a trip to Queens College (see Figure 3.3). One grade 11 class is discussing Mark Twain's *Adventures of Huckleberry Finn*. Their QSI teacher/adjunct professor directs the group's exchange. "I don't think Twain was necessarily racist; he was just showing how people thought about race at the time", states one student; while another concurs "it's a satire, right?" The teacher steers the conversation: "The current acceptable term is black, before it was coloured and also Negro was used." "Does Twain himself", a student remarks, "regret his past where he may have been racist?" I notice how this student cuts a different figure from school. Here he is more attentive, more engaged; his tome is cluttered with yellow post-its. Another student asks: "Why did Twain choose a narrator who is too innocent and ignorant to challenge the topsy-turvy moral universe that surrounds him?" "That's a great question", says the teacher. It's my turn to concur. Students' maturity, independence of thought and reflective capacity are clearly on view. But the teacher demands more than opinions: "Please support your views with reference to the text"; "part of speaking is listening." A brief writing task is presented to formulate evidence-based positioning. It's an exercise to develop critical literacy, to nurture 'ways of thinking' and 'being' in college. At the close of the lesson, one student demonstrates its faculty: "If we take these quotes [she cites two passages], it's as if Twain is commenting on America itself [. . .] giving us the message that youth is very impressionable." Whereupon several classmates copy down her ideas.

The youngest students in college don't stand out; they don't want to. Like others they side-step the busy campus en route to class. In QSI they learn independence (see Chapter 1); here, they must exercise it. There are new skills to learn. In a lesson on 'Orientalism', I witness learning demands that necessitate the adept use of discourse analysis. Drawing on the work of Edward Wadie Said (1979), the lecturer commands: "You are creating, conjuring meaning when you name 'Middle East', 'Muslim', 'War'." The students learn to listen, note-take, pause for thought, question. One wonders how much they can know. In Political Science class, two QSI students blend in with more mature peers. They take in a wide range of concepts such as 'democracy', 'dictatorship', 'fascism' and 'resistance movements'. In this large lecture hall, there's a lot of lecturing, some questions and no hand-outs. Quietly and frantically, the QSI students take notes. They're absorbed in 'capturing' knowledge, but seemingly not overwhelmed. One of the students recently got an 'A' in his university assignment; he also received news of a prestigious college scholarship with four-years' free tuition, board and laptop. It's a fitting tribute to the school's and the student's efforts. "We always read better when the class is over", his friend tells me. Both spend many hours doing homework, helping each other, prepping for lectures and assignments. I am struck by students' own efforts in their 'success' – how *they* engender interest, commit-ment, conviction and resilience. Indeed, similar efforts are self-presented by other QSI students with whom I speak.[90] A grade 9 student spends 3–4 hours each night doing homework; another lives an hour-and-a-half from school and does similar amounts of work upon return. She convinces that the sacrifice is worth it: "One day I'm going to look back and I'm going to say 'I was struggling back then but now I have finally come to a place where I wanted to be all along'." I hear more stories of struggle, sacrifice and pressure. One 9th grade boy confides: "Well I feel pressure because my parents weren't born here and they like expect high of you"; an 11th grade girl adds "I'm absolutely conscious about the financial factor that may affect my college application [. . .] and I'm trying to boost my grades to see if I can get a scholarship." Still 9th grade students feel 'lucky' to be here, partly because "that's what we're told all the time", but also because "we get a lot of guidance and support from our teachers." "Teachers care here", says another, "they care about how you succeed in life, what you're going to do." In college you have more "eccentric professors", one student adds, and "they also want you to be more independent and have more life opportunities."

I am taken by most students' cooperative relations to competition. Certainly, there are individualistic sentiments: "Each of us has a drive" (female 10th grader); "you have to worry about living up to expectations" (male 11th grader); "it's up to me to keep my grades up" (male 12th grader); "we're always trying to see who has the best grades" (female 12th grader). But 'cooperation' is most evident:

- I think competitiveness is what makes people, you know, strive for more. Like your friends get a better grade than you, you have admiration and well you want to be like him [sic.] and then you're like 'let's study'. 'Teach me your ways', you know, and that's how you get a better grade (male 10th grader).
- I think we learnt how to beat the system really ever since 9th grade (male 11th grader).
- She's wearing the NYU T-shirt already. I was there when she got the letter. We were like screaming and jumping around (female 12th grader).
- Like if you're in a course and a lot of kids don't do well in the paper but one kid gets an A, you're going to go to that kid and ask 'can you help me with my paper?' (male 12th grader).
- Like we don't want the worst for each other. We want all of us to succeed, like do better. So we ask each other for help (female 12th grader).

Cooperative competition is a very American fact (Varenne and McDermott, 1998). There will always be students who co-build a 'success' culture, worry about their relative status therein and work hard to become 'successful', avoid 'failure' (ibid.). Beyond individual 'talent' or traits, parents, teachers and students construct 'success' as "a cultural fact": "America is the fact they inherited, and it will frame them for the rest of their lives" (ibid., 10). 'Success' is thus *made* in America.[91] Parents anguish about their children's 'success' in competitions; they display 'teacherliness' at home "making success visible and documentable" (ibid., 17). Professionals anguish about students' 'performance', as well as their own. And students make calculated decisions about who to work with, while earlier 'success' is "continually put on the line" (ibid., 111). In America, 'success' is a shared concern. In New York, it's positively 'transactional'.

Competition is *carefully* managed by the school:

- In chemistry, tests are like every two weeks or every week, compared to monthly in other classes (male 10th grader).
- I still manage to do well in class because of the fact that teachers tell us '10 per cent of the grade is for your homework'; 'do this, do that' (male 11th grader).
- I think what makes a good college student is knowing your priorities. The teachers help us with that (male 11th grader).
- We're focused here on college preparation (female 12th grader).

And competition is *strategically* produced by students:

- Time management is a skill you need to have (female 12th grader).
- We have a chance to win a scholarship to college and that's like an incentive to do well (female 12th grader).
- You have to get peers to help you [. . .] the teacher might go too fast so you're going to have to study, read a textbook, do that chapter yourself (male 12th grader).
- I'm going to go to Queen's College for a year with my credits to save money and then transfer out again (male 12th grader).

Speaking with a representative sample of parents,[92] it's clear that they too are strategic. Their efforts are not without risk since, from the outset, QSI itself was 'an experiment'. While the promise of college presented, there was (up to that point) no 'track record'. Parents acted, according to one, "on gut feeling." More strategic choices were also rationalised: One-to-one supports; an intimate school community; small classes; and the Queens College experience. While the majority of parents I consult do not have a college education, it's clear that they're 'success' literate. Thus, they take on board 'success' messages from social (capital) networks: "My daughter, the teacher"; "my neighbour who has an older son here"; "my son's godfather [who] holds a Harvard doctorate." They are conversant with the language and ideas of learning methodology: "Collaborative environment"; "thinking out problems"; "inquiry"; "independent research"; and "it's not what you learn, it's the questions." And they are keen to display wider meanings of 'success', noting the importance of "belonging", "self-esteem", having "good relationships", developing "as a caring person", being "respectful", "mature", "responsible" and "happy."

All parents assign wider meanings to 'success'. And they acknowledge the need for a more 'level playing field' in education. Indeed, they may have directly experienced this with respect to their own children. It is curious then to see how 'success' is strategically re-positioned in terms of 'advantage gain':

- Personally, if I was opening up a school, I would forget a lottery. I would pick all my students because you want them to succeed. If this school had failed in its infancy, we wouldn't be here.

- My daughter (she's a senior) feels strongly that there should be criteria for admission. If QSI wants to succeed in the future they should really, you know, have a certain kind of student coming in and it's interesting that a student has that perspective.

These insights are not just indicative of failure anxiety, that is, fear of relegation (despite verifiable 'success'). They also appear to demonstrate how "getting unfair advantage [. . .] makes sense for people to do" (Varenne and McDermott, 1998, 108). Why is it that this version of 'success' resurfaces over again? Not for the first time, Bourdieu can enlighten. In his book *Homo Academicus* (1988),[93] Bourdieu refers to 'oblates'. 'Oblates' (habitually from the lower or middle classes) demonstrate intense loyalty to a system that affords them entry to the upper classes and higher forms of 'capital'. Individuals have a 'psychological stake' (Bourdieu, 1988, 167) in becoming 'successful' and so they tend to conserve the (education) system that 'makes' them and are inclined to minimise the risk of status loss. Those who become 'successful', then, are likely to seek and protect 'advantage'. In effect, 'success' is generated by those who experience it.[94] In the words of Michel Foucault, 'power comes from below' (Foucault, 1990).

Not everyone intentionally (or otherwise) protects 'advantage'. Some parents appear less guarded about 'success', particularly those who encounter difficulties. One parent, for example, highlights how QSI teachers 'cared' for her son by providing extra maths supports before and after school. In a highly selective environment, she acknowledges, he could easily have been "left behind." No doubt guided by this experience, this parent appears more attuned to wider meanings of 'success'. Her story rallies some support. One parent speaks of the need for all children to be "well-rounded", to encounter "diverse peoples with diverse abilities." However soon afterwards, this parent returns to a more strategic response:

> I tell my children all the time: 'You used to compete with the kid down the street. You're now competing with the kid in China and Japan, in Spain. Everywhere. You can't stop here in school. You must in order to move on in this country exceed in college education. You've got to go to a graduate professional level.

Another parent is quick to endorse this 'reality'. Yet another points to 'credential inflation' (Coffield, 1999): "Now it's looking like college education is like a high school diploma." By internalising these accounts of 'success', college (naturally) becomes a 'big deal'. And the effects/affects on parents become very tangible. There's financial and career anxiety, mutual sacrifice, strategic responsibility and moral pressure:

- The state university is going to cost 3 times what I make [. . .] never mind if she would choose one of the private institutions. I mean that would be, you know, a mortgage.

- They say the employment opportunity is getting worse for nurse graduates. So we're in a kind of jeopardy, what are we going to do now?
- I say 'you're not the only person in the house in college. Everybody sacrificed for you being in college'.
- There are all kinds of plans we have in this country that you can set up. You're never going to have enough but you most certainly can have a start [. . .] you have to do your research [. . .] The key to college in this country is to get as much education as you can, as far as you can, as free as you can.
- I can't squash her dreams. I can't do that to her, you know.

Parents worry, sacrifice, strategise and care for their children to 'do well'. It is they who routinely escort their children along affective, social and learning journeys (see Chapter 1). It is they who most observe their children's anxieties:

> I try to protect her [. . .] They're requiring her to write 7 papers just for the English course in college. 7 papers is a lot for her. So now I'm in a pretty frustrating and anxious period of time because she's going to enter Hunter and, my God, it's a very tough college [. . .] She started this application process for college and one evening she was sitting there and she just had a meltdown. Crying and crying and I'm like 'what is the matter?', you know. I mean we've been building up to this but we don't realise how much we've been pushing them, you know. College, college, college [. . .] You know, they're nervous about how many credits the college is going to accept. They're nervous about senior year alone. Growing up, leaving school. Leaving QSI behind.

Parents, as well as peers (see Chapter 2), are influential figures in the transition from childhood to adulthood. And parents are central to cultivating educational 'success' (Lareau, 2000, 2003). Habitually, they listen, advise, compensate, model, correct and direct:

- We do a lot of talking and listening. I have to guide her and I have to talk to her. We may need to switch college if she doesn't get that programme.
- I'm a foreigner. I came from a country when I was 20 years old. I told my children 'I don't have any money. I don't have anything to leave you but education; here, there you go'. I spoke only Spanish and I took it upon myself to learn as much English as I could so I can read [. . .] I push and expose him to as much as I could. Museums, let's go. Zoos, let's go. All good things. All the things I couldn't experience.
- My husband is a subway cleaner and I went back to school [. . .] and got my degree. So neither of us were college graduates when our kids started going to school. It's that foundation we were talking about. Did you do your homework? You know, get to school on time. Be prepared, you know. Have a meal before you leave the house.

- She didn't do her homework and the teacher said he can't give her any credits. But we said 'you do it anyway, even if the teacher throw it in the garbage, you do it' [. . .] She never forgets that [. . .] we don't know any other way, but we want them to be where they are.
- Lay the foundation anyway you can lay it. Lay the foundation.

This parenting character appears as another American 'fact' (Varenne and McDermott, 1998). While the stakes are high, conservatism and resilience are binding forces. Parents take their 'success' role seriously. One comments "it's up to me to raise my kid"; another adds "it's not the school's job." That said, the school's work *is* reinforced at home. One parent, for example, demonstrates the need to uphold commensurate language codes (Bernstein, 1971/2003):

> I do say 'young man you're at home. You speak English here. Okay, I don't want to hear that. I don't know what that is. You speak standard English in this house and that's it'.

Correspondingly, home's work is reinforced in school. In a follow-up that evokes Presidential decree:[95]

> You know why our kids are so good? The government took prayer out of school, but we didn't.

While all may not share this view, they connect on home-school patronage. This finds its ultimate expression in school 'choice':

- This is the only school he wanted. This is the only school I put on the application. If he doesn't get in here, yes I'm going to make a fuss because that is what he wants. He will exceed because that is what he wanted.
- He was not picked for QSI. I was devastated. He cried because he was devastated. We did an appeal. We redid the whole thing all over again. I had to do what I had to do and I'd do it again if I had to. That's the hidden story of that lottery.

Parents' work on 'success' doesn't stop there. "It's important", says one, "that everybody plays a part in the education of your child."[96] On behalf of the *school*, parents advocate for "more resources" and the 'freedom' to "stay better" and "teach creatively." And in advocating for their *child*, 'a balancing act' is settled between enabling independence and intensifying direction. "It's a rollercoaster", says one; "up and down, up and down" adds another. Still, when the heaving journey comes to an end, it'll all be worth it. Parents are no different here from students' feedback on 'product'. When they "achieve", "accomplish", they can feel "validated" and "good about themselves." And they can "celebrate their success." "Who", one parent adds, "doesn't like a pat on the back?" Parents are keen here to stress the impact of 'motivation' and 'drive'. And they reserve a special role for the School Principal. "Ms. Ophals" (former Principal), recalls one parent, "had that Harvard handshake" for the students: "Welcome to QSI. I'm glad to meet you. I read your letter. I was very impressed." Another fondly recalls her patiently modelling 'success':

> My son, he's a good kid, you know. But he did some crazy things in the beginning and she didn't throw him out. And that's when my love came for the school, well for Ms. Ophals. He has an IEP [Individualized Education Program]. We're giving him independence, you know, and he is trying. I see it.

My own journey is now coming to an end. There have been plenty of ups and downs in clinging on to *learning success*. I take with me the parting thoughts of Elizabeth Ophals (former QSI Principal), Mary Beth Schaefer (former college liaison officer; now Assistant Professor at St John's University) and Meredith Inbal (present School Principal).[97] It's clear that educationalists want to 'do the right thing', while 'the pressure is on' to prepare for tests and 'care' for students. There may be few parents 'sophisticated' enough to have a nuanced reading of tests (Elizabeth). But beyond judgement, there's an understanding that parents, students and teachers must all cope with the "tyranny of the tests" (Mary Beth). Widespread confusion about measures of 'success' (e.g. school report cards) make nuanced readings more elusive (Meredith), while real life 'success' stories simply do not appear. Elizabeth instinctively records these: The student who surmounted behavioural difficulties; the student who resisted overly demanding academic pressures at home and immersed herself in social activities at school; the student, who despite a distressed home life, eventually found comfort in others and 'success' in the arts. All these stories affirm that "there's so much to a child's growth that has nothing at all to do with test scores" (Elizabeth). They are stories that highlight the need to work with others, and still be independent; to know oneself and figure out (however uncertain) life and work pursuits (Mary Beth). And they are *personal* 'success' stories: "I think everyone in life when they find 'success', they find it at their own level" (Meredith).

Even in an age of school *intensification*, there ought to be "space for kids to hang out [. . .] and just be kids" (Meredith). Persistent supports can, ironically, be 'detrimental' to independence (ibid.). There's also a question around their sustainability: Every subject can claim 'priority'; tasks are regular and multiple; policies can present 'ideal' practice and demand relentless attention (e.g. advisory roles, continuous feedback, extra-school supports, e-mails 'at all-hours', etc.); and some kids may feel overwhelmed by home and school expectations. It certainly appears that high expectations *are* important to 'success': " 'You're not going to fail' is an attitude that we have at QSI" (Elizabeth). And it appears, following the work of Lauren Resnik (1995), that "effort creates ability" (Elizabeth). But questions remain about the nature of expectations and the kinds of efforts that are 'performed' in school. These questions need to be scrutinised in the 'interest' of educational sustainability and effectiveness. For while it's often assumed that it's the student's behaviour and the student's efforts that make the difference, we all have responsibility for the 'performative' conditions of 'success'.

Teachers certainly play an important 'success' role. And they may play an even bigger role as 'leader' practitioners:

> You only get things done I think when everyone feels like they are part of the decision-making process and has a voice that's actually heard [. . .] I mean it's real [. . .] they actually see that they are part of what actually occurs and ends up happening (Meredith).

"You know, a good teacher", remarks Elizabeth, is one who values "children as human beings before curriculum"; who "teaches students, not subjects", adds Mary Beth. All three educationalists rate teachers for their apprenticeship practices; 'innovative' pedagogies; deft management; industry, care and commitment; disciplinary passion; and modelling of 'success'. Head*teachers* continually work on teachers' 'success'. Increasingly, they have to mediate change to balance teacher 'freedom' and autonomy with official measures of 'success'. There's always a 'tipping point' and more official measures can punish the 'best' teachers. Certainly, continuing professional development enhances *learning success*. But we need to ask: How is 'professionalism' so conceived? What is the meaning of 'success'? And are teachers becoming *more* or *less* professional in its pursuit?

Figure 3.4 Anyone for 'success'?

Everywhere, learning success

In America, messages of *learning success* abound. Before I leave, I review a copy of the New York City Education Department's *Expect Success* (NYCED, 2012). It encourages all parents to go beyond graduation requirements, to plan and save for their child's educational future. In one of the biggest bookstores located on 5th Avenue, I pick out titles such as *Cracking the SAT, 10 ACT practice tests* (3rd edition) and *Failure is NOT an option: 6 Principles for making student success the ONLY option*. When I return to Ireland, parallel messages await. 'The Scholarship' (a TV documentary) follows 5 'disadvantaged' students as they compete for limited entry to a prestigious fee-paying school in Dublin. 'Tough Young Teachers' airs on British TV and follows early career (TeachFirst) candidates working for 'success' in low-income communities. The Irish State Examinations Commission's website gives full access to past exam papers and marking schemes. The *Sunday Times* newspaper publishes its annual School League Tables; SchoolDays.ie (an online resource for parents and teachers) publicises them. The *Irish Times*, teaming up with a private secondary and 'grinds' school in Dublin, disseminates *The essential guides to exam success*. Teachers offer 'practical' guidance for exam preparation. The focus is on prediction ('what comes up') and 'performance' ('how best to answer the question'). 'Grinds' are a major industry, offering 'extra' tuition at a price (Figure 3.4). They are not unique to Ireland. For-profit private institutes in South Korea, known as *Hagwons*, are special 'crammers' that steer students towards Ivy League colleges in the States. It is not unusual for children as young as 3 years of age to attend, with senior students spending anything up to 14 hours a day in school. Is this 'sacrifice' worth it? Some will, unproblematically, point to South Korea's 'rise' in the international league tables (PISA, 2012), alongside other Asian regions such as Shanghai-China, Singapore, Japan. But they may not see the real price: Learning intensification, 'high-stakes' testing, and significant levels of youth disaffection. Traditional education systems engender similar effects/affects. In France, for example, Peter Gumbel's *On achève bien les écoliers* (2010) highlights how an elite schooling system creates harsh classroom experiences. 'Success', it seems, always depends on 'failure'. And 'successful' students, 'successful' teachers, 'successful' schools, even 'successful' countries, 'perform' as shining lights for 'others' to follow.

As education becomes ever more commodified and compared, 'innovation' is framed by market 'interests'. Increasingly, spin-off organisations offer training programmes (e.g. Kip McGrath tutor packages) and study services (e.g. Kumon learning centres), providers (*including* universities) engage in more 'relevant' scholarship', online courses proliferate alongside contract educators, researchers and consultants, and teaching itself is reinvented as a technical skills-based science. 'Branding' oneself (e.g. Twitter, individual profiles), one's organisation (e.g. school brochures, university courses) and one's country (e.g. 'Ireland Inc.', 'city of culture') is the order of the day. 'Ratings' yield economic benefits for oneself (e.g. public 'followers', career progression), one's organisation (e.g. student numbers, rankings) and one's country (e.g. high 'skilled' workforce, more 'educational tourists'). And 'success' becomes ever more regulated, often in experimental and authoritative ways.[98] But perhaps the greatest 'selling point' of 'success' is the promise of happiness (Ahmed, 2010). For even in unequal conditions of labour, wealth and power, 'happiness' shadows the ideals of 'success'. And the 'pursuit of happiness' is worth the struggle.[99]

So we are imagined by prospective views on 'success'.[100] How will we make sense of these oft unseen and seemingly indeterminate outlooks? How far can we review their object? How will we look back, and eventually account for, 'success in our time'? Questions for educators, everywhere.

Guiding research (notes)

1 Needless to say, all lists are not exhaustive. In the case of writers, the reader may well add the names of Emily Dickinson, Henry James, W. E. B. Du Bois, T. S. Eliot, J. D. Salinger, Harper Lee, Toni Morrison, etc.

2 The image presented here is one of a 'shooting star' that burns brightly and soon extinguishes. While these 'stars' appear ephemerally, many more follow in their wake. Thus, the cycle itself endures.

3 The tragic deaths of Marilyn Monroe, Grace Kelly and James Dean appear to sublimate their superstar status.

4 This attention can often be intrusive. And it can be unscrupulous, such as in the case in Britain where reporters of the (now defunct) *News of the World* and other *News International* newspapers were shown to have hacked celebrities', politicians' and other high profile persons' phones and to have bribed the police in certain circumstances. This they did in pursuit of selling stories. In the United States, the Federal Bureau of Investigation (FBI) has since launched an investigation into Rupert Murdoch's *News Corporation* to establish whether the voicemails of 9/11's victims were accessed.

5 To demonstrate migrant 'success', one may look to the aforementioned film directors, Frank Capra and Elia Kazan, who were born in Italy and Turkey respectively. Actors Ingrid Bergman and Greta Garbo were born in Sweden; Vivien Leigh in India; and Marlene Dietrich in Germany. All became quintessentially 'American', just like many contemporary artists who present on screen as culturally relevant 'Americans' (both in character and voice). In the world of music, too, Igor Stravinsky and Irving Berlin were both born in Russia but they would quintessentially echo an 'American' sound. Of course *all* (second generation and beyond) Americans identify, to varying degrees, with their migrant past. This may accentuate their own sense of 'success', relative to their family origin status.

6 Many American football, baseball and basketball stars, as well as professional boxers, have risen 'to the top'. Of course, this view of 'success' is largely predicated on material (fame and money) and social mobility ('upward' social and cultural connections) gains. In other sports, such as golf, athletes do not (in the main) elevate themselves from humble beginnings (due to *class* profile), and so do not get as 'tied' to 'upward' social mobility gains – though they do of course benefit from new social and cultural connections. Needless to say, these stars also benefit from high levels of material gain, which remains a significant parameter of 'success'.

7 The bewildering array of 'successful' inventions include the following, limited list: The Ferris wheel (1891), gasoline tractor (1892), (Ford) assembly line (1901), airplane (1903), tea bag (1903), binder clip (1911), fortune cookie (1914), supermarket (1916), toaster (1919), staple remover (1932), transistor (1947), hairspray and hand dryer (1948), the

sport of windsurfing (1948), personal computer and email (1971), handheld mobile (cell) phone (1973), space shuttle (1981), internet (1983), 'Hubble' space telescope (1990), iPod portable music digital player (2001) and the cardboard bike (2013). The vast array of 'successful' military inventions is omitted from this selected list. Of course as inventors (engineers), entrepreneurs, investors and marketers form alliances in this specific field, new 'success' icons emerge.

8   William Edward Burghardt/W.E.B. Du Bois (1903) writes of a 'veil' worn by all African Americans that is both a blessing and curse and that filters their paradigmatic (or worldview) relations to political, economic and social levels of opportunity. In the absence of an inclusive (colour-free) society (a problem Du Bois refers to as the 'colour-line'), the worldviews of African Americans are shown to differ from those of white people. Understanding this distinctiveness is key to combatting society's colour-blindness, that is, where colour is not even seen as an (inclusive) issue. With these *insights*, I am mindful that the term 'American soul' involves both *a priori* and generative meanings of 'whiteness', and that notions of 'freedom', 'democracy', 'human rights' and 'new opportunities' may have different meanings in 'the souls of black folk' or in the souls of marginalised people.

9   The following citation is extracted from the second paragraph's opening lines. The Declaration was originally signed by thirteen United States of America (see www.archives.gov).

10   Later in 1863, in the midst of the American Civil War (1861–1865), Abraham Lincoln directly refers to the Declaration of Independence in his famous Gettysburg Address ("Four score and seven years ago . . ."). In the final sentence of this two-minute speech, he famously declares that ". . . government of the people by the people for the people shall not perish from the earth." (see http://myloc.gov).

11   'Human rights' means different things to different (power) groups. It is important to remind that, at this time, The Declaration was written for a *white* land-owning class population and that the Constitution (later adopted in 1787) effectively sanctioned the system of slavery. Also, there is a stark rejection of the human rights of the 'enemy' Native American people. In a (rather ironic) passage attacking *imperialism*, specifically the King of Great Britain, Jefferson notes: "He [the king] has excited domestic insurrections amongst us, and has endeavoured to bring on the inhabitants of our frontiers, the merciless Indian Savages, whose rule of warfare is an undistinguished destruction of all ages, sexes and conditions." (see www.archives.gov).

12   Despite its 'new world' status, The Constitution of the United States (which is the 'supreme law' of the United States of America) was the first of its kind in the world and has significantly influenced other nations' constitutions. The First Amendment is one of the initial 10 Amendments that comprise the 'Bill of Rights' (to date, there have been 27 changes to the US Constitution).

13   In *Tinker versus Des Moines Independent Community School District* (1969), the Supreme Court adjudged that symbolic speech rights be upheld (provided that symbols are not 'disruptive of school discipline or decorum') for three students who had been suspended for wearing black armbands as a sign of opposition to the US involvement in the Vietnam War (see www.bc.edu/bc_org/avp/cas/comm/free_speech/tinker.html).

14   Following the Battle of Baltimore, in which American troops prevailed against a British attack, Francis Scott Key wrote the lyrics of a victory poem, entitled 'Defence of Fort McHenry'. After its publication in the *Patriot* in 1814, it was popularised and later adopted as the national anthem in 1931 (with its title changed to 'The Star Spangled Banner'). The final lines read: "And the star-spangled banner in triumph shall wave; O'er the land of the free and the home of the brave." (see http://amhistory. si.edu/starspangledbanner/). The Statue of Liberty is perhaps the most famous symbol of freedom in America. Its outline at the entrance to the 'land of the free' proclaims: "Give me your tired, your poor, Your huddled masses yearning to breathe free."

15   Throughout its history America has received many diverse peoples and cultures. Many migrants arrived fleeing political/social persecution and unbearable living conditions. In the case of the Irish, for example, one million people died of starvation during the years of the Great Famine (An Gorta Mór, 1845–1852), with a million more emigrating – the vast majority of whom went to America. At this time, Ireland also received financial aid and support from America, including a donation from the Native American Choctaws in 1847. Of course emigration remains a present-day reality. Of grave concern is the types of emigration highlighted here, that is, where people, at great personal risk, seek refuge from persecution and/or migrate for much improved life opportunities. Poignantly, at the time of writing, close to 360 people (mostly Somalis and Eritreans) tragically lost their lives at sea by Lampedusa (which is 290 kilometres off the coast of Africa and is a key destination for migrant vessels bound for Europe).

16   This was originally informed by a civic rationale and duty to protect the state itself from corruption, to resist oppressive practices and defend oneself and one's family. There are many in America who believe that this 'freedom' ought to be enshrined in practice, as it appears in law.

17   The regulation of gun control is increasingly under question, particularly in the wake of (continuous) high profile tragedies, for example, school shootings. To illustrate, on 14 December 2012, a young man injured two people and killed himself, his mother and 26 other people at the Sandy Hook Elementary School in Newtown Connecticut. Among the deaths included twenty Grade 1 children (aged between 6 and 7 years), four classroom teachers, the school psychologist and the principal. President Obama (2013) has consistently argued for "a common sense" balance between gun rights and gun control (http://articles.washingtonpost.com/2013–09–22/local/42299308_1_gun-rights-gun-control-president-obama). However, it appears that any efforts to enact gun-control legislation will have to countenance the 'freedom' principle attaching to 'the right to bear arms'.

18   Nowhere in the US Constitution is there an explicit mention of the right to own, use or dispose property. There are indirect references to property ownership and rights via both the Fifth and Fourteenth Amendments, where the government is compelled to respect individuals' property with due process of law.

19   Friedrich von Hayek (1899–1992) is probably the most influential economist/political philosopher of neo-liberalism and a supposed favourite of Margaret Thatcher. Post World War II (1947), he assembled and worked alongside American economists: Rose and Milton Friedman (of 'The Chicago School' fame), James Buchanan and Gordon Tullock (of 'public choice theory' fame) and Gary Becker (of 'human capital theory' fame). These economists formed the US vanguard of neoliberalism. In 1955, Friedman wrote an article entitled 'The role of government in education'. The quotes that follow are directly taken from this text.

20   The arts provide an avenue for the cultural endorsement of economic 'freedom' and 'success'. To illustrate, the movie *The Pursuit of Happyness* (2006) takes its title directly from the Declaration of Independence. Inspired by a true story, it stars Will Smith as Chris Gardner, "a San Francisco salesman who's struggling to make ends meet." This aesthetic work has both affective appeal (its story 'touches' audiences) and effective appeal (it 'works' on audiences, generating 'success' attitudes and behaviour). In the end, the protagonist is shown to "rise above his obstacles to become a Wall Street legend" (quotes from the DVD's promotional piece).

21   Vouchers are funding licenses issued by the government that enable parents to 'cash them in' against the costs of private school tuition fees. They are advocated as part of a school 'choice' agenda and have been used before in Main and Vermont and are currently employed in Wisconsin, Florida, Washington, Utah and Indiana (see www.ncsl.org/research/education/school-choice-vouchers.aspx). An Individual Learning Account (ILA) acts as a type of 'life saving account' for one's education. The scheme was launched in Britain in 2000 (under Gordon Brown's administration) and

operated as a reimbursement plan to educational course providers. The scheme soon closed in 2001 following widespread fraud and abuse. Scotland (under a devolved system of UK governance) still operates an ILA scheme. It focuses on those learners on low income, who receive benefits and are not (as yet) in full-time education.

22   However crude the analogy is between schools and restaurants, this type of comparative 'analysis' is typical of certain *economic* commentary. It may also appear in homogenised *political* discourse (perhaps via mimetic or policy-borrowing practices, or more deliberate ideological positioning). Consider the following words, rooted in the neo-liberal zeitgeist, uttered by an Irish (*Labour* party) Education Minister. Here, he exhorts university students to be "critical consumers" of the education they receive: "A bad restaurant doesn't get repeat business. I think there has to be some response from the user of the service provided in an open market economy like ours. People can exercise their choice by moving to another supplier of the service" (former Minister for Education and Skills Ruairí Quinn, in Duggan, *Sunday Independent* 2012, Feb 5, p. 6).

23   For a critique of how education is (economically) represented and how its image and status may be *re-represented*, see O'Brien (2013).

24   Friedman (1955, 11) imagines comparisons between human capital investments (investing in one's 'training') and physical capital investments (investing in machinery). He even imagines a type of venture capitalism, centred on human 'training', where a financial loan is measured against the security of return and eventual productivity of this investment: "The counterpart for education would be to 'buy' a share in an individual's earning prospects: to advance him [sic.] the funds needed to finance his [sic.] training on condition that he [sic.] agree to pay the lender a specified fraction of his [sic.] future earnings. In this way, a lender would get back more than his [sic.] initial investment from relatively successful individuals, which would compensate for the failure to recoup his [sic.] original investment from the unsuccessful." Does all of this seem farfetched? Consider how higher education loans/fees are imagined/effected. From a critical perspective, one must ask if giving students the 'freedom' to bear such costs represents, at the very least, a system of 'control' or, more strongly, if it represents (using Friedman's own words) 'partial slavery'. One may also ask how all of this squares with Friedman's 'voluntary' exchange ideal.

25   ". . . as in other fields, competitive private enterprise is likely to be far more efficient in meeting consumer demands than either nationalized enterprises or enterprises run to serve other purposes" (Friedman, 1955, 5, 6). While this argument appears fashionable (even after all these years), it is of course highly contestable. Besides the problematic comparison of schools with 'other' organisation types, one must consider the *contrary evidence* in relation to numerous private railway operators, banks, prisons, probation services, early school providers (crèches), hospitals, voucher systems and charter schools. In the case of the latter, for example, a Center for Research on Education Outcomes (CREDO, 2009) report at Stanford University analysed 70 per cent of America's charter schools and found that 17 per cent of charter schools perform better than their public school counterparts, 37 per cent perform worse and 46 per cent are approximately comparable in standard. In light of these findings, one must question the supposed delivery of greater 'choice' in a competitive school system. The vast majority of US students attend their neighbourhood school. In so far as they actively choose their local school, and not others (even those deemed to be more competitively 'successful'), they exercise *local* choice. It is important to also recognise that some children have more 'choice' than others, a point that highlights the strong (social) *classed* nature of education (see later discussions in this chapter).

26   The title of Friedman's 1997 opinion piece says it all: 'Public schools: Make them private'.

27   Performance-based rewards for group or individual teachers has been experimented upon in the United States, for example, Kentucky and Charlotte-Mecklenburg Group-Based Performance Reward Programmes, South Carolina Individual and Group-Based

Reward Programmes, The Texas Education Agency Study, and the Dallas Group-Based Performance Reward Programme. In a review of the literature in this area, Harvey-Beavis (2003) concluded that there is limited research in the United States and that there are a number of concerns regarding research methodology, particularly around merit-pay *systems* and *findings* that claim that teacher rewards lead to better student 'outcomes' (Harvey-Beavis, 2003).

28 With the obvious caveats 'if this were even possible' and 'if economics alone was the issue', who would argue with "eliminating the causes of inequality"? The question is, will the alliance of 'competition' and 'incentives' further this cause? Further, 'outright' distribution of income (as Friedman terms it) infers a 'giving away' of income (consistent with critiques of socialism and the so called 'hand-out' welfare state). There is of course a purposeful social (as well as economic) role for degrees of income (re)distribution, for example, it may be used as a means of regulating against the excesses of 'free market' income differentials, establishing and maintaining appropriate social, community and economic services, and contributing to a fairer, more inclusive society.

29 In 1955, the 'choice' was as yet untried since a 'free [education] market' had yet to be partly realised, let alone imagined. All of which points to Friedman's remarkable *inventiveness* and resolute *foresight*. Of course, Friedman *tees up* (to use golfing parlance) the 'choice' – free market or its (polemical) alternative? A type of dualistic thinking is therefore in evidence. No doubt influenced by (and influencing) US anti-communist sentiment, the 'choice' also *appears* stark – this *or* that.

30 Of course neoliberal policies had, and continue to have, a global impact. During the 1980s, Reaganomics and Thatcherism controversially shaped the economic policies of Chile which was then under dictator (General Augusto Pinochet's) rule. Friedman himself had visited Chile in 1975 to deliver lectures on economics and, though he later rejected the political regime, he still lauded its economic model (Friedman, 1991). During the 1990s, neoliberalism was hailed (by proponents) as a 'global success' in the wake of the collapse of communism in Eastern Europe, particularly in Russia. To varying degrees of intensity, neoliberalism shapes world economies and societies.

31 Friedman (1991) emphasises their interconnection, believing that *economic freedom* (more accurately, a neoliberal take on capitalism) is a necessary, but not sufficient, condition for *political freedom*. Friedman (1991, 330) also highlights their paradoxical relationship and suggests that "while economic freedom facilitates political freedom, political freedom, once established, has a tendency to destroy economic freedom."

32 Note how these words resonate with a classical liberal (*democratic*) stance on 'freedom', as it appears in the Declaration of Independence (see earlier discussions). Friedman's later words (in this quotation) resonate with *economic* (or market) versions of 'freedom' and are of course highly contestable. To illustrate, Friedman's reference to how the market enables society "to be organised from the bottom up rather than the top down" fails to recognise the highly authoritative (and oft undemocratic) features of the market, including those that emerge via managerialist/bureaucratic controls (see later discussions in the next section).

33 On another (*political*) level, it is not unlikely. The alliances between neoliberal and neoconservative interest groups within both the Republican Party (US) and Britain's Conservative Party illustrate this point well (see forthcoming discussions).

34 All quotes are from Reagan (1983, 746–9).

35 Thomas Paine was an inspirational figure to the Patriots who later declared their independence from Britain. The Declaration of Independence itself makes a number of references to God and 'freedom': ". . . to assume among the powers of the earth, the separate and equal station to which the Laws of Nature and of Nature's God entitle them . . ."; ". . . that they are endowed by their Creator with certain unalienable rights . . ."; "And for the support of this Declaration, with a firm reliance on the protection of divine Providence, we mutually pledge each other our Lives, our Fortunes and our sacred Honor."

36 All quotes are from Thatcher (1988, 861–4). This speech was dubbed by the British media as 'The Sermon on the Mound' (because of its religious content – hence, its *jeu de mots* on 'The Sermon on the Mount', as well as its location – Assembly Hall, *The Mound*, Edinburgh, Scotland).

37 ". . . intervention by the state must never become so great that it effectively removes personal responsibility. The same applies to taxation; for while you and I would work extremely hard whatever the circumstances, there are undoubtedly some who would not unless the incentive was there. And we need their efforts too" (Thatcher, 1988, 863).

38 See Note 10.

39 President Reagan might have invoked the First Amendment to legitimate freedom of (religious) speech, particularly the government's (and politicians') right to exercise such freedom. For Reagan (the person and statesman), state-church lines are not separate – "Freedom prospers when religion is vibrant and the rule of law under God is acknowledged." (see www.youtube.com/watch?v=FcSm-KAEFFA). An opposing perspective might take the view that the First Amendment acts as a safeguard against the state exercising favours (either directly or indirectly in law, policy, etc.) for any particular religious group, thus making clear the separation between state and church.

40 'The Christian Right' is a collective comprised of such national political organisations as The Moral Majority, Christian Voice, Christian Coalition, Eagle Forum, and The Family. Their widespread allegiance to Republican Party politics (including the Tea Party wing) enables their 'freedom' interests to be politically represented at the highest levels.

41 *Public* schools in the United States are prohibited from conducting religious observances, such as school prayer. The Conservative Right seeks to overturn this 'non-practice'. President Reagan's (1983) stance was clear ("let our children pray"). In his 1983 speech, he highlighted the Supreme Court's practice of opening its proceedings with "a righteous invocation", as well as Congress members' practice of opening sessions "with a prayer", and concluded: "I just happen to believe that the school children of the United States are entitled to the same privileges as Supreme Court judges and Congressmen [sic.]." (see www.youtube.com/watch?v=FcSm-KAEFFA). Note the language of 'rights'/'freedom' infused in the terms *entitled* and *privilege*.

42 In the case of mathematics, for example, Eric Gutstein (2009) demonstrates how it is subject to particular political pressures that seek to improve the educational system. From the Soviet Union's launch of another Sputnik in 1957 to present-day concerns for American competitiveness, the image, status and substance of mathematics instruction are constantly under focus.

43 The phrase 'global order' is borrowed from Stefan Halper and Jonathan Clarke's (2005) book, *America alone: The neo-conservatives and the global order*, which details how US foreign policy was dominated by radical neoconservative voices during George W. Bush's administration (2001–2009), for example, Dick Cheney, Paul Wolfowitz, Jeane Kirkpatrick (who also served in President Reagan's cabinet), Donald Rumsfeld, etc. The advancement of STEM subjects is particularly linked to America's 'global order' status, since it aims to secure (via education) technological, military and economic gains.

44 It is ironic that the Conservatives would preside over "the largest expansion of federal control in the history of American education"; and it is "likewise ironic that Democrats embraced market reforms and other initiatives that traditionally had been favoured by Republicans" (Ravitch, 2011, 21). Internationally, too, there is a surprising political consensus around new corporate reforms, for example, the education policies of coalition governments in Ireland [Fine Gael (centre right) and Labour (centre left)] and England and Wales [Conservatives (right of centre) and Liberal Democrats (social democratic centre)]. In America, a broader political consensus on *educational reform* contrasts strongly with *other partisan policies*. To illustrate, at the time of writing (October 2013), a US

partial government shutdown was effected as a result of Republican and Democrat disagreements on new health care and budget provisions.

45 Among these targets for 2000 are a high school graduation completion rate of 90 per cent and the objective of being the first in the world in *mathematics* and *science* [note the highlighted STEM subjects and their (reputed) competitive role in shaping America's 'global order' status].

46 Charter schools are publicly funded schools that can operate privately. They demonstrate the oft confused/confusing roles of 'public-private' partnerships in education. Thus, *private* school scholarships may be advanced by *public* subsidies (e.g. state vouchers). Also, donation tax credits (tax credits given to individuals or businesses that donate to non-profit organisations) may be offered by the state (*public*) to support *private* individuals and/or *private* organisations (those that support charter schools). In some US states, for-profit private schools are publicly sponsored. Even in the case of non-profit organisations, private providers are often 'outsourced' (to use business lingo) using public (taxpayer) funds. One may therefore ask: What is public and what is private? And what is public-private?

47 This exemplifies a reconfiguration of the (nation) state's role in education – from that of 'provider' to (competitive) 'regulator'. This new state role, which is facilitated by neoliberalism, has a global reception. In Ireland, for example, a recent HEA (Higher Education Authority) report recommends that a portion of the state's core grant be set aside to reward university cluster performances (HEA, 2013). If adopted, it will undoubtedly incentivise 'system reconfiguration' and 'system governance' and embed managerialist practices in Irish higher education (O'Brien, 2012).

48 Common Core standards represent the federal government's attempt to bring state curricular standards more into line with one another. Students are annually tested on 'common' grade standards in English Language Arts (ELA) and Literacy in History/ Social Studies, Science and Technical subjects, as well as Mathematics Practice and Content (see www.corestandards.org/the-standards). This initiative is presently (2013) being adopted by 45 states, the District of Columbia, four territories, and the Department of Defense Education Activity (DoDEA). Common Core standards are actively supported by president Obama, the National Governors Association (NGA) and the Council of Chief State School Officers (CCSSO). Core standards are much informed by the work of the educationalist E. D. Hirsch.

49 More accurately, it presents as a coalescing of *entwined* interests – interests that are strategically inter-related, but not always coherent. To illustrate briefly: Michael Barber, a leading proponent of Individual Learning Accounts (Barber, 1997), was chief adviser to the Secretary of State for Education on School Standards in the UK under Tony Blair's administration. He then served as partner and head of McKinsey's Global Education Practice, was a close advisor to Joel Klein who introduced new accountability and market reforms in New York and is currently chief education advisor for Pearson, a consultancy that provides educational services (publishing and testing products) to American states. David Coleman is the chief architect of the CCSS Initiative and former consultant with McKinsey and joint CEO of an education start-up *Grow Network*. Since, this company has been sold to McGraw-Hill (another educational consultancy) and Coleman has established a not-for-profit agency (*Student Achievement Partners*), which supports (with new data systems and tests) the implementation of the CCSS that, in turn, are aided by the Gates Foundation, etc. (Resmovits, 2013).

50 *Fragile* because there are those that see the benefits of ('high-stake') tests but not a role for federal government in their administration, that is, there is an uneasy marriage between Neoconservatives who want high levels of accountability and performativity and Neoliberals (as well as various 'Neocon' religious and political right interest groups) who do not want federal government to interfere with local schools. *Flawed* because educational 'privatisation', 'choice', 'standards', 'tests' and 'performativity' are all conceptually and practically problematical (see later discussions).

51 As a non-American, I am very conscious of my (in)ability to capture America. In the words of Oscar Wilde: "Perhaps, after all, America never has been discovered. I myself would say that it had merely been detected." While it may be impossible to capture, America's discovery (its 'detection') remains fascinating, exasperating and, ultimately, unavoidable.

52 Many of the statistics in this paragraph are sourced from www.worldpopulationstatistics. com/population-of-new-york-city-2013/ (accessed on 8 November 2013).

53 Statistic sourced from *The Economist* (9 November 2013). See www.economist.com/ news/united-states/21589419-big-apple-has-been-well-run-20-years-mayor-elect-promises-change-where-will

54 Such is the strong relationship between inequality and poor health *across all groups in the metropolitan areas of the United States* that the website inequality.org (2011, 5) cites Lynch *et al.*'s (1998) study that claims that the low-income population living in a low-inequality area has a significantly lower mortality rate than that of the high-income population living in a high-inequality area.

55 One may look to other manifestations of racial inequality, for example, employment. To illustrate, in 2011 a federal judge ruled that a court-appointed monitor oversee diversity initiatives in the New York City Fire Department "because of what he viewed as a persistent and shameful pattern of discrimination against black candidates." (Bellafante, 2011, 2).

56 Conducted on 9–14 March 2005 (N = 1,764), see details www.nytimes.com/packages/ pdf/politics/class-poll.pdf.

57 There are 8 Ivy League schools in the United States and the Russell Group comprises of 24 leading UK universities. At 250 of the most selective colleges in the United States, the proportion of students from upper-income families has grown, not shrunk (Scott and Leonhardt, 2005). This is due in large part to their (highly prized) status value – Ivy League colleges charge around 60,000 dollars each year (2015-). Thus, these institutions present a certain status value, what Bourdieu calls 'symbolic capital', that affords students, alumni and others access to accumulated forms of capital, namely economic, social and cultural. In this way, a 'multiplier effect' frequently emerges in relation to any form of capital accumulation, that is, one capital often exchanges for another (O'Brien and Ó Fathaigh, 2005).

58 At the time of writing, The Affordable Health Care Act (the so-called Obamacare policy aimed at providing universal healthcare insurance in the States) was being effected, debated and vociferously fought against by Republican 'interests'. While it appears as a greater egalitarian step towards universal health insurance, it still validates a *tiered* programme via its platinum, gold, silver and bronze health plans. So it appears that *competition* – and the display of *distinctive* 'products' – renders *universal* healthcare, like universal education, a step too far in America.

59 Thus, one is affected by others' social positioning ('what they do' to be distinctive), not just one's own (what 'I do'). Thus, the aforementioned: *Indeed, the notion of 'distinction', as framed within the market model of education, remains undisturbed. Consequently, the promise of (relative) 'success' is advanced that, in turn, provides for the legitimation of social differences.*

60 *Economic capital* refers to income and other financial resources and assets. It is the most liquid capital in that it may be more readily converted into other capitals (Rudd, 2003). Its potency in the educational field, for example, is manifest in the capacity of some individuals to purchase different types of educational services (e.g. private education, additional grinds/tuitions, distance learning courses) and associated resources (e.g. childcare, transport, books, ICT equipment, etc.). Economic capital on its own, however, is not sufficient to buy 'status' or position; rather, it relies on interaction with other forms of capital (*social, cultural* and *symbolic* – see Bourdieu, 1986).

61 *Cultural capital* comes in three forms: *Objectified, embodied* and *institutionalised* (Grenfell & James, 1998). Each form serves as "instruments for the appropriation of symbolic

wealth socially designated as worthy of being sought and possessed" (Bourdieu, 1977b in Rudd, 2003, 54). The objectified form is manifest in such items as books, qualifications, computers; the embodied form is connected to the educated character of individuals, such as accent, linguistic competence and learning dispositions; and the institutionalised form represents the places of learning one may attend (e.g. library, theatre, different types of schools, colleges, universities).

62   Bourdieu talks about this psychosocial positioning in terms of a mediating 'habitus', captured in the phrase: "The subjective expectation of objective probabilities" (in Jenkins, 2002, 27–9). In other words, the very possibility of 'success' is measured against probable outcomes.

63   In Bourdieuian terms, a 'multiplier effect' frequently emerges in relation to any form of capital accumulation, that is, one capital (economic, social, cultural or symbolic) often exchanges for another (Notes 60 and 61). Thus, those in positions of advantage (those with greater levels of capital) are more likely to accumulate capital than those in positions of disadvantage (those with less capital). Hence, capital accumulation is a more likely outcome than capital redistribution (Bourdieu, 1986). Moreover, those in positions of advantage are more likely to (mentally, physically and socially) engage with 'success' goals, since the possibility of 'success' is measured against probable outcomes (Note 62).

64   Charter schools have increased during the Bloomberg years (2002–2013); there are now close to 200 serving 70,000 students or 5 per cent of the district's total (Sparks, 2013, 2). Bill de Blasio promises to curb their expansion and do away with the city's A-F grades for schools in his first year of office. Moreover, he plans to keep mayoral control but "direct the 13-member appointed school board to 'take into serious consideration' concerns from community education councils, which replaced the former local school boards." (Sparks, 2013, 1).

65   David C. Berliner and Bruce J. Biddle refer to this as a 'manufactured crisis' (Berliner and Biddle, 1996). Among other arguments, they would claim that SAT (Scholastic Assessment Test) scores are stable, while NAEP (National Assessment of Educational Progress) scores show gradual *gains* over the past thirty years. Despite critical responses (Stedman, 1996), Berliner (2011) holds that these claims still stand. Whether 'standards' are really falling, stable or rising (assuming one can tell definitively), this matters little *to a significant minority* that still academically underachieve in the United States. What does matter for this group is the 'achievement gap' (across a range of social indicators) that may be observed via such measurements as school completion rates, attrition rates, college enrolment figures, employment entry points, grade point averages and standardised test scores. Of course each of these measurement standards has its own complications.

66   Michelle Rhee announced in 2010 that, in one day, she had fired 241 teachers, including 165 who received poor appraisals based on students' standardised test scores (Turque, 2010). A latest (2013) release of confidential memos appears to show that Rhee *was made aware of widespread cheating on standardised tests as early as 2009*; however, there was no concerted attempt made to discipline the individuals involved (only 1 educator lost his job because of cheating, while Rhee fired more than 600 teachers overall for low test scores; see www.usatoday.com/story/news/nation/2013/04/11/memo-washington-dc-schools-cheating/2074473/). Diane Ravitch has consistently highlighted the highly suspect nature of test score results during Rhee's time as Chancellor of Washington's schools (Ravitch, 2011, 2013).

67   Within his first few years of office, New York's Chancellor Joel Klein had closed down two dozen large high schools and opened 200 small high schools with financial backing from the Bill and Melinda Gates Foundation, the Carnegie Corporation and the Open Society Institute. Most of these schools were theme schools (centred on a specific speciality or profession) and, by 2009, their total enrolment represented 25 per cent of the city's high school students (Ravitch, 2011, 82, 83). Charter schools increased

during the Bloomberg years (2002–2013) – there are now close to 200 serving 70,000 students or 5% of the district's total (Sparks, 2013, 2). At the start of 2013, the city announced the 'shuttering' of 17 'failing schools' (see www.nydailynews.com/new-york/new-york-city-shut-17-failing-schools-article-1.1235362).

68 Michelle Rhee blamed teacher unions for her leave-taking from her Washington schools post in 2010. As CEO of the *StudentsFirst* lobby group (which has raised over 1 billion dollars in funds), she vehemently opposes tenureship for teachers. In her formative years, she founded an alternative teacher preparation programme called the New Teacher Project. This programme was set up in opposition to university-based teacher education programmes (and, by association, it opposed the role of university teacher educators). Alternative teacher education programmes (TeachFirst, Teach for America) have now extended to the UK (Wigdortz, 2012). TeachFirst, which was developed by management consultant Brett Wigdortz, has received politico-ideological backing from the Conservatives in government (e.g. former Education minister Michael Gove) and by the Chief Inspector of Schools and head of Ofsted (Michael Wilshaw). As further evidence of the university's reduced involvement and status in teacher education, the Department of Education in England and Wales has granted direct responsibility for teacher preparation to certain 'successful' schools (see www.education.gov.uk/get-into-teaching/teacher-training-options/school-based-training/school-direct for details of the School Direct programme).

69 'Private' *management* ('managerialism') is exemplified in neoliberal forms of educational governance (O'Brien, 2012). Friedman (1955, 17) believed that "it is a great virtue of the private arrangement that it permits a gradual transition." But how do these words sit alongside a 'private' *replacement* function, for example, where charter school status takes the place of a 'failing' public school? Also, how do these words sit alongside more disruptive events? For example, after Hurricane Katrina, the number of charter schools magnified in New Orleans (they now comprise nearly 90 per cent of all schools). Naomi Klein (2008) uses the term 'disaster capitalism' to show how entrepreneurs/profiteers/private interests 'piggy back' on the wave of global disasters and *shocks*. Arne Duncan (former Chief Executive Officer of the Chicago Public Schools, presently President Obama's Secretary of Education) is on record as saying: "I think the best thing that happened to the education system in New Orleans was Hurricane Katrina."

70 Rhee may *self*-proclaim but one can discern the (mimetic) appearance of Friedman and other like-minded profiles. In essence, while Rhee is 'invested' in corporate school reform, others (the media included) are 'invested' in her.

71 Lotteries appear to be gaining some policy borrowing traction, as they 'officially' present as a democratic expression of inclusion. To illustrate, a lottery system (with some weighted provision) was proposed by Áine Hyland with respect to selecting students for third level education in Ireland (Hyland, 2011). But how inclusive is a lottery, given that there will inevitably be losers, many of whom may have faithfully followed the 'promise' of college education, with some disproportionately losing out by virtue of their (already) 'disadvantaged' status? A lottery measure may simply act in the 'interest' of the system and present as a systemic solution, whereby (increased) student numbers (once more) are required to adapt.

72 Heilemann (2010) reports on reformers' reactions to *Waiting for Superman*, noting Arne Duncan (former Chief Executive Officer of the Chicago Public Schools; now Secretary of Education) as saying: "The movie is going to create a sense of outrage, and a sense of urgency"; while Joel Klein concurs, "it grabs at you. It *should* grab at you. Those kids are dying." Reformers and their discourse appear to coalesce. Again, Geoffrey Canada in a review of Rhee's (2013) book: "Michelle Rhee is a national treasure [. . .] As told in this important book, her fight against this country's calcified education bureaucracy holds lessons for us all."

73 In his film *Waiting for Superman* (2010), Davis Guggenheim exemplifies this *conservative cognitive up-skilling agenda*: "It should be simple, a teacher in a schoolhouse filling her

students with knowledge and sending them on their way. But we've made it complicated." Would that it were so simple! How important it is *not* to simplify!

74   What follows in the main text is Geoffrey Canada's conclusion to the question, 'what would it take'? as directly quoted from the inside cover of Paul Tough's (2008) book. It's a conclusion that appears to have support from (certain) business 'interests'; for example, Geoffrey Canada was listed as Number 12 on *Fortune* Magazine's list of the world's 50 greatest leaders (2014). It's a conclusion that appears to have support too from (certain) civil rights groups; for example, Geoffrey Canada received the 2013 National Freedom Award from the National Civil Rights Museum (Memphis, Tennessee) in recognition of his significant contribution to the battle for civil and human rights. Other civil rights activists, however, would strongly disagree with Canada's approach, such as Sam Anderson (Black New Yorkers for Educational Excellence and Coalition for Public Education). This demonstrates how 'freedom', specifically that which pertains to 'civil rights', is constantly being (re-)constructed and contested in America.

75   Friedrich Wilhelm Nietzsche's work centres on the 'will to power', and so it offers a valuable critique of 'redemptionist' (O'Sullivan, 2008) ways of thinking about, and acting on behalf of, (for the purposes of this study) the 'educationally disadvantaged'. Specifically, Nietzsche highlights problems with the concepts of morality and charity that are inextricably bound up with Christianity. For Nietzsche, to be 'charitable' (or to even 'save' another) is to command 'virtue' and derive one's own advantage from its powerful authority. Also, the *subjugated* or 'herd' that receive and believe in this 'virtue' are, at once, commanded by it and their 'self-interest' becomes merely a reflection of its power and the 'interest' of those that exercise it (Nietzsche, 1886; 1887). This places the work of 'philanthropies', 'non-profit organisations', 'rescue interventions' and 'scholarship programmes' firmly under the microscope. Nietzsche's own version of *Superman* (Übermensch or 'over-man' from German) fundamentally challenges this 'morality' paradigm, exhorting man [sic.] to become his [sic.] own 'master'; to remove himself [sic.] from the 'herd'. Thus, to 'free' oneself from oneself is presented as the ultimate challenge for man [sic.], as man's [sic.] 'success' depends on his [sic.] own capacity and will to become more Superman-like [sic.] (Nietzsche, 1883–1885).

76   Even those who critique the Global Educational Reform Movement (GERM) and its policy borrowing and transfer work (e.g. PISA) appear to reify the very 'science' of international comparisons. Moreover, they pay insubstantial attention to 'transfer' problems, cultural literacies and diverse traditions. Pasi Sahlberg (2012b), for example, speaks of Finland's 'successful' achievements in the areas of innovation, music, arts, science and gender equity – all worthy achievements in Finland. At the same time, he makes numerous international comparisons – across the fields of health, economics, governance, testing, income equality, environment, etc. These comparisons may (ironically) support the 'science' of global reform by reifying 'benchmarking' values and success 'norms'. This 'slippage' (to make use of a Foucauldian phrase in another context) is evident in such comments as: "In the 1970s we were running behind everyone else; we were running behind in education [. . .] and I'm not just talking about achievement scores but also attendance, equity, efficiency, many other areas of education [. . .] So we can say that the Finnish education system was performing below international averages [. . .] We've been able to improve progress and then gradually pass almost everybody else during the course of the last 30 or 40 years."

77   Sahlberg (2012b) cites the OECD (2012, 64) as unequivocally stating: "[. . .] evidence does not support these [choice] perceptions, as choice and associated market mechanisms can enhance segregation." Funding can also be a source of significant 'inequality', with New York's school funding regarded as one of the most unfair in the nation (National Report Card, 2012).

78   Diane Ravitch (2011, 79) notes how, in 2006–2009, New York State lowered the bar and made it easier for students to pass level 2 in sixth-grade reading and seventh-grade math tests. A new scoring system also enabled the proportion of students in grades 3–6 who reached proficiency on the state math test to rise from 57 per cent to 81.8 per cent in New York City (ibid., 157–8). Moreover, adjusted state scores enabled many more students to pass the Regents diploma exams (ibid., 158). This all produced "the illusion of remarkable gains" (ibid.). Of course, the ultimate illusion is created by test score cheating. Here, Ravitch (2011, 265–7) points to significant cheating incidences in Washington D. C. and Atlanta.

79   There are ethical reasons for resisting a simple reading of 'test scores', since these 'outcomes' can merely fashion an appearance of 'success' and, more seriously, reinforce 'educational dislocation' (Brancaleone and O'Brien, 2011, 515). Dislocation signals the serious loss of the intrinsic worth of things that, as Hannah Arendt reminds, "begins with their transformation into values or commodities" (Arendt cited in Meade 1996, 117). There are scientific reasons too to resist a simple reading of 'test scores'. Diane Ravitch (2011, 160) cites Campbell's law to illustrate this point: "The more any quantitative social indicator (or even some qualitative indicator) is used for social decision-making, the more subject it will be to corruption pressures and the more apt it will be to distort and corrupt the social processes it is intended to monitor" (Original quote from Campbell, 1976, 49). For me, Einstein's dictum sums up *both* ethical and scientific reasons for a cautious reading of 'test scores': "Not everything that can be counted counts, and not everything that counts can be counted" (source unknown).

80   The PISA In Focus report (2012, 2) also states: "In countries with comparatively low teachers' salaries (less than 15% above GDP per capita), student performance tends to be better when performance-based pay systems are in place, while in countries where teachers are relatively well-paid (more than 15% above GDP per capita), the opposite is true. So for countries that do not have the resources to pay all of their teachers well, it is worth having a look at the experience of those countries that have introduced performance-based pay schemes." Of course these statements presume a direct relationship (which elsewhere, as highlighted in the main text, is contradicted i.e. there is *no* relationship between average student performance and the use of performance-based pay). In addition to this confusion, the above statements point to axiomatic faith in a) data systems and b) international comparative indicators (in this case, indicators that pertain to 'teacher performance'). Further, in a review of US literature in this area, Harvey-Beavis (2003) concluded that there is limited research and a number of outstanding methodological concerns around merit pay *systems* and *findings*.

81   A University of Chicago-led study, published as a working paper by The National Bureau of Economics Research (Fryer *et al.*, 2012), claims that teacher 'quality' is increased alongside improved student academic performance once the power of 'loss aversion' is employed to motivate behaviour. 'Loss aversion' involves paying teachers a bonus in advance and demanding the money back should their students "not improve sufficiently." The study also found that there was no 'gain' for students if bonuses were paid at the end of the year. This research, framed within an economic paradigm and reflecting the disciplines of psychology and behavioural economics, is clearly less-than-reliable in capturing the essence of 'teacher performance'. 'Research' on performance-related pay in England and Wales is likewise less-than-reliable (Note 82). Despite fragile evidence, philanthropists (e.g. Bill and Melinda Gates Foundation and the Eli and Edythe Broad Foundation) continue to finance performance-based pay schemes, as well as training programmes that are aimed at managing school 'performance', for example, the urban superintendent certification (Ravitch, 2011).

82   This quote is from Michael Gove, the former England and Wales Education Secretary. His position on performance-related pay is transparent – he is a fervent advocate and has a Populous poll (of 1,723 parents) to 'support' his position. Specifically, three-fifths (61 per cent) of people surveyed thought that schools should be permitted to set

individual staff salaries in accordance with the 'quality' of their performance, which would be decided by annual appraisal (Wintour, 2013). Real policy effects follow this less-than-reliable data. From September 2014, the pay of each teacher in England and Wales is individually determined in accordance with their students' 'progress'. Meanwhile, Michael Gove presents as being 'on the side of parents' (of course, this advocacy position supports *his own ideological views* on civic 'freedom'). The more discerning reader will ask some searching (methodological, ethical and scientific) questions of Mr Gove: How methodologically sound is this survey? How are 'test scores' and 'performativity' so conceived and linked? And how does one categorise this pay proposal – 'evidence-based' policy or 'policy-based' evidence? (Boden and Epstein, 2006).

83 This position is well established in teacher education programmes, for example. In the case of University College Cork (Ireland), teachers' classroom practice is *qualitatively* and *performatively* appraised in accordance with such criteria as planning and preparation, subject knowledge, pedagogical approaches, assessment practices, classroom management and safety, reflective development and professional attitude and values. Formative and collaborative approaches to learning (e.g. mentor and peer feedback) are employed over time to facilitate sustained teacher and student development. Consider how such a model contrasts with a 'payment by results' approach to 'teacher quality'!

84 Diane Ravitch (2011, 211) quotes Bill Gates in 2009 – up to this time, his Foundation had invested heavily in small schools – as stating: ". . . many of the small schools that we invested in did not improve students' achievement in any significant way." In 2009, small schools enrolled approximately 25 per cent of New York's high school students (Ravitch, 2011, 82).

85 Almost a quarter of all (over 120,000 pupils) Irish primary school children are in classes of thirty or more (2013 figure). Many 'supersize' classes are in the commuter belt counties around Dublin (Wicklow and Wexford), though other regions (Cork and Sligo) have very large classes too. As further evidence of (global) bipartisan political support, and the specific conversion around neoliberal education policies, the reform outlined here is advocated by a *Labour* Minister (for Public Expenditure and Reform), supported by another *Labour* Minister (for Education). To be fair to the former Minister for Education and Skills, he had put in place new school and classroom building plans in anticipation of even more school demand.

86 Students in grade 8 (13 years old) may apply for a grade 9 (14 years old) transfer to other high schools in New York. At grade 9, a significant minority of QSI students (anywhere between 20 and 30 students) leave and are 'replaced' by 'new' 9th graders. QSI students tend to leave for other specialised high schools, schools that provide extracurricular activities (like sports), or 'academically successful' institutions like Townsend Harris (where competition for entry is very strong). In the 2011 'transfer window' (to use football parlance), over 5,000 students competed for 270 grade 9 seats in Townsend Harris, an Early College High School that is located *on the grounds* of Queens College. CUNY has plans to open more Early College High Schools and, alongside business partners, is now focused on preparing students for technical careers (e.g. in digital technology). Critics may be concerned about such plans, since they may perceive their remit as supporting functionalist, capitalist 'interests' in schooling (Bowles and Gintis, 1977).

87 "A four-year college graduate earns two-thirds more than a high school graduate does. An Associate Degree translates into earnings significantly higher than those earned by an individual with a high school diploma alone" (Source: Early College High School Initiative, Retrieved from www.earlycolleges.org/overview.html on 8 April 2013). Those with an Associate Degree earn 25 per cent more than people who never attended college (President Obama's 2015 State of the Union address). Indeed, college graduates may earn (on average) more than high school graduates. But beyond the question of

economics, there are other (more *educational*) issues to address, such as to what extent ought college (and career) priorities shape school culture? How can schools nurture wider identity work, especially when college work becomes 'compressed' (see Chapter 1)? What is the impact on college work and life? (The traditional undergraduate is expected to develop as a learner and engage with deeper knowledge over a longer, four-year, term.) And is the 'college and career' journey for everyone – what about alternative pathways to 'success'?

88 My empirical research visit to QSI was conducted between Monday 15th April 2013 and Friday 26th April 2013. During this time, I observed school and classroom life (corridor and staffroom activities, conversations, high school lessons), interviewed key providers (e.g. past and current Principals, past and present college liaison officers) and conducted focus group interviews with a selection of parents and with individual sets of students (grades 9 through to 12). These research methods coalesce to present these findings on the 'lived culture' of QSI.

89 Bennett and Wilezol's (2013) book *Is college worth it* legitimately questions the extraordinary *cost* of college education in the US, relative *insecurity* in acquiring gainful ('remunerative') employment post-college and ubiquitous *faith in the college-route* to 'success'. Discerning readers will note the authors' 'interest' in education, especially their unquestioning support for online 'breakthroughs', elite university 'rankings', economic 'success' values, the educational 'market' and 'conservative' principles of social control.

90 Separate focus group interviews with grades 9–12 students were conducted on 22 April 2013. Each focus group consisted of 8 students from their respective grade and lasted 30 minutes.

91 Hervé Varenne and Ray McDermott (1998) speak of 'success' and 'failure' as properties of American culture. 'Success' is made in America and America is the 'fact' that individuals have inherited ('facere' in Latin is 'to make'). Thus, as outlined in this chapter's earlier discussions, 'success' is already framed and 'successful' individuals (including 'icons', 'innovators') are 'made' in its likeness, its exemplification. For me, this idea of 'making' reflects Martin Heidegger's (1927/2008) concept of 'facticity'. Heidegger believed that individuals are 'thrown into the world'; thus, their ('success') moods, dispositions, relations and practices are already framed in existence, however unconscious.

92 A focus group with 8 QSI parents (1 male, 7 females) was conducted on 23 April 2013 and lasted 1 hour and 15 minutes.

93 Pierre Bourdieu's (1988) *Homo Academicus* is a sociological critique of higher education culture in France. It focuses on academics' social class backgrounds (including their tastes) and links these to their 'scientific' standing and power practices, for example, their knowledge claims, publications, reputations, as well as their social, cultural and political capital networks. One can look to students' social class profiles too. In Ireland, for example, some 99 per cent of Dublin 6 students (living in a high social class neighbourhood) go on to third level, compared with only 15 per cent of young people in Dublin 17 and 16 per cent in Dublin 10 (areas with lower socio-economic standards of living). See Humphreys (2014).

94 I am reminded once more of school 'choice'. What really 'makes' some 'choose' their local public school and others 'choose' the private 'option'?

95 See earlier discussions on the influence of conservative religious conscience in education, as exemplified by Ronald Reagan's (1983) speech.

96 I am reminded of the old African proverb, 'It takes a village to raise a child'. This is often read in praise of *wider social cooperation*. But, in light of earlier discussions on 'cooperative competition', it may also be read (at least from a Western, developed, English-speaking, US cultural perspective) as *social cooperation in shaping individuals' 'success'*. Thus, from Hervé Varenne and Ray McDermott (1998, 107): "It may take a whole village to raise a child, but in America, at the most sacred of times when lives are in balance, the child stands alone for the village to judge. That the village may be

responsible for setting the whole thing up is hard to determine and even harder to change."

97 The interview with Elizabeth and Mary Beth took place on 18 April 2013 and lasted 1 hour and 30 minutes. The final interview with Meredith was conducted on 25 April 2013 and lasted 30 minutes. Time and space do not permit me to fully explore these insightful conversations but, suffice to say, these educationalists' thoughts helped frame the question of *learning success* throughout.

98 Experimental? Authoritative? Take the former Irish Education Minister's statement that "we are moving in the direction" of video cameras being installed for school principals to monitor classrooms (Ruairí Quinn on the *Today With Seán O'Rourke* Radio Show; 3 February 2014). Or Michael Sandel's (2012) case study (which is not unique) of an Israeli day-care centre that fined parents who arrived late to collect their children. In both cases, intrinsic motivation (and trust) appears to be replaced by regulatory forms of extrinsic motivation (and mistrust). This raises an old (yet important) ethical question: 'who watches the watchmen (sic.)?' (in Latin, *Quis custodiet ipsos custodes?*). For while teachers and parents must be accountable (at some authentic level), the same must apply to those who seek to 'manage' them.

99 From President Obama's State of the Union Speech (2014): ". . . here in America, our success should depend not on accident of birth, but the strength of our work ethic and the scope of our dreams. That's what drew our forebears here. It's how the daughter of a factory worker is CEO of America's largest automaker; how the son of a barkeeper is Speaker of the House; how the son of a single mom can be President of the greatest nation on Earth. Opportunity is who we are. And the defining project of our generation is to restore that promise."

100 In the words of the Irish philosopher George Berkeley (1685–1753): 'To be is to be perceived' – in Latin, *Esse is percipi* (see Fogelin, 2001). Thus, while perceptions may appear as 'immaterial' or 'idealist' (e.g. a conscious image of 'success'), they have real material value. Indeed, material objects necessitate being perceived (or 'sensed') by some subject. In this way, ideal meanings of 'success' (e.g. those projected by certain educational 'interests') produce real practices and real objects. And these ideals *imagine us*, often in advance, as *being* 'successful'.

References

Ahmed, S. (2010). *The promise of happiness*. Durham, North Carolina. Duke University Press.

Barber, M. (1997). *The learning game: Arguments for an education revolution*. London. Indigo.

Baudrillard, J. (1994). *Simulacra and simulation*. Transalted by S. Faria Glaser. Ann Arbor, MI. University of Michigan Press.

Bellafante, G. (2011). A diverse city? In some ways, anything but. *The New York Times*. 21 October. Retrieved from www.nytimes.com/2011/10/23/nyregion/a-diverse-new-york-city-in-some-ways-anything-but.html?_r=0 on 2 November 2013.

Bellah, R. N., Madsen, R., Sullivan, W. N., Swindler, A. and Tipton, S. M. (1985/2007). *Habits of the heart: Individualism and commitment in American life*. Berkeley, CA. University of California Press.

Berliner, D. C. and Biddle, B. J. (1996). *The manufactured crisis: Myths, fraud, and the attack on America's public schools*. New York. Basic Books.

Berliner, D. (2011). The manufactured crisis revisited. *School Leadership Briefing*. 01 May. Retrieved from www.schoolbriefing.com/1967/the-manufactured-crisis-revisited/ on 27 November 2013.

Berliner, D. (2013). Effects of inequality and poverty vs. teachers and schooling on America's youth. *Teachers College Record*, 115, no. 2. Retrieved from www.tcrecord.org/PrintContent.asp?ContentID=16889 on 08 January 2014.

Bernstein, B. (1971/2003). *Class, codes and control: Theoretical studies towards a sociology of language.* Volume 1. London. Routledge and Kegan Paul.

Boden, R. and Epstein, D. (2006). Managing the research imagination? Globalisation and research in higher education. *Globalisation, Societies and Education,* 4, no. 2, 223–36.

Bourdieu, P. (1962/1973). The Algerian subproletariat. In I. W. Zarman, ed. (91). *Man, state and society in the contemporary Mahgreb.* New York. Praeger. Cited in R. Jenkins (2002, 27).

Bourdieu, P. (1977a). *Outline of a theory of practice.* Translated by Richard Nice. Cambridge. Cambridge University Press.

Bourdieu, P. (1977b). Cultural reproduction and social reproduction. In J. Karabel & A. Halsey, eds *Power and ideology in education.* New York. Oxford University Press.

Bourdieu, P. (1984). [1979]. *Distinction: A social critique of the judgement of taste.* Translated by Richard Nice. London. Routledge.

Bourdieu, P. (1986). The forms of capital. In J. Richardson, ed. (241–58). *Handbook of theory and research for the sociology of Education.* New York. Greenwood.

Bourdieu, P. (1988). *Homo Academicus.* Translated by Peter Collier. Cambridge. Polity Press.

Bourdieu, P. (1990). *In other words: Essays toward a reflexive sociology.* Stanford. Stanford University Press.

Bourdieu, P. (1996). *The rules of art: Genesis and structure of the literary field.* Stanford. Stanford University Press.

Bourdieu, P. (2004). *Science of science and reflexivity.* Cambridge. Polity.

Bourdieu, P., Chamboredon, J., Passeron, J. and Krais, B. (1991). *The craft of sociology: Epistemological preliminaries.* Berlin. Walter de Gruyter.

Bowles, S. and Gintis, H. (1977). *Schooling in capitalist America: Educational reform and the contradictions of economic life.* New York. Basic Books.

Brancaleone, D. and O'Brien, S. (2011). Educational commodification and the (economic) sign value of learning outcomes. *British Journal of Sociology of Education,* 32, no. 4, 501–19.

Browne, V. (2012). Inequality not on the agenda in US or Republic. *The Irish Times,* January 11. Retrieved from *The Irish Times Archives* on 06 September 2013.

Campbell, D. T. (1976). *Assessing the impact of planned social change.* Dartmouth College. The Public Affairs Centre.

Center for an Urban Future. (2009). *Reviving the city of aspiration: A study of the challenges facing New York City's middle class.* New York. City Futures Inc. Publication.

Chubb, J. E. and Moe, T. M. (1990). *Politics, markets, and America's schools.* Washington. The Brookings Institution.

Coffield, F. (1999). Breaking the consensus: Lifelong learning as social control. *British Educational Research Journal,* 25, no. 4, 479–99.

CREDO. (2009). *Multiple choice: Charter school performance in 16 states.* California. Stanford University. Retrieved from credo.stanford.edu/reports/MULTIPLE_CHOICE_CREDO.pdf on 30 December 2013.

Darling-Hammond, L. (2010). *The flat world and education: How America's commitment to equity will determine our future.* New York. Teachers College Press.

Debord, G. (1967). *The society of the spectacle.* Translated by K. Knabb. London. Rebel Press.

De Tocqueville, A. (1835, 1840) *Democracy in America.* In J. Epstein (2000), *Democracy in America: The complete and unabridged.* Volumes I and II. New York. Bantam Classics.

Du Bois, W. E. B. (1903). *The souls of black folk: Essays and sketches.* In B. H. Edwards, ed. *Oxford's world's classics.* Oxford. Oxford University Press.

Duggan, B. (2012, Feb 6). I haven't a clue if lecturers are doing their jobs, says minister. *Sunday Independent,* p. 6.

Emerson, R. W. (1841). *Essays: First series.* Retrieved from www.gutenberg.org/files/2944/2944-h/2944-h.htm#link2H_4_0002 on 23 January 2013.

Emerson, R. W. (1844). *Essays: Second series.* Retrieved from www.emersoncentral.com/essays2.htm on 23 January 2013.

Finn, J. D. and Gerber, S. B. (2005). Small classes in the early grades, academic achievement, and graduating from high school. *Journal of Educational Psychology*, 97, no. 2, 214–23.

Fogelin, R. (2001). *Routledge philosophy guidebook to Berkeley and the principles of human knowledge.* London and New York. Routledge.

Foucault, M. (1990). *The history of sexuality, Volume 1: An introduction.* Reissue edition. New York. Vintage.

Friedman, M. (1955). *The role of government in education.* New Jersey. Rutgers University Press. Retrieved from www.schoolchoices.org/roo/fried1.htm on 30 October 2013.

Friedman, M. (1991). Economic freedom, human freedom, and political freedom. Inaugural lecture at the Smith Center for Private Enterprise Studies at Hayward, California, USA. In A. Burnet, ed. (329–32). *Chambers book of speeches.* Edinburgh. Chambers Harrap Publishers.

Friedman, M. (1997). Public schools: Make them private. *Education Economics*, 5, no. 3, 341–4.

Gladwell, M. (2013). *David and Goliath: Underdogs, misfits, and the art of battling giants.* New York. Little, Brown and Company.

Grenfell, M. and James, D. (1998). *Bourdieu and education: Acts of political theory.* London. Falmer Press.

Guisbond, L., Neill, M. and Schaeffer, B. (2012). *NCLB's lost decade for educational progress: What can we learn from this policy failure?* Massachusetts. FairTest, National Center for Fair and Open Testing Publication.

Gumbel, P. (2010). *On achève bien les écoliers.* Paris. Grasset.

Gutstein, E. (2009). The politics of mathematics education in the United States: Dominant and counter agendas. In B. Greer, S. Mukhopadhyay, A. B. Powell and S. Nelson-Barber, eds. *Culturally responsive mathematics education.* New York. Routledge.

Halper, S. and Clarke, J. (2005). *America alone: The neo-conservatives and the global order.* Cambridge. Cambridge University Press.

Halsey, A. H., Heath, A. F. and Ridge, J. M. (1980). *Origins and destinations: Family, class and education in modern Britain.* Oxford. Clarendon Press.

Hantzopoulos, M. and Tyner-Mullings, A. R., eds. (2012). *Critical small schools: Beyond privatization in New York City urban educational reform.* Charlotte, North Carolina. Information Age Publishing.

Hargreaves, A. and Braun, H. (2013). *Data-driven improvement and accountability.* Boulder, Colorado. National Education Policy Center. Retrieved from nepc.colorado.edu/files/pb-lb-ddia-policy.pdf on 09 January 2014.

Harvey-Beavis, O. (2003). Performance-based rewards for teachers: A literature review. Retrieved from www.oecd.org/edu/school/34077553.pdf on 20 November 2013.

HEA. (2013). *Report to the Minister for Education and Skills on system reconfiguration, inter-institutional collaboration and system governance in Irish higher education.* Dublin. Stationery Office.

Heidegger, M. (1927/2008). *Being and time.* New York, London, Tokyo and Sydney. Harper Perennial Modern Classics.

Heilemann, J. (2010). Schools: The disaster movie. *New York Magazine*, 05 September. Retrieved from nymag.com/news/features/67966/ on 05 December 2013.

Hochschild, J. L. (2003). Social class in public schools. *Journal of Social Issues*, 59, no. 4, 821–40. Retrieved from scholar.harvard.edu/jlhochschild/publications/social-class-public-schools on 15 November 2013.

Humphreys, J. (2014). Some 99% of Dublin 6 students go on to third-level. Article written in the *Irish Times*, 20 August. Retrieved from www.irishtimes.com/news/education/some-99-of-dublin-6-students-go-on-to-third-level-1.1901885

Hyland, Á. (2011). Entry to higher education in Ireland in the 21st century: Discussion paper for the NCCA/HEA Seminar to be held on 21st September, 2011. Dublin. Ireland.

Inequality.org. (2011). Wealth inequality and other statistics. Retrieved from inequality.org/ wealth-inequality/ on 12 November 2013.

Jenkins, R. (2002). *Pierre Bourdieu*. Abingdon. New York. Routledge.

Kamenetz, A. (2013). System failure: The collapse of public education. *The Village Voice*, April 3, 2013. Retrieved from www.villagevoice.com/2013–04–03/news/system-failure-the-collapse-of-public-education/ on 07 January 2014.

King, J. B. (2013). College and career readiness. Presentation by Dr John B. King, Jr, President of the University of the State of New York and Commissioner of Education on 29 October 2013. Retrieved from usny.nysed.gov/docs/reform-agenda-hearing-testimony-nyc.pdf on 14 January 2014.

Klein, N. (2008). *The shock doctrine: The rise of disaster capitalism*. London, New York. Penguin.

Kozol, J. (1992). *Savage inequalities*. New York. HarperCollins.

Kozol, J. (2012). *Fire in the ashes: Twenty-five years among the poorest children in America*. New York. Crown Publishers.

Lareau, A. (2000). *Home advantage: Social class and parental intervention in elementary education.* Second edition. Oxford, Maryland. Rowman & Littlefield Publishers.

Lareau, A. (2003). *Unequal childhoods: Class, race, and family life*. Berkeley, Los Angeles, London. University of California Press.

Long, F. (2008). Protocols of silence in educational discourse. *Irish Educational Studies*, 27, no. 2, 121–32.

Lynch, J. W. (1998). Income inequality and mortality in metropolitan areas of the United States. *American Journal of Public Health*, July, 1074–80.

McKinsey. (2009). The economic impact of the achievement gap in America's schools. Retrieved from www.hunt-institute.org/elements/media/files/Economic_Impact_of_the_Achievement_Gap.pdf on 03 December 2013.

McNamee, S. and Miller, R. K. (2009). *The meritocracy myth*. Second edition. Maryland. Rowman & Littlefield Publishers.

Meade, E. M. (1996). The commodification of values. In L. May and J. Kohn, eds. (107–26). *Hannah Arendt: Twenty years later*. Cambridge, MA. The MIT Press.

Meier, D. (1995/2002). *The power of their ideas: Lessons for America from a small school in Harlem.* Boston. Beacon Press.

National Report Card. (2012). *Is school funding fair? A National Report Card*. 2nd edn., June 2012. Retrieved from www.schoolfundingfairness.org/ on 30 December 2012.

National Research Council. (2011). *Incentives and test-based accountability in education*. Edited by M. Hout and S. W. Elliot, eds. Board on Testing and Assessment, Division of Behavioural and Social Sciences and Education. Washington D.C. The National Academies Press.

New York City Council. (2013). *The middle class squeeze: A report on the state of the city's middle class*. New York. New York City Council Finance Division Publication.

Nietzsche, F. W. (1883–1885). *Thus spake Zarathustra: A book for all and none*. Reproduced in A. Del Caro and R. Pippin, eds (2006) as part of the *Cambridge texts in the history of philosophy*. Cambridge. Cambridge University Press.

Nietzsche, F. W. (1886). *Beyond good and evil*. Project Gutenberg EBook reprint of the Helen Zimmern translation from German into English. Retrieved from www.gutenberg.org/ files/4363/4363-h/4363-h.htm on 12 December 2013.

Nietzsche, F. W. (1887/2013). *On the genealogy of morals*. Translated by Michael A. Scarpitti. London. Penguin.

NYCED. (2012). *Expect success: A family's guide to preparing students for college and careers*. New York. NYC Department of Education Publication.

NYSUT (New York State United Teachers) (2012). *Taking stock: A progress report on public education in New York State.* Retrieved from www.edweek.org/ew/toc/2012/01/12/index.html?intc=EW-QC12-LFTNAV on 27 November 2013.

O'Brien, S. and Ó Fathaigh, M. (2005). Bringing in Bourdieu's theory of social capital: renewing learning partnership approaches to social inclusion. *Irish Educational Studies*, 24, no. 1, 65–76.

O'Brien, S. (2012). Cultural Regulation and the Reshaping of the University. *Globalisation, Societies and Education*, 10, no. 4, 539–62.

O'Brien, S. (2013). Re-representing education's image and status: In the 'interest' of pedagogical innovation. In G. K. Zarifis and M. N. Gravani, eds. *Challenging the 'European Area of Lifelong Learning': A critical response.* London. Springer Publication.

OECD. (2012). *Equity and quality in education: Supporting disadvantaged students and schools.* OECD Publishing. Retrieved from http://dx.doi.org/10.1787/9789264130852-en on 13 December 2013.

O'Sullivan, D. (2005). *Cultural politics and Irish education since the 1950s: Policy paradigms and power.* Dublin. Institute of Public Administration Publication.

O'Sullivan, D. (2008). Turning theory on ourselves: Some resources and constraints for adult educators. *The Adult Learner.* 2008, 13–32. Dublin. AONTAS.

Perry, G. (2013). Taste is woven into our class system. *The Telegraph*, 15 June 2013. Retrieved from www.telegraph.co.uk/culture/art/art-features/10117264/Grayson-Perry-Taste-is-woven-into-our-class-system.html on 9 September 2013.

Ravitch, D. (2011). *The death and life of the great American school system: How testing and choice are undermining education.* New York. Basic Books.

Ravitch, D. (2013). *Reign of error: The hoax of the privatization movement and the danger to America's public school.* New York. Knopf.

Reagan, R. (1983). The aggressive impulses of an evil empire. In A. Burnet ed. (746–9). *Chambers book of speeches.* Edinburgh. Chambers Harrap Publishers.

Reay, D., David, M. E. and Ball, S. (2005). *Degrees of choice: Social class, race and gender in higher education.* Stoke on Trent, UK; Sterling, USA. Trentham Books.

Resmovits, J. (2013). David Coleman, the most influential education figure you've never heard of: Common Core author is redesigning the SATs and AP Program. The Jewish Daily Forward. 30 August 2013 (Retrieved from http://forward.com/articles/182587/).

Resnik, L. (1995). From aptitude to effort: A new foundation for our schools. *Daedalus*, 124, no. 4, 55–62.

Rhee, M. (2013). *Radical: Fighting to put students first.* New York. Harper.

Rudd, T. (2003). ICT and the reproduction of inequalities: A Bourdieuian perspective. Unpublished PhD thesis. Graduate School of Education, University of Bristol.

Sahlberg, P. (2012a). *Finnish lessons: What can the world learn from educational change in Finland?* Unabridged edition (Series on School Reform). Read by Paul Michael Garcia. Ashland, Oregon. Blackstone Audio, Inc.

Sahlberg, P. (2012b). Finland: An educational phenomenon? Talk at the AEU Federal Conference, Melbourne, Australia, 24 February 2012. Retrieved from www.youtube.com/watch?v=YoMzsaRTW5U on 6 December 2013.

Said, E. W. (1979). *Orientalism.* New York. Knopf Doubleday Publishing Group.

Sandel, M. J. (2012). *What money can't buy: The moral limits of markets.* New York. Farrar, Straus and Giroux.

Scott, J. and Leonhardt, D. (2005). Shadowy lines that still divide. *The New York Times*, May 15 (Retrieved from www.nytimes.com/2005/05/15/national/class/OVERVIEW-FINAL.html).

Sedghi, A. (2013). Which cities do the world's millionaires and billionaires live in? Article written in *The Guardian Datablog*, 08 May. Retrieved from www.theguardian.com/news/datablog/2013/may/08/cities-top-millionaires-billionaires on 12 November 2013.

Sheahan, F. (2013). Schools to decide own class size and teacher numbers. Independent.ie, 03 January. Retrieved from www.independent.ie/irish-news/schools-to-decide-own-class-size-and-teacher-numbers-29884723.html on 08 January 2014.

Skeggs, B. (2010). Class, culture and morality: Legacies and logics in the space for identification. In M. Wetherell and C. T. Mohanty, eds. (339–59). *The Sage handbook of identities*. London. Sage Publication.

Sparks, S. D. (2013). Bloomberg-Era school changes debated in N.Y.C. Race. *Education Week*. 29 October 2013. Retrieved from www.edweek.org/ew/articles/2013/10/30/10nyc_ep.h32.html on 05 November 2013.

Spelke, E. S. (2005). Sex differences in intrinsic aptitude for mathematics and science? A critical review. *American Psychologist*, 60, no. 9, 950–8.

Stedman, L. C. (1996). The achievement crisis is real: A review of *The Manufactured Crisis*. *Education Policy Analysis Archives*, 4, no. 1, 1–11.

Stiglitz, J. (2013). *The price of inequality: How today's divided society endangers our future*. New York. W. W. Norton & Company.

Tavernise, S. (2012). Education gap grows between rich and poor, studies say. *The New York Times*, 09 February 2012. Retrieved from www.nytimes.com/2012/02/10/education/education-gap-grows-between-rich-and-poor-studies-show.html?pagewanted=all&_r=0 on 10 November 2013.

Tough, P. (2008). *Whatever it takes: Geoffrey Canada's quest to change Harlem and America*. Boston, New York. Houghton Mifflin Company.

Truslow Adams, J. (1931). *The epic of America*. New York. Simon Publications.

Turque, B. (2010). Rhee dismisses 241 D.C. teachers; union vows to contest firings. *The Washington Post*, 24 July. Retrieved from www.washingtonpost.com/wpdyn/content/article/2010/07/23/AR2010072303093.html on 28 November 2013.

Varenne, H. and McDermott, R. (1998). *Successful failure: The school America builds*. Colorado and Oxford. Westview Press.

Vargas, J. (2013). The economic payoff for closing college readiness and completion gaps. Boston. *Jobs for the Future* Publication.

Watkin, B. (2013). Performance pay will stop struggling schools attracting top teachers. *The Guardian*, 28 May 2013. Retrieved from www.theguardian.com/teacher-network/teacher-blog/2013/may/28/performance-related-pay-teachers-struggling-schools on 08 January 2014.

Wigdortz, B. (2012). *Success against the odds – Five lessons in how to achieve the impossible: The story of TeachFirst*. London. Short Books.

Wilkinson, R. and Pickett, K. (2010). *The spirit level: Why equality is better for everyone*. London. Penguin.

Wintour, P. (2013). Gove urges 'ideologically motivated' teachers' unions to abandon strikes. *The Guardian*, 24 July 2013. Retrieved from www.theguardian.com/politics/2013/jul/24/michael-gove-teachers-union-strikes on 06 January 2014.

4

LEARNING POWER

The land of Brazil (*Terra do Brasil*) is vast. Covering some 3.3 million square miles, there's plenty of capacity for its approximately 200 million inhabitants. This fertile land offers up timber, sugar cane, gold, rubber, coffee, meat, tropical fruits, oil and gas. With such bountiful resources, *opportunity* is one part of Brazil's land story. *Inequality* is its other divide. Just over 1 per cent of the population controls almost half of the land (Branford and Rocha, 2002) and two-thirds of the nation's arable land is in the hands of 3 per cent of the population (Sadlier, 2008). While millions of arable hectares lie deserted, functional farmland is increasingly (and intensively) worked upon by industry. Goods are mass produced for export, including sugar, coffee, meat, eucalyptus, oranges and soybeans. And hydroelectricity, renewable energies, steel, petrochemicals and high-tech minerals are all mined for domestic and international consumption. This manufacturing of the land attracts signifi-cant foreign direct investment and reinforces Brazil's position as the seventh largest world economy. All of which indicates (economic) 'advancement', at least for its burgeoning wealthy and middle classes.

This is not the reality for the poorest Brazilians. *Conservative* estimates show that 1 in 5 Brazilians live below the national poverty line (a line which is low by international standards), 10 per cent of the population survive on less than 2 US dollars a day and 5 per cent endure the most extreme conditions of poverty (World Development Indicators, 2012). The poor have suffered most from 'modern' industrialisation: in particular, from the displacement of agrarian traditions. Over 70 years ago, Brazil's population was around 80 per cent rural, 20 per cent urban. Now these figures have been reversed. Inner migration (most migration occurs *within* countries) places enormous pressures on the land and its people. Once, small farmers and their families worked large productive farms, maintaining small plots (*sitios*) to consume, produce and sell. Within a short period of time, vast tracks of land were converted for 'monoculture' production, for example, sugar cane for ethanol (used for renewable energy), eucalyptus for paper and razed forests for ranching.[1] As a result, many farmers were forced to work seasonally, to live precariously. Landlords, ever more faceless, administered externally set prices, while payments for small production diminished. The 'deracinated' experienced the most invasive of globalisation effects. Forced to resettle in clogged cities and towns, their hope still centres on survival, providing for their family and changing their life direction.

Land division is firmly rooted in Brazil's history.[2] Ever since Portuguese explorer Pedro Alvares Cabral accidentally 'discovered'[3] Brazil in 1500, the land has been carved up by powerful interests. From the south, the first colonial adventurers (*bandeirantes*) marked out territories in search of Indian slaves and gold while, from the northeast, major landholders extended their concentrated wealth into the backlands of that region (e.g. the *Sertão*). From its original separation into 15 captaincies (*capitanias*), the Brazilian colony subdivided into huge plantations that were eventually worked upon by African slaves.[4] Post-independence (1822) and abolition (1888), large land holdings (*latifúndios*) stubbornly persisted. Brazil's journey then, from Empire (1822–1889) to Republic (1889–1963)[5] to Military Dictatorship (1964–1984) through to present-day Democracy (1985-), is characterised by the (unsettled) *land question*. This narrative is often screened from popular *Terra do Brasil* images. Brazil may have always been imagined from exotic portraits of a 'terrestrial Eden' and 'barbarous land', to gainful exploits in 'scientific expedition' and prospective 'commerce' (Sadlier, 2008). Even now, 'barbarous' images re-emerge in depictions of "a dystopia plagued by corruption, drugs and violence" (ibid., 8), while 'productive' images re-emerge in popular reports on Brazil's global (economic) rise. Still, these imaginaries conceal the *land question*.

Despite obfuscation, land reform has seen some progress. The 1988 Constitution seeks to guarantee citizens 'a right to land'. It also allows for the expropriation of land (subject to fair compensation) once it is deemed to be not 'in use', fails to provide 'a public utility' or 'need' or, in some cases, does not fulfil 'a social function' (Articles 184, 186).[6] To avoid expropriation, 80 per cent of the land must be 'productive', both landowner and worker must profit from its use, appropriate use of natural resources must be employed (e.g. water irrigation) and proper labour and ecological standards must be upheld (ibid.). In 1996, landowners were encouraged to sell unproductive estates via a series of reforms such as raising taxes on *latifúndios*. More money and manpower was given to the *Instituto Nacional de Colonização e Reforma Agrária* (National Institute of Colonisation and Agrarian Reform or INCRA) and a special ministry for Agrarian Reform was established. Presently, direct grants to settlement families[7] are administered via INCRA to help fund schooling (for example) and secure title deeds for such peasants/rural groups (*camponês*). It is also intended that farms be regularly inspected and work practices closely monitored. Real progress, however, is seriously mitigated by the persistence of age-old problems. Land inspections remain restricted and are often prejudiced to match landowner interests. Alarmingly, human rights agencies (e.g. The Inter-American Commission on Human Rights[8]) consistently report flagrant abuses from degrading labour conditions (even 'slavery'); widespread corruption, police collusion, torture and lack of protection; attacks on labour representatives and social activists; murder, repression and discriminatory practices in countering protest; improper judicial investigations; and a common failure to prosecute. *Plus ça change, plus c'est la même chose?*

Even during concentrated periods of land reform (e.g. 1995, 1996), change is ever-shadowed by violence. Within this period, a number of 'landless movement' members (see next section) were killed in the north of Brazil while, in one incident in Pará (christened *Massacre de Eldorado dos Carajás*), 19 were executed by off-duty military police. In the face of grave setbacks, however, land protests persisted. In 1997, 1,300 landless movement members marched to Brasília to highlight their plight. Many students, university teachers, priests and social activists joined them. Totalling 100,000, the crowds pressed President Fernando Henrique Cardoso to commit to greater agrarian reform. This, it seems, is how social reform works in Brazil – protest eventually drives change. And change is further advanced by socially progressive governments. To illustrate, Cardoso's government (1995–2002), though steadfast in promoting privatisation, did commit to universal education and the provision of free AIDS drugs. President Luiz Inácio 'Lula' da Silva (2003–2010) is widely credited for reducing hardship in Brazil via anti-poverty programmes such as *Fome Zero* (a collection of Federal assistance schemes) and, more specifically, its constituent *Bolsa Família* – a direct financial aid to some 11 million poor families who now have access to social services, free vaccinations and schooling and an old-age pension at 70 years (even if there is no history of formal employment). His successor and fellow member of the Workers Party (*Partido dos Trabalhadores, PT*), President Dilma Rouseff (2011–), continues to advance the reformist housing programme *Minha Casa, Minha Vida* ('My House, My Life'). Established in 2009, this scheme provides credit (with small fixed interest rates) to low-income families in need of better quality, affordable homes. It's an ambitious plan with some 2 million builds planned by 2016. In education, too, there have been real attempts to redistribute opportunities. In the last two decades, primary and lower secondary education have become almost universal (some 95 per cent of 7–14 year olds are now in school), while youth and adult illiteracy has been reduced. Most recently, President Dilma announced that 50 per cent of all public university places will be reserved for *public school*-leavers.

Of course there is some opposition to these reforms. Some might argue that direct financial aid to poor families acts as a 'disincentive' to work; low-income families are 'getting houses' for staying below credit thresholds; and reserving university places for public schoolers hinders open and 'fair' competition. Such opposition is often predicated on a particular (neoliberal) political philosophy (see Chapter 3). 'Beyond' ideological concerns,[9] reforms present significant challenges in and of themselves. Thus, it might be argued that the Brazilian government is (inadvertently) promoting profiteering, over-investing in sub-prime mortgages, encouraging more people to migrate to cities (where there's greater opportunity for housing grants) and urging many public schoolers who are not 'college ready' to go to university (Brazil still has high levels of grade recurrences and school attrition). Moreover, 'high-speed' reforms appear to reflect the nation's fixation to stay abreast of modernisation demands.[10] Thus, housing builds are expedited by the latest public-private partnerships, credit-flows and private equity investments.[11] Rapid (private) investment in health is supported by an upsurge in individual insurance schemes. Private schools thrive, spurred on by higher (social class) membership. High-end office and apartment blocks are on the rise, alongside newly secured leisure facilities and hotels. Former state-owned industries (e.g. Vale, Brazil's biggest mining company) are intensively 'downsizing' and concentrating on overseas markets. International investors are rapidly securing assets and appropriating land for 'monoculture' production. And all of this 'progress', so it is presented, is testimony to Brazil's openness to (economic) globalisation. Global free trade is therefore protected. Indeed, it is progressed through bilateral relations with the United States and EU, alongside Brazil's membership of G20 and *Mercado Comum do Sul* ('Mercosul' or 'Southern Common Market').

Brazil imagines itself,[12] *with others*, as a global power. Alongside Japan, it has been elected to the Security Council more times than any other United Nations state. It is internationally respected for its principles of multilateralism and peace-keeping, as well as its donor-giving work and anti-AIDS programmes. Brazilians' celebrated capacity for *jeito* (compromise) and *jeitinho* (being savvy, having guile) is more usefully employed in diplomatic relations, both regionally (Latin America) and internationally (e.g. Haiti[13]). The ability to mimic international art and architecture, and yet produce a distinctive Brazilian quality, is renowned. And Brazil's sporting prowess – in motor racing, martial arts, basketball, athletics,[14] volleyball and, of course, football – is universally acclaimed. The beautiful game (*joga bonita* means 'play beautiful') has produced a long list of icons including Didi, Gérson, Carlos Alberto Torres, Jairzinho, Rivellino, Tostão, Falcão, Zico, Socrates, Júnior, Romário, Rivaldo, Ronaldo, Ronaldinho and – the greatest of them all – Garrincha and Pelé. In 2014, the World Cup returned to Brazil. And new *futebol* artists, like Neymar,[15] carried the highest expectations. But all was not well in Brazil's preparations. Sparked by bus and subway fare hikes, an estimated quarter of a million people turned out to protest in 10 cities (18 November 2013). The tournament, which many hoped would be a unifying event, soon became the focus for division and dissent. Allegations of corruption, failure to invest in major infrastructural projects (such as public transport, hospitals and schools) and massive cost overruns compelled people to protest. Their fury was fuelled by news that Brazilian taxpayers would face a total bill of between 12 and 15 billion US dollars. Footballers in the country protested against an imposed congested calendar. Football supporters bemoaned their global export,[16] low domestic league attendances, FIFA's governance[17] and towering ticket prices. Subway workers in São Paulo and airport workers in Rio de Janeiro went on strike. And more serious protests followed the deaths of construction workers and the forced removal of ('officially' 36,000) persons from *favelas* ('slum dwellings'). The World Cup would become the latest symbol of (globalisation) dissent in a country recurrently at the interface of order and disorder, progress and regress.[18] In Brazil, it seems that protest is 'in the air'. And authorities rule with *jeitinho* diplomacy, as well as military might.

Protest surfaces from the past; retelling history in the present. During Brazil's dark period of slavery (from early-mid 16th century to abolition in 1888), *quilombos* or *mocambos*[19] emerged as symbolic sites of resistance to established colonial powers.[20] These settlements consisted mainly of runaway and free-born slaves and included others fleeing persecution, such as *índios* (Indigenous Indian groups), deserted soldiers and *Caboclos* (those of mixed *índios* and European origins). *Quilombo dos Palmares* in (what is now) the state of Alagoas is probably, not least for its longevity, the most famous settlement. This fugitive commune (1605–1694) grew in size to 20,000 inhabitants and withstood 6 Portuguese efforts at suppression.[21] Eventually it was overpowered and, one year later, its last leader (Zumbi) was captured and beheaded. In time, he would be memorialised as a freedom martyr and hero.[22] Others would follow in his wake. In 1789, the leader of a failed independence movement in Ouro Preto in the state of Minas Gerais – Joaquim José da Silva Xavier (better known as *Tiradentes*[23]) – would likewise be honoured in national memory. And a special place would be preserved for the itinerant preacher and messianic leader Antônio Vicente Mendes Maciel, known to his followers as Antônio Conselheiro ('Counselor'). Between 1893 and 1897, he headed the religious settlement of Canudos in the state of Bahia, counting former slaves, *índios* and landless farmers among its (one time reputed) 30,000 population. After 3 early attempts at suppression, the Brazilian army finally succeeded in razing the settlement (all survivors were mercilessly butchered, including women and children). Canudos is a story first told by the Brazilian sociologist and journalist, Euclides da Cunha in his 1902 book *Os Sertões* (Walter, 1987). It is later retold by the 2010 Nobel laureate Mario Vargas Llosa in his 1981 historical novel, *The War of the end of the world* (da Cunha is the inspiration behind the main journalist character in this book). Vargas Llosa's work is an exceptional narrative that keeps *protest* memory alive. It prompts us to draw out from real characters (like Antônio Conselheiro, Tiradentes and Zumbi) their human qualities (such as strength of will and utopian appeal) that dare to defy authority and seek out freedom. And it starkly reminds of the tragedy of protest as consequences often lead to violent conflict and, ultimately, conquest.

Brazil's indigenous population (*índios*) has suffered most from violent conflict and conquest. Hundreds of thousands were killed by the brutality of early raiders (*bandeirantes*), severe slavery conditions and the primary cause, human disease. A shocking report (*The Figueiredo Report*) commissioned by the Minister of the Interior in 1967 revealed the extent of 20th century atrocities from mass murder, tribal extinction, torture, sexual abuse, enslavement, bacteriological warfare and land theft.[24] In 1968, the then *Sunday Times* journalist Norman Lewis, together with war photographer Don McCullin, brought the story to the world with 'Genocide in Brazil'. It created a huge outcry and prompted the establishment of *Survival International* (a global tribal rights organisation). Yet despite this 'crisis', human rights violations persisted.[25] During the 1960s and 1970s (under military rule), huge networks of roads were built across the Amazon region. The *índios* population plummeted (to just over 200,000) and their homelands (while not 'officially' recognised[26]) were decimated by industrialisation, principally gold mining, logging and ranching. During the 1980s ('the decade of destruction'), millions of Amazonian hectares were deforested and numerous animal and plant species endangered to the point of extinction (scientists claim that the full impact is yet to be felt[27]). To highlight the scale of ecological damage and protect their villages, protestors organised *empates* ('stand-offs') to peacefully resist the bulldozers. Though brutally suppressed, some ultimately prevailed. Of these, the preservationist and social activist Chico Mendes paid with his life (1988). Yet by the mid-1990s, approximately 11 per cent of the original rainforest was lost to the *índios*, the country *and* the world.[28] And in 2005 Dorothy Stang, an American-born nun and social activist, was murdered in Anupu, Pará. Reformists, yet again, would question the futility of martyrdom and the purpose of protest.

But hope is anchored to protest, as it is to change. In the face of great challenges, native populations survived. They even increased in size to approximately 350,000 (more, some 800,000 Brazilians, claim indigenous ancestry in the 2010 Census). With over 200 indigenous organisations, representatives now educate the populace about native traditions in technology, art, culture and language. Communities are being supported to secure greater economic sovereignty, while some are actively involved in *retomadas* – a 'taking back' of old lands from which they had been expelled. Indian affairs are under the jurisdiction of FUNAI (*Fundação Nacional do Índio*), a government agency responsible for demarcating land and preserving settlements (over 50 per cent of Amazonian lands have since been demarcated for protection). And important political and business interests[29] have given their backing to new environmental campaigns. Yet, for all of this, Brazil's tribes still endure invasions and land destruction by miners, loggers, ranchers and settlers. In law from 1996, Decree 1775 permits these groups to challenge the demarcation process. A new Forest Code bill (2012) allows landowners to reforest small percentages of land, but this can often be used to justify large land holdings and demonstrate their 'productive' use. Outside of law, threats, violence and murders against native populations are still not uncommon. As recently as 2013, plans were in train to construct mining and hydroelectric schemes (as well as military installations) on indigenous lands. Though some projects have temporarily stalled, others (like the controversial Belo Monte hydroelectric dam) are on-going. Significantly, all plans were drafted without the free, prior and informed consent of affected communities (Amnesty International Report on Brazil, 2013). Protest in Brazil, it seems, is always incomplete; which may explain, indeed necessitate, its persistence.

Religious figures and artists play prominent roles in keeping *protest* memory alive. The Jesuits were initially successful in empowering *índios* to prevent their enslavement,[30] before they were eventually expelled in 1759. Other religious figures, like Padre Cícero (1844–1934),[31] are still held up as champions of the poor by many Brazilians whose mystic faith blends naturally with their social justice ideals.

In 1968, the Catholic Bishops of Latin America (CELAM) proclaimed a 'Preferential Option for the Poor', which paved the way for *Liberation Theology*. This doctrine set out to (re-)align religious practice with the struggles of the poor and the goals of social justice. But successive US and Brazilian governments, as well as official Vatican administrations and big business interests, strongly condemned its protest 'links' with Marxist thinking.[32] A number of religious figures, at great personal risk, spoke out against subsequent repression. They included Dominican friar and social writer/activist Frei Betto who became a political detainee under military dictatorship, and Hélder Câmara, Catholic Archbishop of Olinda and Recife, who spoke out against state violence and fought for the right of the poor to access low-cost finance. Others would follow their own path to take the side of the poor, like Brazil's leading Spiritist[33] Divaldo Franco. He still lives in the *Pau da Lima favela* in Salvador where he helps resource parenting, housing, education and child-care needs. Frei Betto, Hélder Câmara and Divaldo Franco characterise a long lineage of Brazilian pastors whose (Messianic-inspired) mission it is to connect spiritual activity with social activism. Their mysticism is not entirely 'fanciful' or 'outer-worldly'; rather it appears (necessarily) attuned to world realities. In this sense, it is markedly Brazilian.[34]

Music too is at the heart of Brazilian culture. And Brazilian music is quintessentially choreographed by a *protest* mood. *Samba* – the 'national' rhythm – began in clandestine form before it was appropriated by Vargas's government (1930–1945) and the middle classes.[35] In the 1940s and 1950s, dissent found new expression in Luiz Gonzaga's *baião* rhythms that were popularised in the forró dancehalls of the northeast. Songs, like *Asa Branca* ('White Bird'), lamented the peasant farmer driven from his land by drought, forced to uproot to the city. In the 1960s, the *Bossa nova* singer Nara Leão denounced military repression, while *samba do morro* ('samba from the hill') sounded the harsh conditions of urban life. In the 1970s, Chico Buarque and several artists like Gilberto Gil and Caetano Veloso[36] were briefly exiled, while Milton Nascimento's lyrics were heavily censored. They and other artists would continue to write about despairing social conditions. Chico Buarque's 1981 composition *O Meu Guri* ('Oh My Little Boy') is a powerful example. The narrator, a poor *favelada* ('slum dweller'), professes her love for her (wayward) son. She is proud that he is 'making it' in the world, content to receive his (unlawful) gifts but remorseful for the times she could not provide for him. When his portrait is (inevitably) printed in the newspaper (signifying his death), she sees him again as beautiful, happy. *O Meu Guri* is an iconic protest song. By the 1990s, such records would adopt a more radical tone. Hip hop artists (like São Paulo's *Racionais MC's*) raged against 'the system', remonstrating against poor black youth being kept 'in their place'.[37] Up to present-day, prolific musicians resound the same subject. Their message, as plain as the lyrics of a Bezerra da Silva song, is constant – *A favela é, um problema social* ('The favela is, a social problem').[38]

Protest is performed elsewhere in the Brazilian arts. The photographs of Sebastião Salgado stand out. These black-and-white images speak to the collective subjects of exploitative labour[39] (*Workers*, 1993), migration displacement[40] (*Migrations*, 2000;

The Children, 2000), the landless struggle[41] (*Terra*, 1997), environmental degradation (*Sahel*, 2004; *Africa*, 2007) and the natural beauty of the planet (*Genesis*, 2013; *Le Sel de la Terre*, 2014). Salgado's work bears witness to others' suffering and their search for a better life. The images are compassionate, but not sentimental. Beyond observing, they petition a commitment to change. In this *practical* sense, they appear to educate for a better world.[42] Protest too is to be found in João Câmara's critical paintings of military repression, as well as Gilvan Samico's woodcut engravings and José Borges's prints of protest heroes like Padre Cícero, Lampião and Maria Bonita.[43] In cinema, directors Fernando Meirelles and Kátia Lund chart the stressed and violent worlds of young people in the *favelas* (*Cidade de Deus*, 2002); while José Padilha focuses on the brutality and strained relations between communities, drug lords and the police (*Tropa de Elite*, 2007, 2010).[44] Tetê Moraes's documentaries highlight political struggles, such as that of Rose and her small landless community who occupy an abandoned farm in the state of Rio Grande do Sul (*Terra para Rose*, 1987). These and 'other' political struggles are bravely recounted by some committed journalists.[45] In the world of academia, too, there are a number of protest voices, including cultural theorist and sociologist Antonio Candido, whose theory of *literature as a social project* (Candido, 1995) inspired many critical writers in Brazil, and anthropologist Darcy Ribeiro, strong defender of *índios* culture and co-creator (with educator Anísio Teixeira) of *Centros Integrados de Educação Pública* (CIEPs) – centres that cater for children's needs and their recreational and cultural interests. These and other academics, like sociologist Gilberto Freyre, physician/ geographer Josué de Castro and educationalist Paulo Freire,[46] critically represent 'other' Brazilian narratives.

I'm now on my way to visit Recife, the birthplace of Gilberto Freyre, Josué de Castro and Paulo Freire. With a metropolitan population of 1.6 million, this is the primary city of the state of Pernambuco. Pernambuco is one of 9 states in *Região Nordeste*. The northeast region occupies almost one-fifth of Brazil's landmass, with 2 of its 4 climate zones made up of semi-fertile terrain (the *Agreste*) and arid 'backlands' (the *Sertão*). It is Brazil's poorest region, where illiteracy levels are highest (over 25 per cent in the over-15 age group; 2010 Census). It is also one of Brazil's most diverse areas. The majority of *Nordestinos* (northeasterners) are of mixed race (*mestiço* or *pardo*), while a significant minority describe themselves as black (*preto* or *negro*).[47] Many practise syncretism – a fusion of religious beliefs (see Endnote 33). Created from African, Indian and European cultures, Nordeste cuisine comprises of national (*feijoada, pães-de-queijo*) and regional delicacies (*buchada, bolo de rolo*). And *Nordestino* music is also regional (*forró, xote, baião*) and national (*mangue beat, samba*, rap and hip-hop) in taste. Over the next two weeks,[48] I learn much more about the people and their culture from my welcoming host, Professor Alfredo Gomes of the Federal University of Pernambuco, Recife.[49] He has come to meet me at the *Recife/Guararapes–Gilberto Freyre International Airport*. As we travel through the city at night, he explains that the traffic is always this dense. This has much to do with urban migration, poor public transport and expansive car sales. Driving at angles, he manoeuvers between lanes with *Capoeira*-like agility. I am exhorted to try the local *cachaça* and *peixe ao molho de maracujá*. We stop at a main road restaurant, where an 'unofficial' parking attendant guides us to our spot. Upon leaving, we will pay him 3 or 4 R$ (Brazilian *Reais*[50]).

It's my first cultural lesson. Alfredo tells the story of a parking attendant at university campus. All through his student years, he had come to know this young man. Sometime later, even after further study and work abroad, Alfredo returned to university to work. Each time he observed the (older) man still attending to cars. It's a poignant story about the challenges of social mobility in Brazil, made all the more so as it's set within a dynamic educational environment. "Should we be surprised then", Alfredo asks, "if we see the informal economy everywhere at work?" It does appear everywhere – unofficial parking attendants roam the roads; beach vendors, the strand; and traders cling to busy intersections and travel stops. They work hard (often for others); some are quite old; all need to be fit and strong. They make pitches (*pregão*[51]) for all types of services, including illicit ones.[52] Most of those that work the informal economy are naturally creative and resilient. Many don't have a choice. Their presence is an everyday reminder of how 'others' live in the city. This may be my own cultural bias but there is a mundaneness, a certain subjection, attaching to their existence. Certainly, their way of life reminds of the necessity to survive. It is but one of a number of Brazilian contradictions that I encounter. On the one hand, Brazil appears *inclusive*. Education and health developments are imagined for all; recent governments have introduced socially progressive policies; the people are culturally sensitised to diversity (e.g. they celebrate together[53] and welcome their inter-racial heritage[54]); and they appear unified in their regional and national identities and in their support for Brazil's global ambitions. At the same time, my visits to the poorest areas of Recife (e.g. *Casa Amarela*, the *Capibaribe* river basin) reinforce an 'other' *exclusive* Brazil.

Rooftop satellite dishes resemble upturned umbrellas dotted on the hills above Recife. But scattered signs of progress cannot shelter from the burning segregation that must be felt in such *favela*-like[55] communities. Social needs loom large: Clean water and sanitation; safer houses and streets; more educational, health and leisure facilities; better public transport; and the need to address high levels of racial poverty.[56] Juxtaposed with gated communities,[57] new apartment blocks, shopping centres, businesses and sporting facilities, there are clear land and class divisions on view (Figure 4.1). Everywhere I go in Recife, there are barriers, fences, cameras, shutters, sentry towers. Each private residence and apartment block is secured. In Brazil, land and social division go hand-in-hand. And in cities like Rio de Janeiro and São Paulo, in particular, it's the source of extreme levels of violence.[58] Brazil has one of the highest gun death rates in the world and has the largest number of crack cocaine addicts (estimated at over 1 million people[59]). Children are caught up in gun, drug and sexual violence. While concentrated more in working-class areas, violence can spill over into middle-class spaces.[60] This is extensively covered by the conservative press and by *telenovela*-like[61] programmes that fuse theatre with (doctrinaire) politics. While social apartheid[62] is not always broadcast in Brazil, it still endures. And it hardens through widespread elitism, white-collar benefits, political scandal and corruption.[63] Brazil is undoubtedly making political, economic and social advances. The country is moving forward. Still, many are left behind. Are they the 'inevitable' price of 'progress'?

History appears as a more inescapable force. The past presents ripe conditions for social confrontation and exclusion. *Terra* ('land') is central to the cycle of inequality, insecurity, degradation, migration, poverty and violence.[64] At the same time, *protest* resurfaces to tell 'other' stories. Those that speak with, and on behalf of, the *landless* still offer hope (however fragile), idealism (however motivated) and change (however elusive). This is their story.

Figure 4.1 Land settlements 'on the edge' (Capibaribe River, Recife)

Movimento dos Trabalhadores Rurais Sem Terra (MST): The Landless Movement

What provokes revolution? 'Necessity', argues Hannah Arendt (1963/2006). This is what led "[. . .] the poor [*sans-culottes*], driven by the needs of their bodies, [to] burst on to the scene of the French Revolution" (Arendt, 2006, 49). In suffering poverty, they (like many *descamisados* after them) were put "under the absolute dictate of their bodies, that is, under the absolute dictate of necessity" (ibid., 50). In revolution they could question their *fate* – albeit briefly – and dare to *hope* that their futures might no longer be determined by (inevitable) circumstances. Over time, many would use (and 'misuse') poverty to secure power; while others would articulate their complex relations. Marx, as Arendt reminds (ibid., 53), helped to liberate the poor "by persuading them that poverty itself is a political, not a natural phenomenon, the result of violence and violation rather than of scarcity." Still, much less is known about Marx's (later) views on how *necessity* (more so than *freedom*) stirs revolution:

> [For Marx] the role of revolution was no longer to liberate men [sic.] from the oppression of their fellow men [sic.], let alone to found freedom, but to liberate the life process of society from the fetters of scarcity so that it could swell into a stream of abundance. Not freedom but abundance became now the aim of revolution.
>
> (Ibid., 54)

While freedom surrenders to necessity (ibid., 55), it cannot be overlooked. History teaches us (e.g. the French Revolution, Soviet Socialism) that liberation from tyranny spells freedom for the few and (still) misery for the many. Rather depressingly, no revolution has solved 'the social question' or liberated people from 'the predicament of want' (ibid., 102). Yet revolutions endure whenever those who suffer can no longer endure. And revolutions ignite when *les Malheureux* (the 'wretched'/ 'destitute') become transformed into *les Enragés* ('the enraged'):

> . . . both together, necessity and violence, [make the poor] appear irresistible – *la puissance de la terre*[65] ['the power of the land'].
>
> (Arendt, 2006, 105)

It's hard to imagine the poor as powerful. In his novel *Vidas Secas* ('Dry/Barren Lives'), Graciliano Ramos (1939/1999) presents another reality. Ramos's style as a writer – natural, economical with words, elemental practitioner – reflects the *Nordeste* characters he knows and portrays so well. And the book's title, *Vidas Secas*, reflects the scorched region (the *Sertão*) they inhabit.[66] Ramos connects the land with its people and communicates (as far as possible) the experience of poverty, its 'inner world' and affective qualities. Like Arendt's account on poverty (1963/ 2006), the body suffers. In *Vidas Secas*, the family members endure weariness, hunger, aches, migration, tireless working of the land. The land also works on the body. *Vitória* (the mother) is constantly fearful and anxious. She entreats higher powers to fend off (inevitable) drought and protect the family's (fragile) existence. She has needs beyond subsistence and, above all, wants a real bed and home.[67] Meanwhile, Fabiano (the father) wanders between providence and escapism; his patriarchal pride constantly bruised by paucity.[68] He teaches their boys about what they *need* to know in order to survive – they have "to be hard, like armadillos" (Ramos, 1999, 21), avoid being "curious" (ibid., 17, 57) and behave like "the kind of people" they are (ibid., 22). They must be just like their father who always obeyed (ibid., 24) and was used to violence and injustice (ibid., 29). For Ramos's characters, imagining another reality is ultimately futile; it isn't real. In essence, hardship just is. Such fatalism has appeal. It can free oneself from (unnecessary) mindfulness. It can liberate oneself from an existential void.[69] It can even say something heroic about one's survival in adversity. So Ramos's novel concludes, as it began, with the family migrating. Its closing words appear as a prophetic statement on rural displacement: "They were on their way to an unknown land, a land of city ways. They would become its prisoners" (ibid., 131).

The family in this semi-fictional novel does not present as a "force of elemental necessity" to spark revolution (Arendt, 2006, 100). Nor does it appear to possess the power to change its own circumstances. *In reality*, many poor Brazilian families face a similar fate. To change their realities, these families may need to directly challenge fatalism; to become a force, they may need to organise themselves politically; to become empowered, they may need to commit to collective action. One group stands out to protest on behalf of the rural landless, to fight for their right to land, to advance their access to a better quality of life. Following Marx, this group contends that poverty is not a natural phenomenon; it is not the consequence of a scarcity of resources. Rather, poverty is political, the product of violence and dominance that directly attaches to Brazil's land division, its modern industrialisation programme and lack of real agrarian reform. For this group, *O problema do Sertão não é a seca, é a cerca* ('The problem with the *Sertão* is not the drought, it is the fence').

With over 1.5 million members from 23 of Brazil's 27 states, *Movimento dos Trabalhadores Rurais Sem Terra* (or MST for short) is the largest social movement in Latin America (Branford and Rocha, 2002[70]). Officially founded in 1984 in Cascavel, Paraná, it is inspired by a history of land protest – Canudos in the late 19th century; the Mexican revolution at the beginning of the 20th century; the Cuban Revolution in 1959; and the Peasant Leagues (*Ligas Camponesas*) and Landless Farmers' Movement (*Movimento dos Agricultores Sem Terra*, MASTER) of the 1950s and 1960s. Of particular influence is the Pastoral Land Commision (*Comissão Pastoral da Terra*, CPT), which was set up in 1975 by the Catholic bishops of the Amazon basin to help peasant families defend themselves against increased violence, intimidation and eviction. The movement was kindled by early land occupation successes in Rio Grande do Sul (in Macali, 1979 and Brilhante, 1980). And it established itself as a political entity when landless families eventually (after almost 3 years) defeated the brutal suppression of the *Encruzilhada Natalino*[71] encampment in 1983. From the outset, the MST garnered crucial support from a range of academics (e.g. the sociologist José de Souza Martins), social activists (e.g. João Pedro Stédile, former seminarist and key member of the national leadership), liberal theologians (e.g. Dom José Gomes, former bishop of Chapecó and senior member of CPT), lawyers (e.g. Darci Frigo, founder of *Terra de Direitos*, TDD or 'Land of Rights') and trade unionists (e.g. 'Lula', former trade union leader, PT head and President of Brazil). Despite support from liberal factions of the church and the political left, the MST resolved to be an independent 'grassroots' body. And in contrast to unions like the National Confederation of Agricultural Workers (*Confederação Nacional dos Trabalhadores na Agricultura*, CONTAG) that sought to solve land disputes only by legislative means, the MST employed a different (more radical) strategy. Using people's knowledge in towns and villages, its members would learn about unproductive *latifúndios* and public lands. Then they would plot their *occupation*.

Local MST committees organise occupations in new states and experienced campaigners (known as *militantes*) are sent to assist. Men, women and children arrive unarmed, in numbers and in the early hours of the morning to surprise landowners and the authorities. Support groups follow – MST settlers, MST lawyers, religious figures, politicians and the press – to raise spirits, win over public opinion (a process known, interestingly, as *territorialisation*) and help steer the changeover from 'occupation' (camp) to 'settlement' (community). Transition is rarely smooth. Life in the camps is arduous: Living (sometimes for years) in black polythene tents and other temporary shelters, under poor sanitary and health conditions, with no immediate food supply, constant intimidation and violence and no ultimate guarantee of a legal right to stay. Children are particularly at risk. All 'camp dwellers' (*acampados*) live under strict disciplinary 'rules' – there are clear committee structures in place; stealing, prostitution, domestic violence and substance abuse are all prohibited. They share what little resources they have, harvest courage from one another and persevere in collective 'struggle' (*luta*) – they may even need to 'reoccupy' following forced eviction by hired gunmen and inimical authorities. These are 'landless' people fighting for the right to legally attain and work their own land. Their organisation and mobilisation, so the MST claims, has as much to do with democratic inclusion as it does with land procurement. And their struggle seeks to provoke wider debate about agrarian reform – change for all Brazilians, not just for the landless. In setting out this political purpose, the MST reaches out to like-minded national and transnational partners, including The Homeless Workers Movement (*Movimento dos Trabalhadores Sem Teto*, MTST) and The International Peasants Movement (*La Via Campesina*).

Acampados elect a camp coordinator who, together with the *militantes*, divides people into cells (*núcleos*); these cells then elect two representatives to the camp coordination committee (Branford and Rocha, 2002, 252). This committee, which effectively runs the camp, oversees the formation of commissions that deal with education, health, crop cultivation, tent construction, etc. (ibid.). *Acampados* – just like *assentados* ('settlers' or those who have attained a legal right to land through the courts) – are integrated into the MST's organisational structure. The camp coordination committee elects two representatives (a gender mix is encouraged) to form part of the regional coordination committee, which then elects two members to the state coordination committee (Branford and Rocha, 2002, 253). In turn, a smaller state council (*direção estadual*) is developed to elect two representatives to the national coordination committee that oversees the election of the 21-person national council[72] (*direção nacional*) (ibid.). In addition to these structures, a number of elected *coletivos* ('collectives') – focusing on education, health, food production, human rights, youth affairs, etc. – are established to cultivate national policies (ibid.). These seemingly tight, democratic-led structures have fashioned the MST as a well-organised body. According to João Pedro Stédile (2011), there is no centralised fund. People pay for food and shelter when they occupy land, though they may be helped by trade unions and churches (ibid.). Farmers pay 2 per cent of their encampment's production to become MST members but funds are reallocated to support people and train activists in the region (ibid.). And the MST helps finance communities' basic needs: School, teacher, health resources, electricity networks, etc. (ibid.). Preferably, and where possible, the organisation links with (progressive) state agencies. Thus, a number of universities bear the cost of educating teachers and agronomists, while the MST retains significant autonomy in deciding upon the learning and curriculum direction (ibid.). In extraordinary circumstances, such as the case of its flagship national school in São Paulo (*Escola Nacional Florestan Fernandes,*[73] ENFF), projects are co-funded with other international bodies (in this instance, the European Union).

Despite its radical ideological image, the MST is a practical organisation. In the interest of small farmers, it needs to work closely with (progressive) government policies, for example, with Lula's (2004) Programme for Technical, Social and Environmental Advising (*Programa de Assessoria Técnica, Social e Ambiental à Reforma Agrária*, ATES). It has learned from experience in the earlier settlements that collectivisation does not typically work[74] (Branford and Rocha, 2002). It has learned that it is impractical to replicate the practices of big landowners and farmers (ibid.). And it has learned to win over people with an 'other' mode of food production (*agroecologia*) that compensates with increased profits, taxes and employment (see next section). Still, practical developments are overshadowed by ideological ascriptions. MST members are commonly referred to as (interchangeably) 'Marxists', 'socialists', 'revolutionaries', 'criminals', 'trouble-makers', 'violent', 'invaders'. In commemoration of *Massacre de Eldorado dos Carajás*, most occupations and marches occur during (what the media now dubs) 'red April'. Many landowners, farmers, Congress politicians and right-wing activists (especially *União Democrática Ruralista*, UDR) view the MST as dangerous 'ideologues' and 'anti-capitalists'. Such groups powerfully mobilise to protect individual property rights and the land market system. Of course in directly opposing expropriation and land reform, they perform ideologically. But the MST stands out – prominent occupations, marches and protest banners (Figure 4.2) hold higher visibility. And through its ritual practices (known as *mística*), the MST (literally) stages revolutionary performance. These rites draw upon Catholic spirituality, as well as protest music and folk hero traditions. Performed daily in camps and settlements, they recollect past struggles, strengthen group spirits and deliver hope for the 'promised land'. Black polythene tents are reconstructed to retell (to schoolchildren and new settlers) the struggles of their forbears, and shanty town visits are organised to articulate present realities. Songs and slogans are chanted in moving tribute to the movement's martyrs. And celebrated freedom fighters are summoned to the cause: *Che, Zumbi, Antônio Conselheiro; Na luta por justiça nós somos companheiros!* ('In the struggle for justice, we are all comrades!').

Sacrifice is stirred by religious sentiment. And protest is pronounced in Marxist language. To some, more critical onlookers, *mística* are mawkish ceremonies, indoctrinating rituals. To others, the sight of peasants with red hats and flags shouting

Marxist slogans simply demonstrates the democratic right to remonstrate. Certainly, it's important to critique the seductive images[75] and practices of revolutionary thought. But MST leaders defend *mística* as important social and communicative events. As spokespeople for a (traditionally) lowly educated and politically under-represented population, they value the literacy and civic power of these rituals. Cultural and political symbolism appears just as important to the MST, as it does to other organisations. I want to explore this, among other issues, with Jaime Amorim, a very senior MST figure. Jaime has lived an extraordinary life. A former seminarian, he left the priesthood to help set up the movement. Alongside José Rainha Júnior, he established the MST in the northeast and since 1987 has helped organise numerous protests and occupations. He currently serves on the *direção nacional*, gives frequent talks, writes for the *Sem Terra Journal*, meets strategic partners and holds information and advice sessions in MST's headquarters in Caruaru. It is here where Alfredo and I meet him[76] – up narrow cobbled streets with their hugging low-rise houses, down from a sex motel, beside the foreboding prison. Jaime has been to jail a number of times. He does not appear easily intimidated or threatened, though he has experienced both. A portrait of the revolutionary Che and a Sebastião Salgado photo adorn his office walls. We are introduced to his young son, Paulo Ernesto (*Paulo*, after Paulo Freire; *Ernesto* from Ernesto Che Guevara). Perhaps in another context, such symbolism might mean less. But I remind myself that over the course of three decades of MST membership, close to 1,000 of Jaime's *comrades* have been murdered or killed. His symbolism means more.

Jaime recalls the critical phases of MST's development. Initially, especially in the *Região Nordeste*, there was "violent struggle." Despite "many difficult times", the MST became a mass movement, focusing its political efforts (via protests, land and public building occupations) against the "implantation of neoliberalism." During this second phase, the media began to "criminalise" the movement, presenting its image "through negative discourse." This had the effect of sidelining "the political viewpoint" and realigning "justice issues" with "law enforcement." Landowner and agribusiness affairs were advanced and the media, in "close alliance with the government", began to "silence the movement" by presenting little or no coverage. 'Interests' conspired (once more) to conceal the *land question*; but then there appeared more hope for real agrarian change. This third phase coincided with Lula's government's efforts (especially in 2003–2006) to invest in land reform and ratify increased community settlements. Resurgence did not sustain, however. Though Cardoso's anti-land occupation policies adopted in 2000 ended, Lula's government still advanced neoliberalism, albeit "with a gentler face" (Ondetti, 2008, 202). Overall, occupations under Lula "returned to levels comparable to those of 1996 and 1997, but shy of the peaks attained [ironically under Cardoso] during the 1998–99 period" (Ondetti, 2008, 210, 211). Paradoxically, then, a 'soft' political relationship with Lula's (and subsequently Dilma's) government led to slower progress. At this time too, as Jaime highlights, globalisation had a "quietening effect" on the working class. There appeared (in postmodern fashion) to be greater "political participation in society" but less "political movement." Accordingly, the

MST is now entering its fourth development phase – "recuperation." This, Jaime asserts, involves "restarting the process of mobilisation in society", "placing the big [land] question back on the table." Already the MST has reignited. In 2014, for its 30th anniversary, some 15,000 activists marched to Brasília to set up camp outside the World Cup stadium. And the 6th *Congresso Nacional do MST* led with the chant *Lutar, Construir Reforma Agrária Popular!* [Struggle, to Construct Popular Agrarian Reform!].

Protest in Brazil, it seems, is always incomplete, which may explain, indeed necessitate, its persistence. The MST acknowledges the important role that education plays in sustaining land protest. There are over 2,000 public schools in encampments and settlements that afford over 160,000 landless children (*sem terrinha*) and adolescents free access to education (dos Santos, 2014, 2). In addition, some 50,000 adults and youth have become literate in recent years and over 100 graduate courses, in partnership with 54 Brazilian universities, have been created (ibid.). While basic schooling and training are facilitated in camps and communities, programmes in 'political formation' are facilitated in the national school in São Paulo (ENFF) and in other locations, such as *Normandía* (see next section). In a relatively short period of time (e.g. two months in ENFF), students learn how political and technical knowledge is bound up in the study of political philosophy, international relations, rural sociology, social history of Brazil, the political economy of agriculture, etc. University partners (such as *Universidade Federal Rural de Pernambuco*, UFRPE) now offer a number of graduate and postgraduate courses in such disciplines as agricultural science, education, health and engineering. MST leaders are encouraged to participate to empower them to exercise the requisite 'cultural capital' (Bourdieu, 1977; see Chapter 3). Indeed, all members are encouraged to partake in education and training. It is often assumed, Jaime asserts, that *camponês* have only 'hard hands' (like, I later reflect, those embroidered depictions in a Cândido Portinari painting[77]). But while it is important to be "linked with the land, [they] also need to have technical knowledge and political formation." This model of education is not without its challenges. Universities, for example, can be "very conservative", even when they are located (via 'outreach' work) *in* the countryside. There is a presumption too that MST students are somehow "less able", even if (as Jaime informs me) assessments indicate otherwise.

Teachers and professors are challenged, therefore, to overcome systemic and ideological prejudices. With familiarity, they can and do and they can even, says Jaime, "become engaged with the movement." The MST actively "seeks out" those practitioners who are more conversant with its "philosophical values." MST students are supported by their communities who put them forward for education/training and by mentors ("political pedagogical coordinators") who 'scaffold' them in different courses and programmes of study. They are also given financial support by the movement (board and subsistence, not fees). In this way, Jaime contends, students' "will to learn" is positively (and "successfully") influenced by "collective" responsibility and patronage. To understand this model of education, then, is to understand its (political) change purpose. The study of *agroecologia* ('agroecology'), for example, goes beyond curriculum content (e.g. knowledge of different systems of agricultural production and their ecological practices). It also engages how to critique such systems and, with newfound knowledge, effect changes to one's own practices (see next section). Is this transformed way of being and thinking nothing more than contrived indoctrination? Does this approach, as argued in some critiques of *mística*, not serve to dilute educational 'freedom'? Jaime counters with the following: "Are students not presented with ideological beliefs [already]?" Should they not contest "dominant knowledge" forms? Doesn't 'freedom' come from questioning that knowledge "which does not speak to you and your community?" Reverting to the *agroecología* exemplar, students may come to question the (dominant) use of industrial fertilisers and toxic pesticides; they may critique monoculture practices that produce soil erosion, saltation and deforestation. Only through understanding this 'reality', the (counter) argument runs, can they begin to access an 'other' reality – crop diversification, rotating harvest schemes, natural fertilisers and complex cultivation systems (that use native Brazilian seeds). In this way, technical (or practical) knowledge is allied to 'political formation'. And an 'other' discourse – in resistance to the 'dominant' syntax of agribusiness – is (literally) named. Moreover, the *ideas* attaching to new language terms like 'food nutrition and security' and 'food sovereignty' can begin to articulate *the landless* 'reality' (see next section).

Education can empower us; we can be empowered through education. As a social activist movement, it's unsurpising to see identity transformation at the heart of MST's educational mission. The movement, after all, seeks to arrest rural exodus to the city – where violence, poverty and ill-health (including mental health) loom. It seeks to challenge the classical model of agrarian reform (including redistributive efforts which clearly have not worked in places like Zimbabwe and Venezuela) in order to re-present an 'other', 'more inclusive' way (see next section). And, definitively, it seeks to provide healthy, sustainable livelihoods for rural landless communities. Nearing the end of our interview, I ask Jaime why he perseveres in protest. He does not hesitate: "The main reason is that you can believe that you can change society for the better." Ultimately, the MST's success is measured against this social justice ideal. There are now over 222 settlements in Pernambuco alone. In Brazil, more than 350,000 families have been enabled to secure land[78] (dos Santos, 2014). These families have developed cooperative farms, healthy food and water supplies, adequate housing, schools and health clinics. In addition to subsistence farming, many small landowners provide healthy food products at affordable prices to village, town and city markets. A number of small farmers supply their own fresh fruit, vegetables and animal products to the poorest school communities (specifically via the *School Nourishment and Food Acquisition* programme, PNAE). This demonstrates, as Gabriel Ondetti (2008, 228) notes, that occupation-based movements can "sometimes contribute to broad policy changes that benefit even people who did not participate in protest initiatives." It shows how in democratic times – though often difficult, these are *not* revolutionary times – land reform can be successfully achieved for the *descamisados*.[79] And it demonstrates how *local* economic development can be stimulated and sustained (Ondetti, 2008, 238). But perhaps the biggest success of the movement is its power to effect *social* change. Here, the MST claims to (trans-)form more than 'small landowners'. It creates a critical citizenry, landless people who become the subjects of their own history (dos Santos, 2014).

Still, numerous obstacles hinder this 'movement': The ever-presence of corruption, injustice and violence; the strength of counter-ideological messages and their public reception; 'soft' partnership[80] with PT governments (12 years at the time of writing), poor (land and living) conditions and indebtedness of some settlements; continued lack of structural support for communities (especially in terms of education, health, technical and financial assistance); some members' 'readiness' (especially among young people) to migrate to cities for 'better' life opportunities (often in chase of the 'informal' economy); an associative lack of wider educational opportunities in the countryside (especially beyond elementary/primary level); and a dearth of credit and infrastructure to expand small rural production. The importance of land reform cannot be undervalued, not least because it can enhance rural families' security and self-sufficiency, as well as augment Brazil's agricultural production. But how wide-ranging can land reform be given that there is an effective Constitutional ban on expropriating *productive* land? (Ondetti, 2008). Does this not essentially shield large commercial producers, with smaller ones being "doubly protected"? (ibid., 237). How 'relevant' is the MST in an era of ('politicised') globalisation? What 'interest' is it of an increasingly modernised, industrialised and urbanised population? How far can the so-called 'green revolution' present as

Figure 4.2 MST: Land protest banner

an 'other' reality? Given its higher production costs (including its labour protection measures), how can this model ever compete with 'high-profit-low-cost' agribusiness? Accordingly, how can the MST counter its 'anti-modernisation' and 'anti-foreign direct investment' image? Within its own ranks, how will leadership engage more critical voices who might challenge 'collective' ideals and strategic direction? How, even once land is secured, will the movement further deliver on 'freedom'? Specifically in relation to its schools, does the MST have the 'right' to interpret social 'reality' *for*, as well as *with*, 'others'?

Praxis – critical pedagogy in action

It's early in the morning when Alfredo and I set off to visit the MST's training centre in Pernambuco. Named after the Brazilian educator Paulo Freire (*Centro de Formação Paulo Freire*),[81] this is located in the *Normandía* settlement of Caruaru, some 150 kilometres west of Recife. On the car journey to the semi-arid interior (the *Agreste* region), I take in the Brazilian countryside. With its oversized tropical plantations, its lattice of forest and *caatinga* ('desert' vegetation) and its blanket of reddened soil, it paints an impressive scene. Now and then, tracts of land bordered by colourful flags catch my eye. These, Alfredo tells me, are development lands. 'Progressively', middle class families are investing in 'country homes', retiring from city life at the weekends. It's odd to think of the rural poor flocking to the sprawling towns and cities, while the better-off depart to the sparsely populated countryside. But, for the MST, this is further demonstration of the 'invasion' of rural Brazil and the direct impact of globalisation on population migration.[82] We stop for breakfast at a roadside restaurant that caters for a mixture of *índios* and Brazilian cuisines. On display, a smörgåsbord of delicacies from *Tapioca, Manioc, Cuscuz* and *Tucupi* beside an extensive range of meats ('obligatory', even at breakfast time). More than satiated, we head for Bezerros. Once a small town, it has swollen to almost 60,000 people. Tile-fronted houses are silent and gated, in contrast to the busy open streets and corner bars. Bare sewers and passing traffic emit a tangible pollution. And congested heat rises with the day. We meet Alfredo's affable colleague, Professor André Gustavo Ferreira da Silva from the *Centro de Educação, Departamento de Fundamentos Sócio Filosóficos da Educação*. André teaches, researches and writes on Paulo Freire. En route, he passionately shares his ideas on illiteracy (*analfabetismo*) and Popular Education (*Educação Popular*). As a former director of *Centro de Formação Paulo Freire* and as recent co-organiser of the *Colóquio Internacional Paulo Freire* (it takes place every two years), André is well versed and has many connections. A trusted confidante of the movement, he expedites access to the *Normandía* settlement. Winding our way up the former plantation's dusty road, past the Norwegian-styled church, around the back of the *casa grande* ('big house'), we eventually arrive.[83]

There to greet us is the imposing, tranquil figure of Greisson Izidorio (MST state education coordinator). He shows us around and informs that at least 4 adult learner groups (aged 16 upwards) are facilitated here each year. These students are specifically nominated by their communities for political and *agroecologia* training (without formal qualifications). On average, they stay for 6–8 weeks. Some bring their partners and children. All avail of the basic dormitory and communal refectory facilities. The day we arrive, 10 students are preparing for an upcoming protest that coincides with President Dilma's visit to Recife. They are constructing a giant effigy (symbolising fascism) and deliberating upon its use (and destruction) during the march. Greisson explains, following Freire, how education necessarily involves dialogue. In *Normandía* dialogue is aimed at "democratising knowledge" in order to mobilise "committed action." Thus, in support of Freire's theory of *praxis*, learners not only share knowledge about their 'reality', they consciously set out to act upon their world, to collectively transform it (Freire, 1970/1996). This cycle of critical reflection, dialogue and action clearly takes time and demands *commitment*. For the teacher's part, he/she needs to be patient, mediate enquiries, seek elucidations and, above all, listen to students' views and concerns. I observe this now in practice (in accordance with the theory), including how the words that emerge from dialogue appear to litter the blackboard – this exemplifies a Freirean approach to literacy ('read the word, read the world'). I imagine how *self-transformation* (a new way of seeing one's reality) can never be too far away. And I contemplate education's (ultimate?) transformative quality. While it's clear to me that education involves some 'conversion', I wonder how much of this can be truly student-centred, ever voluntary?

Greisson's own story may be illustrative. He vividly recalls his first encounter with the movement – 3 brightly-coloured columns marching abreast through his hometown. For a number of years, he was a seasonal worker on a sugar plantation, while his mother toiled for long hours in a factory. At that moment, the MST started to build relations with his community (*territorialisation*) and he was chosen to coordinate supports for some 10 families. He was later given responsibility for education and training across a number of areas in a southern region of Pernambuco. Now, some 15 years later, he has his own plot of land and is state coordinator responsible for liaising with 52 of his regional *comrades* on all education and training matters. Greisson explains this "ascendency" in terms of the movement's standards of "fairness", "democracy and leadership." Leaders, he asserts, "come from below, then they decide, then they go back down", that is, they are replaced. This two-way structure empowers others to be leaders and provides continuity and democratic accountability. Collective identity is also strengthened since those who 'ascend' undergo political formation, usually a 30-day *Pé No Chão* ('Feet on the Ground') course. The idea, as Jaime already noted, is that 'hard hands' will lead the way in learning. People in the movement, Greisson reminds, don't generally go to university – "that's for the wealthy class." Progressively, however, the MST is connecting with (technological) universities through their 'interior' programmes, for example, *Instituto Federal de Educação, Ciência e Tecnologia do Sertão Pernambuco*, IFPE. We meet 3 students in *Normandía* who are studying for an agricultural science degree in IFPE but who are here specifically to engage political formation. André explains that while the movement co-constructs certain curricula with certain third-level institutions, it retains full autonomy for learning instruction in places like *Normandía*. This sense of 'bi-location' (being both *within* and *without* the system) is very interesting. Does it not present, I ask, a number of identity issues for teachers and students? André sees dual benefits: It provides an opportunity to "reach out to others and learn more" and "communicate your values", as well as "create your own space, with your own professional identity." But there are tensions too. Sometimes, André translates on behalf of the students: "You feel different", "under pressure to do well", "not understood." It must be very challenging, I reflect, to move between 'cultural worlds', to experience a sense of distance, confusion or alienation, to be a 'cultural stranger' (O'Sullivan, 1995, 2005).

Greisson tells us that in *Normandía*, "the curriculum adapts to particular learner groups." Thus, depending on the region (e.g. the *Agreste* or the *Sertão*), there are different needs for "different land producers." The curriculum here, like a Graciliano Ramos (1939/1999) novel, connects the *land* with its *people* and communicates (as far as possible) the 'reality' of their lives. In very practical terms, it engages students' needs, desires, interests and knowledge gaps. The majority of students learn about basic environmentally friendly farming practices, such as sourcing one's own seeds and fertilisers, protecting local biodiversity, harvesting organic produce, organising crop complementarity, diversity and rotation, etc. *Land recuperation* features strongly in students' learning: Reclaiming contaminated soils (in advance of organic transferal), planting multiple crops in one area (to circumvent drought and disease), creating natural fertilisers (from chicken and cow manure, as well as weed material) and maintaining plots (using dried sugar cane mulch and rubber irrigation systems). Greisson shows us around the working farm. There are 4 productive units – medicinal herbs, pigs, cows and chickens. Students learn very practical skills from driving a tractor and feeding animals to tending to crops and cleaning out shelters. This is a collective endeavour, demanding individual energy and commitment. Naturally, for these young adults, there's some resistance to early morning rises and shared living (*alojamentos compartilhados*) duties. Greisson reminds that they are faced with real change. Everyone must clean their own clothes, wash their own dishes and show consideration for others in the collective. *Machismo* is confronted and females are given an equal right and voice in determining *agroecologia* practices. All students are challenged to *unlearn* through 'hidden' (e.g. rejecting *machismo*) and 'formal' (e.g. rejecting pesticides) curriculum messages. Ultimately, says Greisson, this 'other' way makes sense to them. Passing through semi-arid fields, we come across 3 large rainwater capture systems. Each has a capacity of 16,000 litres used for crop hosing. "Sustainable design makes sense to them", he repeats.

The science of ecology, Denis Owen (1980/1991, 18) contends, is (simply) "concerned with the relationships between plants and animals and the environment in which they live." But another (complex) facet is "more concerned with man's [sic.] place in nature and threats to the quality of life" (ibid., 20). Accordingly, human activities (including agricultural practices) are perceived to be just as 'ecological'. Learning about agriculture, then, (necessarily) involves 'thinking ecologically' (ibid., 23), for example, how naturally diverse environments can be damaged by agribusiness or how increased demands for food production affect livelihoods. Murray Bookchin (1921–2006) takes a particular (critical) position. He uses the term 'social ecology' to demonstrate how "the very concept of dominating nature stems from the domination of human by human" (Bookchin, 1980/ 1991, 59):

> . . . as long as hierarchy persists, as long as domination organizes humanity around a system of elites, the project of dominating nature will continue to exist and inevitably lead our planet to ecological extinction.
>
> (Ibid., 60)

The bigger social task alluded to above contrasts with that of 'environmentalism', which merely seeks to develop techniques to 'engineer' nature (e.g. solar and wind power) and reduce hazardous fall-out, but which ultimately serves to accommodate existing dominant relations (ibid., 61). Many others (to varying degrees) critique this 'engineering' outlook and, in so doing, *commit* themselves to 'other' ways. Evelyn Barbara Balfour (1943/2006, 1977/1991), for example, long championed the cause of organic farming. Her supporters still promote personal, as well as collective, responsibility for environmental change. They believe that you can 'train' yourself and others to foster life energy (e.g. enhance soil fertility), protect natural eco-systems, use renewable resources, practise organic farming and avoid the monoculture of crops and animals. Rewards are both self-sacrificing and self-seeking since 'by us giving to nature, nature gives to us'. Land is not perceived as 'property', less still as 'property of the few'. In its place, 'a land ethic' is cultivated that sustains the 'right' of resources to their "continued existence and, at least in spots, their continued existence in a natural state" (Leopold, 1949/1991, 239). Such a worldview *connects to real* issues of 'sustainable development', such as over-farming, deforestation, climate change, community (re)settlements and poverty problems. It naturally exhorts us to establish a sound grasp of the technical science of *agroecologia* (Altieri, 1995; Gliessman, 1998). But it also challenges us to use that knowledge *purposively*, to mobilise a 'green education'[84] (Figure 4.3) which, at the very least, counters dominant knowledge forms.

In *Normandía*, training reflects the 'lived realities' of its students and their communities. And by linking technical and political knowledge, wider 'world' connections are also forged. To illustrate, take the (rather lacklustre) topic of seed production.[85] The 3 largest seed companies (they are also pesticide producers) control more than 50 per cent of the global market[86] (Berne Declaration and EcoNexus, 2013). They are also involved in consolidating control over intellectual property and patent rights.[87] Such concentrated power in the hands of a few corporations presents a number of (technical and political) concerns. Farmers are now faced with increased, more volatile seed prices.[88] They are effectively compelled to re-pay those increased prices, since they cannot reliably replant hybrid seeds year-on-year.

And by diverging evermore from diverse crop varieties,[89] they are pressured to produce more of the same in order to compete and survive. In Brazil specifically, the world's largest seed company (Monsanto) expects that its genetically modified (GM) soybean strain will exceed 80 per cent of crop production (Kassai and Moura, 2011).[90] Indeed, Monsanto's seeds are the only biotech varieties that are sold in the country (ibid.). From an ecological perspective, such monoculture crop practices are highly problematic since "complexity (in terms of species diversity) is correlated with stability" (Owen, 1980/1991, 23). Other serious technical (as well as humanitarian) problems relate to the very limit of this production mode, specifically its ability to source suitable food for an ever-expanding population (ibid., 24). From a political perspective, too, monoculture crop practices raise considerable questions about *food and nutritional security*,[91] as well as *food sovereignty*.[92] How can unelected forces, disconnected (though not by lobby) from political institutions, exert such control over food production?[93] Who has the 'right' to grow seeds? How can farmers become self-reliant if their primary role is just to sow and reproduce?

The teachers and students in *Normandía* ask such technical, humanitarian and political questions. They are not alone. In France, for example, a similar exchange of ideas is being generated by activists like Guy Kastler (of the *Farmers' Seed Network*), Dominique Guillet (of *Kokopelli*) and José Bové (of *La Confédération Paysanne, La Via Campesina* and the *European Greens*).[94] Influenced by environmental campaigners like Pierre Rabhi, they advocate just 'land and people' relations (see Rabhi's *Manifeste pour la terre et l'humanisme* (2008). Their political slogans protest against the prevailing power of agribusiness: *Le monde n'est pas une marchandise!* (Bové et Dufour, 2000); *Non à l'usine à vaches!*; *Trois petites fermes valent mieux qu'une grande!* And their vision is of an 'other' world, a more just global order, as imagined each year by civil society organisations that present at the *World Social Forum*. Collectively, these groups form part of a diverse alter-globalisation movement, one that embraces the 'spirit of Porto Alegro', not the 'spirit of Davos'[95] (Wallerstein, 2009). In practical terms, they seek to raise social consciousness (often through protest) and stimulate social change (often through progressive and integrated government policies). In Brazil, civil society groups (like the MST) have been successful in helping to advance real change, for example, the establishment of the National Council of Food Security and Nutrition (CONSEA), the Zero Hunger Strategy (*Fome Zero*), the National Food and Nutritional Security Policy (PNSAN), the removal of basic food taxes and the 2010 Brazilian Constitutional amendment that makes the 'right to food' a 'social right'. Nevertheless, change is qualified; incomplete. Notwithstanding the power of pressure politics and the achievement of some very positive outcomes, one must question the extent to which an 'other' global order is really being advanced? Explicitly, if capitalism *is* the crisis and there's no revolt against it, how can revolution ever be possible?

Naomi Klein, Canadian writer and social activist, is unambiguous – capitalism *is* the crisis. Speaking on climate change (Klein, 2014a), she asserts that it's impossible to take action without directly confronting historical injustice and wealth distribution in society. Real change, she argues, is not in the 'interest' of big business and neoliberal factions. They, alongside their policymaking allies, do not represent those who are disproportionately affected by climate change, that is, the poor or *descamisados*. While they are not omnipotent, as demonstrated by a growing number of resistance movements (e.g. Occupy and *Indignados*), they remain all-pervasive (Rose, 1999). Protest against these external forces is therefore necessary, though we also need to *change within* (Klein, 2014b). Thus, in the 'interest' of climate justice, *each one of us* is obliged to re-think economic urgency,[96] consume less and reclaim some knowledge of the land:

> Shielded from the elements as we are in our climate-controlled homes, workplaces and cars, the changes unfolding in the natural world easily pass us by. We might have no idea that a historic drought is destroying the crops on the farms that surround our urban homes, since the supermarkets still display miniature mountains of imported produce, with more coming in by truck all day [. . .] Climate change, meanwhile, is busily adding to the ranks of the rootless every day, as natural disasters, failed crops, starving livestock and climate-fuelled ethnic conflicts force yet more people to leave their ancestral homes. And with every human migration, more crucial connections to specific places are lost, leaving yet fewer people to listen closely to the land.
>
> (Klein, 2014b, 3)

'Modernisation', a concept tenaciously branded by agribusiness 'interests', leads to fewer people 'listening to the land'. For farmers, in particular, many traditional 'ways of knowing' are being lost (e.g. seed production). In order to reclaim this *lost knowledge*, modern 'ways of knowing' need to be 'unlearned'. This presents a significant educational challenge. First, learners need to name the problem, that is, disrupt the common-sense ('progressive') logic of the market. And second, they need to re-name the problem by re-presenting the past and re-instating (i.e. acting upon) an 'other' way. Thus, in developing its own organic producer (*Rede Bionatur de Sementes Agroecológicas*), the MST commits to countering common-sense and reclaiming *lost knowledge*. This empowers members to cultivate ('other') organic ways. And it makes (new) 'sense' to farmers, not least because *they* can sell back their seeds through this alternative source.

Transformative learning is neither smooth nor certain. In 'reality', farmers see that markets, bureaucratic systems, state investments and food export licenses are all geared towards the big companies (Branford and Rocha, 2002, 224, 225). In an 'other' reality, some farmers see that *agroecologia* works – seasonal workers can be given security, cooperatives can be established alongside individual plots, natural manure and seed production can develop, and mixed farming methods (including medicinal cultivation) can offer new possibilities. Still, it's not easy to move from one 'reality' to an 'other'. It's not easy to align one's education to 'change'. And it's not easy to look beyond oneself, to embrace *social* change that has yet to be 'realised'. Despite these real difficulties, change *does* happen. Freire (1970/1996) contends that when we experience learning as connected to the world, we become caught up in transformation. Thus, when farmers experience functional, sustainable food systems, they begin to imagine a more progressive, humanising, alter-globalisation model. And their own 'reality' changes in parallel with this social transformation (Branford and Rocha, 2002). Ultimately, the MST seeks to mobilise this change (Figure 4.3). There are now over 400 associations and cooperatives that work collectively to produce foodstuffs without transgenics and without pesticides (dos Santos, 2014). In addition, 96 agro-industries operate under much-improved health and labour conditions to provide low-priced, quality goods (ibid.). And in centring its focus on small farmers, the MST and others (like *Centro de Apoio ao Pequeno Agricultor*, CAPA) support self-sustainability and new food markets.[97]

Still, Brazil has very high levels of food insecurity and poverty. The food insecure population is estimated to be in the region of 66 million, with 12 million experiencing extreme food insecurity (Oxfam, 2010). The proportion of food-insecure Brazilians living in northern and north-eastern Brazil is estimated to be as high as 60 per cent (ibid.). And it is thought that 16 million Brazilians live in extreme poverty, while 47 million avail of free daily school meals (ibid.). A 2010 report from the Brazilian health sector's System of Food and Nutritional Surveillance (SISVAN) reveals that just under 4 per cent of those children below 5 years of age who used the health services had low or very low weight-for-age, while over 7 per cent were overweight (Chmielewska and Souza, 2011, 7). Another 2009 Ministry of Health report found that 7 per cent of children below the age of 5 had insufficient height-for-age, with close to 15 per cent recorded in the northern regions (ibid., 7, 8). Despite these (and other) reports that highlight high levels of food insecurity and poverty, agribusiness food production in Brazil has expanded and remains largely monocultural and export led. Characterised by *latifúndios* that occupy more than three quarters of the rural land area, agribusiness accounts for 15 per cent of the 5.2 million rural establishments (ibid., 15). In contrast, family farmers (representing some 4.4 million families) account for nearly 85 per cent of rural establishments (ibid.). They make up three quarters of rural labour (over 123 million people) that work one quarter of the rural land area (ibid.). And they comprise (most notably in the northeast) a significant share of the population's poor and food-insecure (ibid.). To compound their unequal status, agribusiness received in excess of six times more resources than family farming in the 2009–2010 public budget (ibid.). Most recently, President Dilma's 2013–2014 agricultural plan allocated 115 billion R$ to agribusiness while family farming was given an 18 billion R$ share (Araujo, 2013). Further, successive governments have supported the growth of genetically modified organisms (GMOs). Brazil is now the second largest GMO production area in the world (Chmielewska and Souza, 2011, 15, 16), which, for some, (literally) pays dividends.

Against this context or (more accurately) *because* of this context, the MST engages in political formation. As an independent, grassroots social movement, it advocates on behalf of its main constituents – landless people, rural workers and small farmers. And it forms close alliances with like-minded groups that support other uprooted communities, such as Movement of People Affected by Dams (MAB) and *Movimento dos Trabalhadores Sem Teto* (MTST). Collectively, these groups confront capital by disputing agribusiness and industrial models that dictate more social, economic and land divisions. As a distinct collective, the MST prompts us to question *what kind of society do we want to live in?* It presents sound ecological, civic and democratic reasons for critiquing big business 'interests'. And its educational project 'makes sense'. It makes sense to resist deregulated urbanisation, not least because this migration has high social, economic, health and security costs (Vidal, 2014). It makes sense to empower marginalised rural groups to question their own 'reality' in the midst of social transformation. And it makes sense to activate individual and social consciousness, to galvanise *wider debates on educational inclusion*. Thus, we are provoked to question. Does the formal (or 'official') curriculum speak to marginalised learner groups? Does education adequately consider the context within which, through which, learners come to know and 'realise' change? In short, *do non-traditional learners demand non-traditional forms of learning?*

Free of the 'danger' of poverty, Graciliano Ramos (1939/1999, 22) writes in *Vidas Secas*, "the boys could talk, ask questions, and do anything they liked." Education is presented as something of a luxury (especially to 'hard hands'), as something removed from necessity. But an 'other' view is to see education as *necessary*, to see it as a means of liberating society from paucity, as a means of releasing more 'abundant' opportunities and resources (Arendt, 1963/2006, 54, 55). Clearly, it is not enough to just own land. The MST also argues that *land reform* is needed to enable greater educational sustainability. In this way, education is not seen as an isolated field of social and cultural production. Education both reflects and generates greater social inclusion. Education is *connected* to the land.

On the return journey from *Normandía*, Alfredo, André and I stop off in Gravatá (75 kilometres from Recife). As we share coffee and sugary desserts, the Easter Passion goes by. It's a dramatic scene with hundreds of palm-bearing pilgrims reciting in hymn and prayer. Astride a donkey, a life-like Christ figure leads the way and completes the pageantry. I reflect on the devotees. It's hard not to draw parallels with followers of *critical pedagogy*. Paulo Freire (1921–1997) – Brazil's foremost educationalist and the world's leading advocate of critical pedagogy – actually writes of the 'Easter Experience' (Freire, 1970/1996). He uses the metaphor to refer to those who authentically commit themselves to 'other' people. Their conversion, he argues, is so radical, it cannot involve ambivalence – 're-birth' necessitates a new ('committed') way of being (ibid.). This transformative perspective is no doubt informed by Socratic philosophy. But it is also shaped by strong Christian beliefs – Freire, after all, once worked for the World Council of Churches and hails from the *Nordeste* where religion is absorbed in *protest*. Alfredo and I discuss these Freirean ideas on the final leg of our journey. How many teachers, we wonder, are authentically committed to 'others'? How many are committed to a change of 'self'? What does it take to become 'converted'? The radio hums in the background. It's

Figure 4.3 Mobilising *agroecologia*: Education as praxis

the semi-final of the Pernambuco state championship. The match has gone to extra-time, now to penalties. Players are on their knees praying for a goal or a miss. The commentator is hyper-animated. We tune back in to 'reality'. Meanwhile, the MST is planning to march on the governor's office in Recife to demand greater land reform. A week later, a television news station covers the event. How many, I wonder, tune in to this 'reality'?

Learning *power*

Education can empower us; we can be empowered through education. Educators would surely agree. But how many are really tuned in to learning *power*? Freire (1970/1996) contends that it is man's [woman's] *raison d'être* (his/her 'ontological vocation') to become more fully human. It is our duty to know and empower ourselves such that we may collectively shape a more just, humane society. Educators can make this real difference with 'others'. But how exactly?

The first thing to recognise is that it's not easy to know ourselves or 'others'. Martin Heidegger (1927/1996) presents this fundamental challenge: How to recognise one's being, much of which is unseen, removed from our immediate senses.[98] 'Thrown into the world', we are bound by our own 'facticity' (our material environment, our history), capable (at best) of only interpreting our 'being-in-the-world' (Collins and Selina, 2012). For Heidegger, our 'being-in-the-world' is further entangled in our practices, emotions, dispositions and, crucially, in our 'being with others' (ibid.). Even the most enlightened (who he calls *Dasein*) is not assured of his/her understanding of being, let alone the being of 'others'. What we can take from Heidegger, then, is that one's 'being' is certainly complex, perhaps impossible to comprehend. Still, the question of being holds value. We must grapple with it. Many of us carry out our existence and have little time and space for critical reflection. It is rare for us to become aware of our own 'reality', let alone be in tune with the 'reality of others'. What's it really like to be uprooted? To live with poverty with all its material, affective and relational consequences? We can empathise, show some awareness, tolerance, love and respect (Freire, 1970/1996), but can we ever know an 'other' body? And what about those who are marginalised, oppressed and silenced? Can they ever know themselves? In essence, what is our 'reality' (looking in mirrors)? And what is theirs (looking through windows)? It's not easy to confront appearances. It's not easy for dominant groups to recognise how their white, male, ethnic-majority, classed, able, heterosexual body excludes 'others'. And it's not easy for subjugated groups to embrace 'outsider' status and embody protest. In fact, taking these steps can lead to *more* exclusion. Thus, one can reach out to like-minded 'others' for collective support, but this risks alienation from more powerful groups. Most absurdly, powerful groups (including the media) can re-present (even 'demonise') *others* as exclusionary forces.

Educational discourse (saturated as it is in political, policy, class, gender, culture, ability, sexual orientation and racial values) generates convincing 'realities'. *Real* power is mobilised when discourse is organised (Foucault, 1977), when it *produces* inclusionary/exclusionary identities and practices 'on the ground' (Ball, 1990; Apple, 2006; Willis, 1981; Youdell, 2011; Grant and Sleeter, 2011; Slee, 2010; Gillborn, 2008). For Michel Foucault (1977), powerful social forces behind/aligned to particular language and knowledge forms critically shape thoughts and behaviours. Thus, teachers and students are 'caught up' in (even 'committed' to) certain governance practices that include/exclude, for example, ability setting, banding, exam scores, performativity and comparative judgements. Such practices pressurise individuals to govern them 'selves' and 'others' in particular ways (see Chapter 3). Governance is hard to see, since power remains typically invisible, particularly to those under its gaze. For Foucault, power does not exist on its own; it is not held or possessed. Instead, it relies on complex strategic relations that provide limitations and 'conditions of possibility' to our very being (Gordon 2005, 236). In Foucault's own words, "power is not primarily the maintenance and reproduction of economic relations, but is above all a relation of force" (Foucault interview in Gordon, 2005, 89). Moreover, power is dispersed: It "invests itself in institutions", becomes "embodied in techniques", "in direct and immediate relationship", "in our gestures [. . .], behaviours" (Foucault interview in Gordon 2005, 96, 97). Sarah Ahmed (2004) adds 'affective economies', where emotions and dispositions are shown to constantly shape, and be shaped by, what is a 'normal' and what is an 'other' person. Thus, impressions are *made* of working class kids, feelings are *generated* with lower ability students, etc. (Kitching *et al.*, 2014). Further, Judith Butler emphasises individuals' 'reflexive/psychic' positioning and the freedoms and limits that *they* exercise in their *own* formation (Butler, 1997). These insights uphold the

Foucauldian position that individuals (including teachers, learners) "are the vehicles of power, not its points of application" (Gordon, 2005, 98). In effect, 'power comes from below' (Foucault, 1990). In learning *power*, then, we encounter our own limits and possibilities. In both we find *hope* (Freire and Freire, 1994/2004). Since there are "no relations of power without resistances", there is always the possibility of conflict and opposition (Foucault interview in Gordon 2005, 142). And the question of how one "transforms oneself into the ethical subject of one's behaviour" (Schaff, 2004, 61) assumes real purpose.

Foucault's powerful work chimes with Freire's transformative learning: "Men [sic.] not only set themselves rules of conduct, but also seek to transform themselves" (Foucault quoted in Schaff, 2004, 61). For Foucault too, critique has a purposeful role, one that is concerned with concrete social and political problems. And like Freire, Foucault challenges us to rethink critique as 'virtue', specifically as a practice that offers the right and power to question, as well as the prospect to act upon limits of being and knowing (Butler, 2002). Thus, critique sets forth the challenge

> how not to be governed *like that*, by that, in the name of those principles, with such and such an objective in mind and by means of such procedures, not like that, not for that, not by them.
>
> (Foucault, 1997, 26)

So from critique comes (some) freedom. Both are constrained by our limited knowledge of 'being' and our limited awareness of the 'invisibility' and penetrability of power. Identity questions present 'newer' challenges: 'Who am I'? 'Who are others'? Postmodernists, in particular, emphasise our ever more fragmented and obscured identities (Baudrillard, 1981, 1994). We are, for example, more likely to find ourselves both 'inside' and 'outside' the system. How then can we identify with a 'collective'? How can *we* protest against the system? For whom, by whom, and in whose name, do we protest? Inevitably, to identify with a cause means to risk (at least) part of our 'selves'. But perhaps this is exactly what commitment entails – 'doing risk' to our 'selves' (Kitching, 2011), 'troubling' our identities with 'others' (Youdell, 2011). Followers of critical pedagogy might appear like processional devotees. Indeed, leading figures (like Freire) might be putting many through their paces. But *committed* followers choose to mobilise them 'selves' with 'others'. And they look to leaders (like Freire) to authentically guide them with the ideas and practices of pedagogical resistance (Giroux, 2001).

Commitment is not easy of course. Teachers who seek change, for example, often have to work with tensions, contradictions and uncertainties. Teachers work both *with* the system (teachers are 'state workers') and *against* it (teachers are 'cultural workers') (Freire, 1998/2005). In having to think 'outside the box', they often work creatively, resiliently and in isolation. It takes courage, self-sacrifice and openness to profess an 'other' (alternative) reality. I recall witnessing, on our second visit to *Normandía*, a young teacher at practice. Amélia teaches, tutors, cooks, cleans, supervises, lives and administers MST affairs on site. She does not work for money or certification; hers is (literally) a vocation. I struggle to understand how she remains so committed. Taking guidance from Heidegger, this may never be resolved. I wonder what else she could do with her life. I have to check myself – it's not for me to say. It's clear that Amélia has committed herself to those with whom she struggles (Freire, 1996). Her political identity is very strong. Perhaps, as Grayson Perry (2014) presents, "the more we cleave towards one type of identity, the less it leaves for anything else." But perhaps too, in this context, Amélia's political identity exemplifies commitment. Her convictions form a 'way of life' (Freire, 2000). They don't appear naïve. She speaks passionately and authentically about the problems of 'liberatory' education (Shor and Freire, 1987), how it's very difficult for some teachers and students to openly dialogue and how democratic classrooms, like democratic societies, are hard to create (Freire, 2000). I see her with the students; there's great care in her work, in their relations. Her hope, she tells me, is for them to "make positive changes to their communities." *Social change* is a journey; it takes small steps and more time (Horton and Freire, 1990). Amélia works *with* the students; she engages (in some depth) *with* their 'lived' realities. This, it seems, is a different kind of commitment, the commitment to 'others'. I contemplate how an even commitment to students has contradictory effects; it may benefit some, even a majority, but *not* every 'body'. And I recall the words echoed by Thomas Jefferson:[99] *There's nothing so unequal than the equal treatment of unequals.*

How can teachers *differentiate*, that is, relate differently with different learner groups? How can they *empower* working class groups, individuals with special educational needs, minority culture circles, *as well as* the mass of mainstream students? For Freire, the starting point is knowing (in some depth) one's 'reality'. We have seen in *Normandía* how the curriculum (e.g. *agroecologia*) reflects the students' 'lived' realities. We have seen how technical and political knowledge is inter-linked. And we have seen how 'other' ideas are (re)named to articulate protest and mobilise change. Powerful words appear on classroom blackboards. Powerful symbols surface in the fields (e.g. rainwater capture systems, herb mandalas[100]). And powerful rituals are routinely rehearsed (*mística*, meals in the refectory/*refeitório*[101]). Imagery is central to MST education; it conveys not just a struggle for land but a struggle "for the right to know" (Branford and Rocha, 2002, 112). For Roseli Salete Caldart (1997, 2000), a key member of the national collective of the Educational Sector of the MST, imagery expresses self-creativity and self-reliance. And imagery is crucial in breaking a 'culture of silence' among the oppressed (Freire, 1970/1996). Through powerful words, symbols and rituals, students develop a new 'critical consciousness' or *conscientização* (Freire, 1974/2010). This empowerment process is best encapsulated by Freire's approach to literacy (1970/1996), especially his use of 'generative themes'. Words like 'land', 'occupation' and 'seed cultivation' reveal concrete representations of the world. Students recognise their meaningful presence. At the same time (following Marx's treatise on 'dialectics'), each theme interacts with its opposite meaning and set of relations – '*latifúndios*', 'invasion' and 'seed companies'. Through inter-dialogue/contestation, students come to acknowledge a number of social and political contradictions. This leads to a deeper understanding of *agroecologia* and the world. And it leads to self-change, not least because 'others' can choose *not* to imitate dominant beliefs and practices.

Conscientização then is a journey of coming to know 'others' and one's 'self'. It begins by 'codifying' (or building up a picture of) real situations, problems and needs. Thereafter, students develop a clearer picture of themselves *in* social 'reality' (a process Freire calls 'decodifying'). Throughout, the teacher (like an experienced photographer) helps bring a distorted picture into focus. This role, however, is far from straightforward. Many questions linger. Does any teacher have the 'right' to interpret social 'reality' *for*, as well as *with*, 'others'? Temptation for the former must surely be strong. Is there not a danger that teachers might replace one dogma with an 'other'? And what of other challenges posed by postmodernism? If discursive relations of power simultaneously produce both free and constrained individuals (e.g. 'you have a right to protest'/'you have no right to protest in that way'; 'you have a right to speak'/'you need to speak this way'), how can oppression ever be seen? How can you name oppression if it appears everywhere and yet nowhere? How can teachers bring it back into focus? These are just some (critical) questions. They appear to reflect Freire's own stance on dialectic enquiry and, more specifically, his use of 'problem-posing'. In 'problem-posing' we come to know through enquiry (by being 'curious'), we come to be critical, and we come to know and enquire again. In essence, we follow a kind of critical hermeneutic circle that opposes dualistic thinking ('right-wrong'; 'this way constantly, not that'). Of course, this circuitous enquiry challenges any absolute standpoint, including certain MST opposition to big-business (*and* vice versa). But it also strengthens the powerful case for critique. Without some concerted effort to become critically aware, it seems, oppression can easily be lost. In mainstream education (note the term 'mainstream'), oppression is readily suppressed. But in 'other' places like *Normandía*, it is (made) visible.

Making oppression visible is an important (critical) step to reclaim the voice of 'others'. And developing *critical literacy* skills enables 'other' knowledge forms to come out from the shadows. Ira Shor (1999), a close associate of Freire, writes about the power of critical literacy: It enables individuals to more fully understand how they are positioned in the world (ibid.); and, in tandem with the power of imagination, it enables individuals to re-position themselves and act upon their world (Shor and Freire, 1987). Framed within critical pedagogy, critical literacy embodies a specific learning approach. A critically literate person, it is reasoned, is better able to understand language, specifically its underlying meanings and knowledge connections. A critically literate person is better able to critique 'common-sense' (e.g. seed production) and reconstruct new forms of social change and collective action (e.g. organic farming). And a critically literate person is better able to develop in conjunction with more enlightened educational structures. Thus, following the work of John Dewey (1916/1966), critical literacy is central to a democratic vision for schooling (Freire, 1970/1996). Indeed, it is *necessary* to help free the system from (further) elitism, exploitation and exclusion. Inasmuch as it questions, defies, re-imagines, critical literacy signals a power challenge to 'authority'. Accordingly, there's a fragility to its stature and visibility. Placing limits on critical literacy furthers learner docility. This serves some interests more than 'others'. Conversely, cultivating critical literacy furthers learner empowerment. This serves 'others' more, though mainstream interests need not be excluded (see later discussions). Critical literacy, then, is a key feature of transformative learning. Ultimately, this learning leads to cognitive (psychological) change, as established habits of mind, assumptions and expectations are all challenged (Mezirow, 2009). It enables social democratic change, as established traditions, identities and practices are likewise confronted (Apple and Beane, 2007). And particularly to those who are silent, marginalised and written out of education, transformative learning offers personal hope (Freire and Freire, 1994/2004).

In *Normandía* transformative learning is neither smooth nor certain. This is even more evident elsewhere. In mainstream schools, teachers and students are caught up in a number of power change struggles. This is due in large part to the nature of schooling which both enables and disables or, in Freirean terms, generates dominant and oppressed values (Freire, 1970/1996). To illustrate, the 'official' curriculum (Apple, 2000) produces 'correct thinking' (Freire, 1970/1996) and 'classed' language codes (Bernstein, 1977). And because it is written outside the 'lived' experiences of 'others', the official curriculum demands that individuals 'fit the system' (not the other way around). Empowerment, then, is often predicated on access to a whole set of codes,[102] which leaves 'others' at a distinct disadvantage. While all 'others' struggle, some succeed in accessing/assimilating these codes (see Chapter 3). Thus, even though the official curriculum misrecognises 'others' (or doesn't recognise them at all), it can still 'empower' some. These individuals are often held up as 'success stories'. Of course we should celebrate their achievements and acknowledge their efforts in overcoming power obstacles. But, critically, we should also enquire where the real *learning power* lies. 'Others' may feel they have no choice but to partake and enact the official curriculum. 'Others' again, not conscious of their own 'reality', may simply be following the (known) powerful route. Both (mimetic) responses are legitimated against dominant value systems. Is this justified? Freire defends the right of 'others' to learn 'official' (dominant) knowledge precisely because this is *the* powerful convention. But he is quick to point out the perils of this power surge, especially to teachers. Mimetic responses are themselves power acts that assume the dominant paradigm, that perceive *it* as the only way of seeing, speaking, thinking and acting upon the world. Real *learning power* lies in its denial of an other's existence, in its denial of an 'other' human's right to learn contextually, uniquely. While unofficial codes need not replace official ones, for Freire they must nevertheless be validated, even prioritised. Teachers still have the choice to affirm 'other' students' words, ideas and 'lived' experiences. And teachers can still choose to cultivate critical literacy, to enable students to recognise themselves, that is, to name those political and social contradictions that locate them as society's 'oppressed'.

How hard it must be for *teachers* to enable students to name their oppression. Shouldn't 'caring' professionals do the opposite? Is naming oppression not a 'disabling' act? What is the point of naming oppression if you can't change it? All questions to test the teacher's power position and remind him/her that with empowerment, comes responsibility. Certainly, a teacher's responsibility is to *all* students, not just to 'others'. Indeed, for political and social transformation to take root, a teacher's critical work necessitates fuller participation. Take, by way of illustration, the MST's metaphor of the 'fence' (*cerca*). It's clear that some groups can't get in because others are keeping them out, while almost everybody else in society is affected. For Freire, this represents a 'teachable moment' – a chance to communicate on this issue with all students, not just the 'landless'. Consciousness-raising for all, Freire argues, serves a greater interest and is a necessary step towards the collective shaping of a more just, humane society. From a critical pedagogy perspective, *all* students are challenged to develop their critical literacy skills alongside deeper (cultural, historical, modern policy) constructions of Brazil's land question. Of course this presupposes awareness/commitment on the part of the teacher to engage students in a subject that appears to matter more to 'others'. It presupposes the teacher's capacity to dialogue. And it presupposes the teacher's capacity to see that 'education *is* politics', that he/she is personally (and politically) implicated in the classroom (Shor, 1987). Thus, teachers are challenged to (critically) know: Who am I favouring when I teach? Am I working in favour of something and against something else? (ibid.). Much of this self-knowledge may never be fully known, as Heidegger reminds, but teachers can still work on *their own* critical literacy. In everyday school settings, much of this work is intuitive, outside of consciousness (Mezirow, 2009). Teachers continually listen to 'other' views and channel conflicting/disorienting feelings, such as fear, anger, resistance or shame (ibid.). This is the messy dialogical process of classroom teaching. This is where teachers learn to care, enable and give hope to their students. This is where they can make a virtue out of critique.

How hard it must be for *students* too to name their oppression. Many may never know their 'reality'; 'others' may (instinctively) know, but not wish to name, their lowly status (see Chapter 1). Certainly, some 'leap of faith' is required to overcome power obstacles and embrace newfound opportunities. At another (rational) level, 'others' habitually measure the possibility of 'success' against likely (or unlikely) outcomes (see Chapter 3). Risk-taking has its limits, therefore, while change remains uncertain and elusive. A particular challenge for teachers, then, is how to positively (read, 'critically') engage the power of the 'hidden curriculum'. This focuses teachers' work away from 'content' (Freire disparagingly refers to this as the 'banking concept' of education) to (re-)centre the person. From this humanistic perspective, the teacher commits to challenging fixed mind-sets, low expectations and run-down levels of school confidence. This is not a straightforward task. Learning is immensely personal, spiritual and emotive (see Chapter 2; Goleman, 1995) and there's a real possibility that learners reject (or act in defiance of) the organised learning experience. Enabling students to find their own voice is especially challenging. And even if students do find their voice, they may lose it again once they 'become' educated.

I am moved to revisit Willy Russell's powerful play *Educating Rita* – a story popularised by the 1983 film of the same name, directed by Lewis Gilbert and starring Michael Caine (as Frank, a lecturer of comparative literature) and Julie Walters (as Rita, a 26-year-old working-class hairdresser from Liverpool). Rita has just enrolled in the Open University and, as a non-traditional adult learner, enters university for the first time. Frank, disillusioned by the affected world of academia, has been assigned as Rita's tutor. As the play evolves, both characters experience significant changes in their learning relationship:

> *Rita:* But when I first came to you, Frank, you didn't give me any views. You let me find my own.
>
> *Frank (gently):* And your views I still value. But, Rita, these aren't your views.
>
> *Rita:* But you told me not to have a view. You told me to be objective, to consult recognised authorities. Well that's what I've done; I've talked to other people, read other books an' after consultin' a wide variety of opinion I came up with those conclusions. (Russell, 2000, 89: Act 2, Scene 3)

Rita rejoices somewhat in her newfound learner status. She has battled hard to access the grade. Like many 'other' (female) adult learners, she has had to commit a form of 'cultural suicide' (Brookfield, 2006), rejecting her former life and those close to her. For Frank, there is serious trepidation over his role in Rita's transformation. She had once ('subjectively') voiced her opinions, honestly and intuitively. Now she appears to be more knowledgeable ('officially') and can speak in authoritative ('objective') ways. But, for Frank, Rita's new learner identity signals a 'cultural loss'.[103] His own academic identity likewise resembles self-compromise. Rita reacts strongly to Frank's feelings. She is resolved to develop her 'own' views on literary texts. She is no longer dependent upon him. He must feel threatened, she intimates; how comfortable he would be if only she stayed 'where she was'. During the learning journey, neither is ever fully aware of each other's state of mind. But when Rita's course finally comes to an end, she expresses her gratitude to Frank (it's clear that he too is indebted to her). That final scene elevates the curious, contradictory and powerful qualities of learning:

> *Rita:* [. . .] I had a choice. I did the exam.
>
> *Frank:* I know. A good pass as well.
>
> *Rita:* Yeh. An' it might be worthless in the end. But I had a choice. I chose, me. Because of what you'd given me I had a choice. I wanted to come back an' tell y' that. That y' a good teacher. (Russell, 2000, 104: Act 2, Scene 7)

There are (learning) lessons throughout the learning process. While many (including Freire) extol the virtues of transformative learning,[104] it is well to remind of potential conflicts. Change is ultimately 'for better or worse', or both. And change involves power struggles (both within and without).

In an increasingly 'credential society' (Collins, 1979), where do 'others' fit in? This is a question of (power) access. Do systems emancipate or do they merely institutionalise? This is a question of (power) accessibility. Finally, how can one exercise learning power if one hasn't been learner-empowered? This is ultimately a question of (power) effect. Critical literacy, it seems, depends on one's 'education' which, in turn, depends on the form this takes. If the education system does nothing more than require 'others' to adapt, then the system itself needs to be critiqued. Herein lies the real power of 'other' forms of education. In *Normandía*, education is centrally positioned to critique the system and one's place therein. It draws heavily upon Marxism since, as Greisson puts it, "the logical focal point is on the political economy." Marxism too guides the Centre's pedagogical principles. Anton Makarenko (1888–1939), a lesser well-known Soviet educator,[105] is particularly influential. His 1936 book *Road to Life*, written about his work in the Poltava Colony for young offenders (Ukraine), presents a number of pedagogical ideas that are loosely adopted in *Normandía*. They include: A person's past/present difficulties should not adversely affect his/her relationships, teachers must share the life of the students as far as possible; students respond best to peer pressure; students can largely set their own rules and govern themselves; and productive labour and self-respect are centred on the *collective* good. The 'collective', a central tenet of Marxist thinking, is a particularly interesting concept. Following Makarenko (1936), it supersedes individual freedom since, as Greisson puts it, "liberty is something that cannot compromise the organisation of the collective." Thus, with freedom comes (social) responsibility. This does not mean that the collective is against individual freedom. Rather, freedom is generated *from* collective power. Thus, in reference to another (more celebrated) Soviet educator, Lev Semyonovich Vygotsky (1896–1934), self-reliance and independence can only come about *through* others (Vygotsky, 1978).

Many may well be sceptical about this 'collective' idea, pointing pejoratively to its Marxist (historical) connotations.[106] They, like sociologists and former MST advisors Zander Navarro and José de Souza Martins, may even argue that a Marxist group like the MST is anti-democratic, anti-state; that its education programme is tantamount to indoctrination. These critics may also point disapprovingly to the MST's adoption of militaristic symbolism (*militantes*, *mística*, *coletivos*, marches, occupations), radical thinkers (e.g. Karl Marx, Friedrich Engels, Antonio Gramsci, Florestan Fernandes, Paulo Freire) and revolutionary figures (e.g. Che Guevara, Zumbi, Antônio Conselheiro). Of course it is right that critical social movements be (justly) critiqued. And it is right that they (authentically) 'turn theory' on themselves (O'Sullivan, 2008). Problem-posing demands this reciprocal critique. What is the real purpose of the MST – merely to protest or to govern? Does group advocacy compromise the *science* of agrarian reform? (Kuhn, 1962/1996) How can the MST protect itself from 'commanding' the 'virtue' of critique? (Nietzsche, 1886; 1887)?[107] 'Others' may 'positively'[108] critique the MST. They, like international development scholar Miguel Carter (2011, 2014), may argue that the MST's 'tough touch' is fundamentally democratic, that this is *necessary* (note Arendt, 1963/2006) to advance social equality in Brazil (ibid.). They may also point to the MST's visibility, politicisation and non-violent stance as being compatible with civil society (ibid.). And while the MST stands for 'anti-capitalism' (seeing its present form as *the* problem), they may argue that it is *not* 'anti-capital' (seeing cooperatives and social corporatism as viable alternatives). There are practical (as well as ideological) reasons too for supporting the 'collective' idea. Together, 'others' may: Avoid being over-powered; name and question disadvantage; and forcefully organise for change. Marxism is one framework (feminism, multiculturalism, queer theories are others) that unifies a particular discourse and pedagogy for resistance (Shor, 1999). The Landless (*Sem Terra*) may naturally join in this protest. Others may not share the same political platform, or profess hope for a democratic socialist alternative to capitalism. But they can still evoke the virtues of Marxism, without being Marxist. And they can draw upon its equity values to powerfully advance democratic forms of education.

The work of the landless movement, then, may signify an important democratic space that is dedicated to advancing social inclusion. Dominant common-sense values that exclude 'others' and label them 'non-traditional' can be opposed. And an 'other' way can be proposed to re-present marginalised 'realities'. In an increasingly multi-ethnic, diverse, globalised society, many new (inclusive) challenges present. But the primary challenge is in many ways an old one: How can governments support (and not oppose) the 'general will' (*volonté générale*)? If the social contract (Rousseau, 1762/1997) is to be meaningful, how can self-interest give way to the 'collective' good? How, as democratic citizens, can we surrender our 'selves' to a popular, sustainable unity that secures civic freedom for all? The education choices we make are analogous. In the 'interest' of democratic education, we can choose to treat public schools as a *public good*. We can uphold the right and duty of a learner-citizen to become critically informed, to serve the 'interests' of 'others' and one's 'self'. And we can value a teacher's work in accordance with inclusive principles and values, acknowledging that there isn't any one 'democratic classroom' or 'democratic school' template to follow (Apple and Beane, 2007, 25):

> Democracy is not something out there waiting to be reached. Rather it is in the work itself as we create ways to promote human dignity, equity, justice and critical action.
>
> (Ibid.)

Critical action, then, is as diverse as the learner population it serves. It reflects *Realpolitik* concerns as much as ideological convictions, since 'others' (in particular) can experience positive changes in their lives. Action centres on developing critical literacy to access real learning power. And, framed within critical pedagogy, learning holds out the promise of personal and social *re-form*.

> My philosophical conviction is that we did not come to keep the world as it is. We came to the world in order to remake the world. We have to *change* reality.
> (Paulo Freire's last public interview, 1996 World Conference on Literacy, Philadelphia[109])

Figure 4.4 Paulo Freire: An educational model

Shortly after I leave, this proud country is rocked by the manner of its 2014 World Cup exit. When the dust settles, the mood shifts to anger and frustration as profligate social investment takes its toll. The World Cup project seems so much at odds with President Dilma's invocation: *País rico é país sem pobreza* ('A rich country is a country without poverty'). But it signals something depressingly familiar about all political cycles in Brazil. Following her re-election to power (2015-), Dilma controversially appointed Kátia Abreu to the agriculture portfolio (Abreu is a former right-wing party member, a key agribusiness lobbyist, and an outspoken critic of land reform and environmental regulation). Unsurprisingly, the MST, Greenpeace, *índios* and *quilombo* communities criticised the appointment. The Homeless Workers Movement (*Movimento dos Trabalhadores Sem Teto*, MTST) also censured the appointment of Gilberto Kassab to the cities ministry (Kasseb is a former right-wing party colleague of Abreu's and, as former mayor of São Paulo, is accused by the MTST of representing the 'interests' of the construction industry). And there was general disquiet among critical social movements regarding the Worker Party's

(PT) decision to yield its control of the education ministry. To add to unease, the new administration was shaken by a huge corruption scandal involving Petrobas, the largest multinational energy corporation in the Southern Hemisphere. A 2014 federal investigation resulted in charges against 39 people, including top executives from Brazilian (engineering and construction) companies. Unsavoury accounts of fraud, bribery, money laundering and tax avoidance schemes emerged, while a number of politicians (including those in the present coalition) were implicated. Their potential prosecution is seen as yet another test case for Brazilian justice.

But justice transcends the land of Brazil (*Terra do Brasil*). It is ubiquitous. And its critical action is as diverse as the global population it serves. A brief review reveals the need for constant vigilance and resistance. In Russia, a 2013 law, intended to 'protect minors', bans the 'propaganda of non-traditional sexual relations'.[110] In Uganda, a new law enforces harsh jail sentences for 'aggravated homosexuality' – it is one of 37 African countries to legislate against same-sex relations. In Pakistan, at least 132 students and 9 teachers are killed in an attack by Taliban militants on a high school. In France, 12 people are shot in a Paris newspaper office in 'revenge' for its published caricatures of the Prophet Muhammad; 4 hostages are later killed in a related attack on a kosher supermarket in the city. In Nigeria, 23 people are killed by 3 female suicide bombers (one is only 10 years old); attacks in the North East leave as many as 2,000 people dead. The surge of religious fundamentalism (e.g. Islamic State, al-Qaeda, Boko Haram) is an affront to democracy, to racial, cultural and spiritual unity. And the reaction and rise of right-wing political ideology also discords with long-standing democratic principles (e.g. National Front in France, FN; the Freedom Party in Austria, FPÖ; the Finns Party; the Party for Freedom in the Netherlands, PVV). The moral position of the United States remains weakened by Guantánamo torture cells and Edward Snowden's revelations about National Security Agency policies. Within its borders, mass demonstrations protest against the deaths of unarmed black men at the hands of the police. In Turkey the President, Recep Tayyip Erdoğan, announces that "you cannot put women and men on an equal footing." Pakistani activist and Nobel peace laureate Malala Yousafzai protests, calling for urgent gender equality reform and the right of all young girls to go to school. The European Court of Human Rights (ECHR) finds in favour of Louise O'Keefe whose case against the Irish State is upheld many years after she suffered sexual abuse at the hands of her primary school principal. Other protests emerge over the inhumane treatment of adults with intellectual disability in care homes, the homeless crisis and direct pro-vision conditions for asylum seekers. Throughout the world, citizens sustain their protest against displaced migration, prejudice, class poverty, neoliberal privilege, exploitative working conditions, abuse, corruption, and increased restrictions to land, food, water, shelter, security, health and education. Protest is always *necessary*, while injustice persists.

The smallest protest acts make a difference;[111] while education (*praxis*) lies at the heart of change. I finally reflect on Freire's model in *Normandía* (Figure 4.4).

Education's (purposeful) role is to change reality. We don't 'possess' knowledge; we experience it, enact it with others. Through self-experience in the world, we develop both as people and as critically literate beings. And we become empowered since, in the words of Francis Bacon (1597), *ipsa scientia potestas est* ('knowledge itself is power'). Even if we resolve *not* to use our knowledge, we still act powerfully, usually in concert with how things stand.[112] But if we do engage with knowledge, we can keep protest memory alive and change our world for the better. This is what makes education, essentially, a political act. At the same time, we need to recognise that education itself is *politicised*. Neoliberal 'interests', in particular, capture contradictory, more dominant knowledge meanings. These are encapsulated in various terms/concepts: 'Human capital', 'research commercial-isation', 'educational privatisation', 'skill exchange', 'student-consumers', 'teacher-producers', 'benchmark standards', 'accountability', 'performativity', etc. (see Chapter 3). Converted words, symbols and rituals cultivate a leading learning consciousness. Knowledge is ever more diverted from a (public) sharing of ideas/values towards a (private) focus on individual 'possession' (e.g. 'human capital', 'accreditation') and collective 'ownership'[113] (e.g. 'knowledge Ireland', 'knowledge economy'). Knowledge is still about change; but this has more to do with 'entrepreneurial' drive, 'innovation' and 'strategic' purpose (see Chapter 3). And contrary to 'other' curious, creative and critical meanings, knowledge is ever more objectified, measured and transferred.

Once you see knowledge in 'other' ways, it's hard *not* to imagine (and identify with) an alternative 'reality'. Of course there are dangers in seeing oppression everywhere. But there are greater dangers in seeing it nowhere. Since my return from Brazil, I have begun to experience a different relationship with the 'land'. We all share this earth together. We share a social responsibility with 'others'. And we bear personal responsibility for civic, social and political change. In 2014 the world remains in a fragile state: At least 18 million people die each year from preventable diseases, mainly due to a lack of access to medicine (World Health Organization, 2014); an estimated 2 billion suffer from a lack of essential food nutrients, or 'hidden hunger' (2014, Global Hunger Index); and rising temperatures continue to adversely affect food security, natural habitats, human health and population migration (Intergovernmental Panel on Climate Change, 2014). Global neoliberal relations, poor governance structures, state violence and political/ideological conflicts all intensify unstable conditions. And with the population projected to grow to between 9 and 10 billion people by 2050, we are pressed more than ever towards 'problem-posing': *How best can we use this land together? What kind of a world do we want to live in? How will we leave it a better place for our children?*

At 'home' in Ireland, I reflect on our complex relationship with 'land'. Positive North-South and Anglo-Irish relations have created much-needed stability and hope for the future. But the unfettered neoliberalism of the Celtic Tiger years (1995–2007), the subsequent collapse of the property market, bank bailouts, mass youth unemployment, family emigration and years of managed economic austerity have exposed the brittle social fabric of the country. The resultant low supply of housing (particularly affordable social units), high levels of homelessness and mortgage arrears, increased repossessions, lack of rent control systems, and accumulative investments (by international and vulture fund financiers), deliver salient Irish lessons on spatial justice. Unsurprisingly, the broadsheets report news of a rising property market. There's a headland retreat in West Cork for sale – a piece of the Irish coastline for sale. Elsewhere I note signs of the privatisation and management of coastal commons, while communities continue to resist inland developments (most notably the 'Shell to Sea' campaign in the West of Ireland). I see that the Irish state, in line with its European 'partners' (e.g. United Kingdom, Belgium, Netherlands, Spain), operates a 'knowledge-development box' scheme. This enables companies who 'settle' here to pay less tax on the profits they make from their patents. There is tax relief too for individual citizens, specifically those with 'key talents' to offer.[114] I read about the 3 teenagers from Cork who win the 2014 BT Young Scientists of the Year Competition. Their exceptional work with naturally occurring bacteria (rhizobium strains of the diazotroph grouping) demonstrates how crop germination (barley, oats, wheat) can be significantly accelerated. The discovery "could play a crucial role in solving the global food crisis", the *Time* magazine covers, and the teenagers are already reported to be "planning to commercialize it."[115] In most information broadcasts, a powerful *economic value* permeates; shaping our common-sense knowledge of the world and our place in it. The consumer society, it seems, is everywhere, even impacting on our leisure needs and desires (Debord, 1967). That Christmas of 2014, Monopoly, the world's bestselling board game, is translated into an estimated 40 different languages and is sold in over 100 different countries. Invented during the American Great Depression, the object of the game is to become the wealthiest player. Even in recessionary times, it seems, we are urged to buy, rent and sell 'land'. Those with the most reserves ultimately profit.[116] And they are venturing into new frontiers for greater takings. Has there ever been a more timely 'teachable moment'?

Guiding research (notes)

1 In the Amazon alone "some of the [land] areas to which companies laid claim are the size of small nations" (Sadlier, 2008, 277). The majority of the large estates in Brazil are to be found in the Amazon and northeast regions.

2 See Boris Fausto's (1999) book *A concise history of Brazil*, which charts the country's development from 'establishment' (1500) to the end of Military Dictatorship (1984), and Robert M. Levine's (2003) work *The history of Brazil*, which outlines Brazil's origins as 'an earthly paradise' (inhabited any time from 12,000 and 40,000 years ago) to modern democratic times (up to 1998).

3 Cabral had been en route to India and the Spice Islands. Of course he would have 'discovered' that other peoples had been there before him. Brazil had long been inhabited by Indigenous Indian groups (*índios*), such as the Tupi-Guarani, the Arawaks and the Caribs. The *Instituto Brasileiro de Geografia e Estatística* (Brazilian Institute of Geography and Statistics, IBGE) shows, from its last Census in 2010, that over 800,000 Brazilians claim Indigenous ancestry (see www.ibge.gov.br/english/estatistica/

populacao/censo2010/). The *Fundação Nacional do Índio* (National Indian Foundation, FUNAI), which is the agency responsible for protecting the rights and cultures of Indigenous populations, claims that there are still a number of uncontactable Indian tribes in Brazil (see www.survivalinternational.org/about/funai).

4   In the mid-16th century, slaves were purchased and imported from the slave market of Western Africa (they included many Sub-Saharan Africans, as well as Africans from the colonies of Mozambique and Angola). In 1853 (over 300 years later), slave importation ended in Brazil. And in 1888, all slaves were officially 'freed'.

5   Since Pedro II's overthrow by the military in 1889, subsequent presidents within the so-called new 'Republican' era (e.g. Getúlio Vargas 1930–1945 and 1950–1954) were propped up by the military regime.

6   Article 184 states: "It is within the power of the Union to expropriate on account of social interest, for purposes of agrarian reform, the rural property which is not performing its social function, against prior and fair compensation in agrarian debt bonds with a clause providing for maintenance of the real value, redeemable within a period of up to twenty years computed as from the second year of issue, and the use of which shall be defined in the law." Article 186 reads: "The social function is met when the rural property complies simultaneously with, according to the criteria and standards prescribed by law, the following requirements: I – rational and adequate use; II – adequate use of available natural resources and preservation of the environment; III – compliance with the provisions that regulate labour relations; IV – exploitation that favours the well-being of the owners and labourers." [Source: Government of Brazil (2010). *Constitution of the Federal Republic of Brazil 1988.* Brasília. Documentation and Information Centre.].

7   Once land is expropriated, settlement families need help in 'starting up' their communities, such as securing adequate housing, health and education facilities. Note that the term 'peasants' (which appears later in the sentence) is not widely used in other languages/cultures; yet, in the Brazilian context, it presents as a close and accepted translation of *camponês*.

8   See The Inter-American Commission on Human Rights website www.oas.org/en/iachr. See also The US Department of State (2008) *Human Rights Report: Brazil* and *Amnesty International Report on Brazil* (2013) – both are available at www.state.gov/j/drl/rls/hrrpt/2008/wha/119150.htm and www.amnesty.org/en/region/brazil/report-2013 respectively.

9   It's hard to go 'beyond' ideological concerns because many views *are* predicated on particular political philosophies. In Brazil, it's especially hard because views are shaped by the *real* presence of opposing political philosophies (there is a genuine distance between those on the 'left' and those on the 'right'). This difference is played out in political history, for example, governments that promote more popular programmes (e.g. Goulart's brief Presidential reign; Lula's presidencies), that exercise military repression (e.g. the Presidency of General Costa e Silva) and that foster increased levels of privatisation (e.g. President Cardoso's government), etc. Of course in (post)modern times, distinctions (in political philosophy) become somewhat blurred. What government, for example, wouldn't claim to be 'socially progressive'?

10   This has historical resonance. In the 1930s and early 1940s, Getúlio Vargas led a period of intense modernisation via centralised industrialisation. Most notably, in taking office in 1956, President Juscelino Kubitschek famously promised "50 years of progress in 5." True to his word, massive (state-sponsored) infrastructure projects were undertaken (mills, hydroelectric plants, roads, factories) and a great deal of foreign money was invested in Brazil (especially in manufacturing). Kubitschek's most exuberant project was that of Brasília, which became Brazil's new Federal capital city in 1960 (see Maram, 1990). Ultimately, Kubitschek's administration (1956–1961) presided over a period of rapid growth, spiralling public debt and mass corruption.

11 Note how 'modernisation' *is itself* caught up with political philosophy, as exemplified here by neoliberal understandings of 'progress' in housing, health, education and commerce. See related discussions in Chapter 3 on neoliberalism's (paradigmatic) framing of 'innovation', 'reform' and 'success'.

12 I am borrowing this phrase from Darlene J. Sadlier's (2008) book *Brazil Imagined*. It is indeed useful to think of nationhood as a discursive representation or idea. Sadlier's (2008) work has helped me deliberate upon Brazilian culture, 'Brazilianness'. Of course, Brazilian culture, 'Brazilianness' is also shaped by practice, by life experiences. In sections 2 of this chapter and thereafter, discussions focus on how *practice identifies* some Brazilians over 'others' (namely, 'the landless').

13 The largest contingency of Brazilian international peacekeepers is in Haiti. Since 2004, Brazil has held the military command of the United Nations Stabilisation Mission in Haiti.

14 Rio de Janeiro was selected to host the 2016 Olympic Games and the 2016 Paralympic Games.

15 At the time of writing, the World Cup (Brazil 2014) was about to commence. My own research visit to Brazil (11–27 April 2014) coincided with close preparations for the tournament. I visited one of the World Cup stadia (*Arena Pernambuco*) to see the regional final between *Sport Club do Recife* and *Clube Náutico Capibaribe* (*Sport* beat *Náutico* 1–0 in the decisive game). I witnessed first-hand the passion of Brazilian football supporters, haphazard preparations (e.g. no public transport arrangements or ticket map finders) as well as some street protests aimed at highlighting the (social) cost of the World Cup (see further discussions in the text). Neymar played well in the World Cup but both he (injury) and Thiago Silva (suspension) missed Brazil's semi-final match with Germany – they were sorely missed.

16 Some 500 Brazilian professional footballers ply their 'trade' in Europe (2014), while only 1 national team member plays in the domestic league ('Fred' plays for Fluminense FC). Thus, Brazilian footballers exemplify the global 'transfer' system. Many football commentators, post Brazil's shock exit from the World Cup (Germany beat Brazil by a record 7–1 in the semi-final), have now seriously questioned the global export of players and the demise of domestic league talent. This appears as a new globalisation protest in Brazil.

17 The Sunday Times (1 June 2014) ran an explosive investigative story entitled *Plot to buy the World Cup* in which the decision to award Qatar host nation status in 2022 was claimed to be corrupt. This provoked an outcry among many football supporters in Brazil and around the world.

18 The national motto of Brazil is *Ordem e progresso* ('Order and progress'). Closer to reality – and the twin-edged forces of globalisation – Brazil appears at the interface of order *and* disorder, progress *and* regress.

19 *Mocambos* is a term originally derived from the Ambundu people of North West Angola – it roughly translates as 'hide-away'. Other (more contemporary) meanings variously associate the term with 'slums', 'urban decay' and a specific artistic and cultural 'identity' (Tavares Correia, 1999). Quilombola communities are still fighting for land. In Maranhão state (in the northeast), at least 9 communities are facing constant threats, violence and eviction at the hands of gunmen hired by landowners (see Amnesty International report, 2013).

20 Brazil's colonial powers included the French who built a garrison in (what is now) Rio de Janeiro in 1555; they were later expelled in 1565. The Dutch ruled large parts of the northeast (Pernambuco) from 1624 to 1654. And the Portuguese ruled the whole country thereafter, first as a colony (even when moving court to Rio during the Napoleonic war in 1807) and subsequently as an empire (1822–1889).

21 See Palmares (2014). *Encyclopaedia Brittanica*. Retrieved on 17 June 2014 from www.britannica.com/EBchecked/topic/440136/Palmares

22   A bronze bust is erected in Brasília with the inscribed words: *Zumbi Dos Palmares, O lider Negro de todas as raças* ('Zumbi of Palmares, Black leader of all races').

23   *Tiradentes* means 'Tooth-puller' in Portuguese, so-named because Joaquim José da Silva Xavier worked latterly as a dentist before leading a failed rebellion against the Portuguese, called the *Inconfidência Mineira*. See Joaquim José da Silva Xavier (2014), *Encyclopaedia Britannica*. Retrieved on 17 June 2014 from www.britannica.com/ EBchecked/topic/544736/Joaquim-Jose-da-Silva-Xavier

24   The report was mysteriously destroyed by fire only to resurface again some 45 years later. It details a number of horrific incidences that include poisoning of hundreds of *índios* with arsenic-laced sugar, numerous mutilations of children and mothers, and 'the massacre of the 11th parallel' where dynamite was thrown from a plane killing thirty *índios* in the village of 'Cinta Larga' (two survived to tell the tale). Genocidal-level repression of indigenous groups is not unique to Brazil; for example, following the communist-led uprising in El Salvador in 1932, the nation's indigenous Pipil population was virtually annihilated.

25   Survival International's director Stephen Corry is on record as saying: "The Figueiredo Report makes gruesome reading but, in one way, nothing has changed: when it comes to the murder of Indians, impunity reigns. Gunmen routinely kill tribespeople in the knowledge that there's little risk of being brought to justice – none of the assassins responsible for shooting Guarani and Makuxi tribal leaders have been jailed for their crimes. It's hard not to suspect that racism and greed are at the root of Brazil's failure to defend its indigenous citizens' lives." See www.survivalinternational.org/news/9191

26   Brazil is only one of 2 South American countries that does not recognise tribal land ownership (see www.survivalinternational.org/tribes/brazilian).

27   In 2012 scientists at Imperial College, London claimed that the Amazon's extinction rate has yet to be fully felt; for example, spider monkeys that feed on high canopy fruit are becoming seriously endangered due to the expansion of roads and razed farmlands, and the giant otter faces more challenges from increased levels of agricultural and mining pollution of the rivers (Wearn *et al.*, 2012).

28   The Amazon maintains the world's largest river basin (holding over two-thirds of all the earth's freshwater); over 20% of the earth's oxygen is produced there. It is home to the world's largest rainforest, which comprises the most bio-diverse environs on the planet. Below its surface, there is enough iron ore to supply the world for the next 500 years while, above ground, there are untold potentials to advance research in science and medicine. See www.wcupa.edu/aceer/amigos/cd/rainforest.htm

29   Resistance requires the backing of political 'interests' and big business. For example, in 2009 Bertin (Brazil's top leather exporter and second-largest beef exporter) signed a pact with Greenpeace to refuse purchase of cattle reared in parts of the Amazon that have recently been deforested.

30   The *empowerment* role played by Jesuits is of course a moot issue. On the one hand, they helped *índios* resist enslavement; on the other, they supplanted *índios* culture with religion and hard labour and (inadvertently) spread human disease.

31   Hundreds of thousands still flock each year to the giant Statue of Padre Cícero in the city of Juazeiro do Norte in the state of Ceará (his birthplace). It is thought that the miraculous priest, inter alia, could convert the dry backlands (the *Sertão*) into lush green pastures for the benefit of poor farmers.

32   Under military dictatorship, tens of thousands of (mostly young) 'revolutionaries' lost their lives. Protest was brutally quelled by military might and many more 'freedom martyrs' were memorialised.

33   Spiritism, a phrase first coined by the French writer Allan Kardec in his 1857 work *Le Livre des Esprits* (The Spirits' Book), is a doctrine that believes in the existence of Spirits and our capacity to communicate (mediate) with them. Many Brazilians practise religious *syncretism*, that is, they follow two or more religious beliefs/customs. Hence, it is possible (and not 'contradictory') to be a Catholic and a Spiritist or an Evangelist

and a Candomblé follower (an Afro-Brazilian religion) or have any other faith combination(s) in Brazil.

34   This (noticeably Brazilian) mysticism resounds in the popular writing of Paulo Coelho. The reader is presented with mystical prose (e.g. biblical-style parables) that offers lessons/relief on how to overcome real-life problems and hardship.

35   See BBC 4's excellent series on Brazilian music, entitled *Brasil, Brasil* (2007), written and produced by Robin Denselow. Many of the ideas presented in the main text reflect the musical insights of this three-part documentary (for full descriptions of the episodes, see www.bbc.co.uk/musictv/brasilbrasil/episodes/1/).

36   Caetano Veloso and Gilberto Gil invented *tropicalismo*, a fusion of Native Brazilian sounds and Western rock.

37   Just imagine one city – Rio de Janeiro. One-third of its population live in the *favelas* and the vast majority are black.

38   Some *musical* projects attempt to combat the social problem of the *favela*. Notably, the Afro Reggae movement has had limited success in encouraging kids to take up music and turn away from drug gangs and crime. However, the rise of *Funk ostentação* (a musical genre that glorifies flashy lifestyles) appears to (ironically) divert this protest message.

39   One of Salgado's most iconic images is that of *Serra Pelada* ('Bald Mountain'), a cavernous pit in the northeast state of Pará. Its sharp focus on exploitative labour appears in a still shot of tens of thousands of ant-like gold miners (*garimpeiros*) scrambling up and down its slopes (*Workers*, 1993).

40   I was first exposed to Sebastião Salgado's work when his exhibition *Exodus* came to Cork as part of the European Capital of Culture programme in 2005. The images, taken from his *Migrations* and *Children* series, demonstrated to me the power of the arts to connect with humanity and challenge consciousness.

41   Salgado posthumously photographed the massacre in Pará (mentioned earlier in the main text) of 19 landless movement members, executed by off-duty military police. He also produced images of landless people's work practices, migration journeys and occupations (including the largest ever occupation in 1996 on the Fazenda Giacometti farm in Paraná, which held some 200,000 acres of good fertile land). Notably, musicians Chico Buarque and Milton Nascimento collaborated with Salgado for his *Terra* collection (1997).

42   In 1998, Lélia Wanick Salgado (in partnership with her husband) established the *Instituto Terra* in the state of Minas Gerais. Returning the land from a 17,000 deforested acreage to a natural subtropical rainforest, the Salgados committed themselves to environmental change. As well as overseeing the planting of millions of trees and cultivating the return of numerous wildlife species, the *Instituto Terra* project enables environmental research to be conducted (e.g. in ecosystem restoration and seedling production). Moreover, it provides resource supports to small neighbourhood farms (e.g. in milk production and nursery planting). In this practical sense, the *Instituto Terra* appears to educate for a better, more sustainable, environment (see www.institutoterra. org/eng/#).

43   During the 1920s and 1930s Lampião and his *cangaceiros* (his 'bandits', which later included his wife Maria Bonita) ruled over the *Sertão* ('backlands') region, raiding many towns and land estates across the northeast of Brazil. Despite his bloody deeds, people looked favourably on Lampião's 'religious' character (he revered Padre Cícero) and 'generous' disposition (he gave much to those who had little). Consequently, he was immortalised as a 'folk hero' (Jaynes Chandler, 2000). The three Nordestino (north-easterner) artists mentioned – João Câmara, Gilvan Samico and José Borges – come from a long tradition of *folk poets/artists* that preserve *protest* memory.

44   Of course in 'semi-fictional' cinema work, such as *Cidade de Deus* (2002) and *Tropa de Elite* (2007, 2010), there is a real danger that violence becomes glamourised (a type of *favela* 'pornography', if you will). Dystopic images are not uncommon in

Brazil (Sadlier, 2008) and can divert from deeper causal explanations of poverty, exclusion and violence.

45 The self-styled *Mídia Ninja*, for example, is a group of independent reporters who present themselves 'in the protestor's shoes' and in opposition to mainstream media (see their recent reportage in social media on world cup protests). Critics may argue that this form of activist journalism is (paradoxically) 'partisan'. Proponents may counter with the assertion that marginalised voices are given greater exposure. Certainly, *Mídia Ninja* is provocatively challenging older modes of media reporting in Brazil. Presently, *Globo* is the largest media group in Brazil (it is the second largest commercial TV network in the world). The federal government also operates a news agency that includes radio and television stations (though audience figures are quite low). And there's a one-hour state radio programme that is (mandatorily) broadcast every weeknight.

46 Gilberto Freyre's 1933 book, *Casa-grande E Senzala* ('The Big House and the Slave Quarters' or, as it is known by its English publication title, 'The Masters and the Slaves'), argues that all Brazilians need to identify with their inter-racial roots; that what sets them apart (from 'The Deep South' in America, for example) is their (positive) socio-cultural and political relations to race. Freyre's life contribution (1900–1987) to a 're-Africanisation' of Brazil is noteworthy, though his supposition (rightly or wrongly attributed to him) that Brazil is a 'racial democracy' is highly controversial. Josué de Castro connects the disciplines of ecology and politics and demonstrates (de Castro, 1946/1952) that hunger is not a natural result of overpopulation; rather it is a man-made phenomenon that *causes* overpopulation and social inequalities. Paulo Freire (1921–1997) is Brazil's foremost educationalist – Sections 3 and 4 of this chapter deal extensively with his pedagogical ideas. For an overview of his work (as a good first text), see Freire and Macedo (eds., 2001).

47 Skin colour is often confused with race in Brazil and self-descriptions can deny 'blackness'. This is despite an increased awareness (and celebration) of African-Brazilian heritage. Census 2010 shows that people of mixed race (self-described as *mestiço, pardo* or other terms) and black people (self-described as *preto* or *negro* or other terms) now make up the majority of Brazil's population (just over 50 per cent). The Census also shows that social inequality is directly linked to race. Shockingly, three quarters of Brazil's poorest 10 per cent are black; black people are 50 per cent more likely to be unemployed than their white compatriots and black men earn 60 per cent less than white people (black women fall further behind); black people live an average of 6 years less and 4 out of 5 Brazilian youths murdered each year are black (Hennigan, 2014).

48 My research visit to Brazil took place from Friday 11th April to Sunday 27th April 2014.

49 Professor Gomes is an authority on Brazilian Higher Education and a highly respected scholar of critical forms of pedagogy. His writing on, and access to, the landless movement was invaluable to my own research study. I am forever grateful to Alfredo for sharing his cultural and pedagogical insights and for personally overseeing my translation and photographic needs on research site.

50 As of July 2014, 3 R$ is equivalent to 1 euro. Such payment is usually given each time one encounters 'unofficial' parking attendants.

51 When slaves were 'freed' in Brazil, they desperately had to make money to survive. The term *pregão* (meaning 'cry') is thought to derive from post-slavery times when black people 'proclaimed' their goods for sale.

52 During broad daylight in the centre of Recife, I witnessed a number of homeless people taking and offering crack-cocaine. Brazil has the highest number of crack cocaine addicts in the world (estimated at 1 million – Note 59). Prostitutes (legal in Brazil if over 18) also work the streets by day and night. Shockingly, child drug use and child prostitution is a real social problem in Recife and beyond. *The National Forum for the Prevention of Child Labor* (2012) estimates that Brazil has half a million child sex workers (second in the world only to Thailand) [Brasileiro, 2013].

53 This can be witnessed in the *forró* dance halls of the northeast or during the annual Easter carnival in Recife, Olinda and surrounding areas.

54 Black Awareness Day is celebrated each year on the 20th November (marking Zumbi's birthday). There have been a number of recent black appointments to powerful state positions, including Joaquim Barbosa (the first black president of the Supreme Court). Also, Pelé and Gilberto Gil have served as Ministers for Sport and Culture respectively. Such equality developments, while welcome, have not significantly disturbed racial gaps in income, health, education, housing, occupational status, etc. See Notes 47 and 56.

55 The term *favela* ('slum dwelling') is more widely used in the cities of Rio de Janeiro and São Paulo. In Recife, the Spanish derivation *bairro* is used (meaning 'municipality' or city 'division'/'suburb'). Some *bairros* (like *Casa Amarela*) are more significantly disadvantaged than others. Of course I cannot really know what it's like to 'feel' segregation in these communities (see later discussions in the main text on Martin Heidegger). Moreover, many therein may not identify with my own feelings, nor might they identify with a 'need' to recognise their (racial) poverty (as I present in the next sentence of the text).

56 In the 2010 Census, white inhabitants were shown to earn approximately two-and-a-half times more than their black counterparts. More black Brazilians, especially young men, die as a result of accidents or violence compared to their white counterparts whose deaths are predominantly concentrated in old age and are as a consequence of cancer (ibid.). As mentioned previously (Note 47), almost three quarters of Brazil's poorest 10 per cent are black (ibid.). Black people also make up the majority of *favela* populations and are seriously under-represented in the professional occupations.

57 During my time in Recife, I stayed in a gated middle-class apartment complex in the *bairro Madalena*. Next to this building, there was a strip of land occupied by a *favela*-type community. All over the city, this juxtaposition can be found. Even by *Boa Viagem* beach (where property commands the highest prices), or by the *Caxangá Golf & Country Club*, *favela*-type accommodation exists alongside more affluent residences.

58 In 2008, the Brazilian government began a campaign (called 'pacification') to reclaim the *favelas* from violent drug gangs. Their efforts to restore social stability has not been without problems (including violence), though there has been limited success. In Rio de Janeiro alone, there are an estimated 1,000 *favelas* – less than 50 have been 'pacified' (2014). Before 'pacification' many residents would not have officially paid electricity or property tax. Many of these *favela* residents remain suspicious of authorities; after all, there have been numerous incidences where police have been indicted for collusion with criminal gangs and where the judiciary has failed to administer justice.

59 This is a 2014 estimate (see www.bbc.com/news/world-latin-america-24903446). In 2012 FIOTEC (*Fundação para o Desenvolvimento Científico e Tecnológico em Saúde*) found that there were approximately 370,000 urban users (in the 26 capitals of Brazil and in the Federal District) of crack and similar drug substances (paste, merla and oxy) [see www.fiotec.fiocruz.br/institucional/index.php?option=com_content&view=article&id=2028:the-worlds-largest-research-on-crack-is-supported-by-fiotec-number-of-users-is-over-300000&catid=133:noticias-en&Itemid=364&lang=en].

60 In February 2014, a black teenager accused of being a mugger was beaten, stripped naked and tied to a lamppost by his throat by a group of vigilantes in the (middle-class) Flamengo area of Rio de Janeiro. In a scene reminiscent of slavery times where black people were punished against a pillory (*Pelourinho*), it reminds of the cyclical nature of (racial) violence [see www.mirror.co.uk/news/uk-news/vigilantes-tie-mugger-lamppost-bike-3110391]. It must be further acknowledged that, while violence is mostly concentrated in working-class communities (such as *favelas*), those who benefit from criminal activity are often (white, faceless) people living 'outside'.

61 *Telenovela* literally means 'television novel' (otherwise known as 'soap opera'). *Telenovelas* are extremely popular in Brazil and Latin America and they are a powerful

medium for addressing and shaping social issues/problems. In this regard, they can empower or disempower, be educative or ill-informed.

62 Former Minister of Education, Cristovam Buarque (born in Recife), has used the phrase 'social apartheid' to argue that in Brazil there is a clear division between those that are included and excluded, between those who are rich and poor.

63 In the year of her Presidential inauguration (2011), Dilma compelled a number of ministers to resign on foot of corruption allegations brought to light by press investigations and formal police submissions.

64 There's an old joke in Brazil that plays on Stefan Zweig's (1941) celebrated book title *Brazil – Land of the future*: 'Brazil is the country of the future – *and always will be*'. Zweig borrowed the phrase 'Land of the future' from the French *une Terre d'avenir* (which was used by the Austrian diplomat Graf Prokesch Osten in correspondence to Gobineau in 1868).

65 Earlier in her book *On revolution*, Arendt (2006, 49) fully quotes Saint-Just (1767–1794), political and military leader in the French First Republic: *Les malheureux sont la puissance de la terre* ('The unhappy ones are the power of the land').

66 I wish to acknowledge Ralph Edward Dimmick's introduction to *Barren Lives* (Ramos, 1999) for these insights into Graciliano Ramos, the writer.

67 Ramos describes Vitória in thought: ". . . they were getting along, by the grace of God. The boss trusted them. They could almost consider themselves fortunate. All they lacked was a bed. That was what tormented Vitória. Since she was no longer worn out with hard work, she spent part of the night thinking. That business of turning in as soon as it was dark wasn't right though. People aren't the same as chickens" (Ramos, 1999, 42).

68 Ramos describes Fabiano in thought: " 'Fabiano, you're a real rancher', he exclaimed aloud. Then he restrained himself, noting that the boys were nearby. They would surely be surprised to hear him talking to himself. Besides, thinking better of the matter, he wasn't a rancher after all; he was just another half-breed hired to look after other people's property. He was red-skinned and sunburned, had blue eyes and a ruddy beard and hair, but as he lived on other people's land and looked after other people's cattle, he considered himself a half-breed, taking off his hat and feeling ill at ease in the presence of white gentry. He glanced around, fearful that someone besides the boys might have heard his imprudent remark. He amended it, murmuring: 'Fabiano, you're a crack ranch hand' " (Ramos, 1999, 14, 15).

69 As Samuel Beckett might comfort: 'Nothing is more real than nothing' (Beckett, 1951/1956, 16).

70 See Sue Branford and Jan Rocha's (2002) text, *Cutting the wire: The story of the landless movement in Brazil*. In researching the MST, this was a very valuable text for me to draw upon. I wish to acknowledge these authors' deep ethnographic knowledge of the movement and their close attention to individual members' life experiences.

71 The President, General Figueiredo, sent the army to destroy the settlement under the command of the (infamous) Major Sebastião Curió. The occupiers of *Encruzilhada Natalino*, so-named because the camp lay at the junction (*encruzilhada* means 'crossroads') of three counties (Sarandi, Ronda Alta and Passo Fundo), suffered enormous levels of hardship, intimidation and abuse. After almost three years, those families that desperately held out finally won legal rights to the land.

72 As Branford and Rocha (2002, 253) note, however, there are a few *permanent* members on the *direção nacional* (João Pedro Stédile being one). The MST justifies this situation on the grounds that some degree of continuity and experience is necessary in the organisation. But as Branford and Rocha (ibid., 254) challenge: "The real test of the MST's internal democracy will come when there is a serious leadership contest. Will the old guard eventually hand over power to a new generation of democratically elected leaders? Or will João Pedro Stédile, like Fidel Castro, see himself as irreplaceable and decide that he cannot step down?"

73 Named after the radical Brazilian sociologist Florestan Fernandes (1920–1995), the school took over 5 years to build with the aid of over 1,000 landless workers and supporters. In its first 5 years of existence, some 16,000 *militantes* from Brazil, Latin America and Africa studied a range of college-level courses in the areas of political philosophy, international relations, rural sociology, social history of Brazil and the political economy of agriculture (see http://amigosenff.org.br/site/node/23).

74 I am reminded of former French Prime Minister, Aristide Briand's, reputed words: "The man who is not a socialist at 20 has no heart, but if he is still a socialist at 40 he has no head." This is not to deny 'socialism' ideals; or even suggest its name removal, as Manuel Valls (French Prime Minister from 2014) did in 2009 in relation to his own political party. Instead, one might (practically) question: What does socialism mean now? And can socialism legitimately reject some (and not other) aspects of capitalist 'freedom'? Of course, it is also important to (conversely) question: Does *capitalism* have a future? (Wallerstein *et al.*, 2013).

75 Take the seductive images of revolutionary art, for example. As a young boy, I was always fascinated by Seán Keating's (1889–1977) *Men of the South, 1921–1922* painting in the Crawford Art Gallery, Cork. It shows a group of strong steely-faced IRA (Irish Republican Army) revolutionaries at the time of the war of independence in Ireland. William Orpen (1878–1931), who was Seán Keating's mentor for a brief period in 1915, paints another image in the Crawford Art Gallery (*The Revolutionary*, c.1902). This work unsettles the reader via its apparent questioning of the sacrifices of revolution and the costs of nationalism. Figuring a bare chested revolutionary in Christ-like pose, it nevertheless (ironically) presents as a romantic ('suffering') image.

76 The interview with Jaime Amorim took place on Wednesday 23rd April 2014 in his Caruaru office. Professor Alfredo Gomes kindly acted as interpreter and the interview lasted one hour.

77 Cândido Portinari (1903–1962) painted numerous images of uneducated Brazilian workers – using a style known as 'social realism' – with subjects' hands and feet exaggerated in size to emphasise their 'labouring role'. His fresco *Guerra e Paz* ('War and Peace') adorns the United Nations building in New York.

78 The MST does not account for all land occupations and settlements in Brazil – estimates vary: Up to one fifth of total expropriated farmland may be due to direct MST actions, or maybe as much as 45 per cent of Brazil's agrarian settlements are in some way connected to the MST (Carter, 2011). The Brazilian State can directly expropriate land (usually if it is 'undisputed'; if private landowners are open to a straight sale; if land is more freely available, especially in frontier regions; or if the federal government or state governments already own it). Also, other grassroots organisations, such as trade unions, MST dissidents, The Homeless Workers Movement (*Movimento dos Trabalhadores Sem Teto*, MTST), carry out land occupations and oversee settlements. Within the 'grassroots' category, however, the MST is by far the biggest, most organised and most successful organisation for occupying and securing land. In the last 2 decades, it has motivated the Brazilian government to expropriate approximately 50,000 square miles – a territory the size of Ireland (Carter, 2011).

79 Gabriel Ondetti (2008, 230) makes the important point that land reform in Latin America has been very difficult to achieve "under democratic conditions." In Cuba, Mexico and Nicaragua, for example, major land reform was achieved only through "violent upheavals" (ibid.). Columbia still endures over five decades of violence since the war with FARC (*Fuerzas Armadas Revolucionarias de Colombia* or 'Revolutionary Armed Forces of Colombia') began in 1964.

80 The MST attempted just 110 land occupations in 2013, while only close to 160 families were settled.

81 I visited the Paulo Freire Centre twice over the course of my two-week research visit (11–27 April 2014). I was accompanied by Professor Alfredo Gomes on both occasions and by his colleague Professor André Gustavo Ferreira da Silva on the first visit. In practical terms, the 300-plus kilometre round trip prohibited any more visits.

82 From *outside* Brazil too, one may critically reflect on the global movement of capital and people, for example, the (temporary) migration of those who desire 'a place in the sun'.

83 For a visual of Normandía, see www.youtube.com/watch?v=BvLM0_rLgP4 (accessed on 4 October 2014).

84 Advocates have argued for many years that we need a wider, more integrated approach to 'green education': "An understanding of ecology does not necessarily originate in courses bearing ecological labels; it is quite as likely to be labelled geography, botany, agronomy, history or economics. This is as it should be, but whatever the label; ecological training is scarce" (Leopold, 1949/1991, 240).

85 It may appear (especially to those of us 'outside' agriculture) as a rather lacklustre technical issue. Yet seed production is all important to our food consumption, life-styles, lifechances and even survival (especially in the Global South).

86 "For sugar beet, the market share of the 3 biggest seed producers is 90%, for Maize 57% and for soya beans 55%" (Berne Declaration and EcoNexus, 2013, 10).

87 "In Europe, 5 companies (Monsanto, Dupont, Syngenta, BASF and Bayer) own half the patents on plants" (Berne Declaration and EcoNexus, 2013, 10).

88 "For example, prices for cotton seed have increased by 3 or 4 times since genetically modified (GM) cotton was introduced in the US" (Berne Declaration and EcoNexus, 2013, 10). Also, ". . . global trade has a disproportionate influence on prices. On the stock market, batches of the same soya and maize may be traded speculatively several times over, thus increasing price volatility" (ibid., 2).

89 "The worldwide erosion of diversity is massive. An estimated 75% of all crop varieties were irretrievably lost in the 20th Century" (Berne Declaration and EcoNexus, 2013, 10).

90 Multinationals' share of the hybrid maize seed market in Brazil is over 90 per cent (Monsanto has over 60 per cent of this total; Branford and Rocha, 2002, 176). Take France as another example: 95 per cent of all corn seeds in the national catalogue are hybrids (A *Flór Scéal* Irish language documentary, *presented by John Paul Lepers*, broadcast on TG4 on 21 October 2014). Monsanto, the world leader in seeds and genetically modified organisms (GMOs), has its biggest European plant in France. It supplies one third of all the corn seeds sold on the French market (ibid.).

91 *Food and nutritional security* as defined by the Organic Law of Food and Nutritional Security (LOSAN) in 2006 and as directly quoted in Chmielewska and Souza (2011, 3): ". . . food and nutritional security is the realisation of everyone's right to regular and permanent access to quality food in sufficient quantity, without compromising access to other essential needs, based on health-promoting food practices that respect cultural diversity and that are environmentally, culturally, economically and socially sustainable."

92 The definition of *food sovereignty* by the National Council of Food Security and Nutrition (CONSEA) in 2009 and directly quoted in Chmielewska and Souza (2011, 4) is ". . . the right of a people to define its own policies and strategies for food production, distribution and consumption."

93 In the 2009–2010 public budget, for example, agribusiness food production received in excess of six times more resources than family farming (Chmielewska and Souza, 2011, 15). Further, in President Dilma's 2013–2014 agricultural plan, 115 billion R$ was allocated for agribusiness while family farming was given an 18 billion R$ share (Araujo, 2013). These figures are repeated later in the main text to illustrate the unequal treatment of family farming vis-à-vis bigger agribusiness 'interests'.

94 I made these significant connections after watching a *Flór Scéal* Irish language documentary, presented by John Paul Lepers and broadcast on TG4 on 21 October 2014. I am grateful to this programme's makers and contributors. Since its viewing, I began to understand how 'seed production' (a seemingly tame technical issue) is so politically connected to an 'other' way of 'seeing' and 'being' in the world.

95 The World Social Forum (WSF) was first held in 2001 in Porto Alegre in the Brazilian state of Rio Grande do Sul. Taking place each year in January, it deliberately coincides with the meeting of the World Economic Forum (WEF), which takes place annually in Davos, Switzerland. The primary function of the WSF is to develop a global justice presence to discuss, organise and campaign for 'other' ideas and solutions that directly oppose capitalism, specifically its neoliberal form with its attendant ideological and material effects. In this way, the 'spirit of Porto Alegre' is in direct opposition to the 'spirit of Davos' (Wallerstein, 2009). Incidentally, at the inaugural meeting of the WSF in Porto Alegre in 2001, a number of activists (including José Bové and the MST) were involved in destroying a crop plot belonging to Monsanto, the world leader in seeds and GMOs. Also, Immanuel Wallerstein (originator of 'spirit of Porto Alegre' versus 'spirit of Davos' phrase) was one of 19 signatories (alongside Frei Betto) to the 2005 *Porto Alegre Manifesto*. This 'manifesto' (it is still a moot point whether this is representative of all WSF groups) sets out an 'other' way to progress economic reform, peace, climate change and democracy (there are 12 clauses in total).

96 Naomi Klein (2014c) argues that we need to move away from the economic urgency of resource production, for example, drilling and fracking practices aimed at securing more (gas) fuel. This specific production, she ironically notes, actually emits more methane, thus 'heating up' our warming climate! Existing (conventional) oil and gas resources, Klein believes, are more than sufficient for our needs *alongside* a much-needed expansion in renewable energies (ibid.). Klein's argument appears to be fully supported by a new 'forward-thinking' IPCC (the Intergovernmental Panel on Climate Change) report (IPCC, 2014). Drawing on the work of some 800 scientists already published since September 2013, the report claims that world emissions would have to fall to 'near zero or below in 2100' if the world has any chance of staying below a 2 degree Celsius heat rise. This effectively means that fossil fuel power generation without new Carbon Capture and Storage (CCS) technologies will have to be almost entirely phased out by then (ibid.). If we fail to act on climate change, the report warns, there is a high risk of 'irreversible' global disasters, for example, large ice melts, coastal erosion, town, city and land destruction, and widespread health, infrastructure, food and water crises.

97 João Pedro Stédile argues that more significant land reform could happen in Brazil if there was a widespread alliance between small producers and urban working class consumers. Thus, the MST is not opposed to markets or capital per se, rather it opposes dominant *agribusiness* markets and *neoliberal* forms of capital. Through its own modern (market) logic, the MST argues that it is keeping alive (in line with cultural historical traditions) Marxist *protest*.

98 To quote the fox in Antoine de Saint-Exupéry's *Le petit prince* (1943/1995, 82): "L'essentiel est invisible pour les yeux" ("What is essential is invisible to the eye").

99 Thomas Jefferson's words derive from Aristotle's insights into distributive justice (see *Nicomachean Ethics*).

100 'Mandala' derives from the Sanskrit word 'circle'. Mandalas are to be found in sacred art and are used as meditative rituals designed to teach about the impermanence of all beings and objects. Buddhist monks, for example, can spend weeks/months working with elaborated (symbolic) patterns of coloured sand. Upon completion, the art object is deliberately destroyed. In *Normandía*, Greisson showed us the herb garden, comprising of concentric circles with a pond at its epicentre. He explained the specific purpose of this mandala. The circles signify the transformation journey that students and 'others' must undertake if they are to arrive at the spiritual centre. This life centre (signified by water) depicts a place that is free of all ignorance and slavery.

101 A refectory (*refeitório*) is usually found in boarding schools, higher education institutions and monasteries. The connection with monasteries is particularly (symbolically) significant since: Many of the MST founders and leaders are ex-seminarians; Brazilian protest is intrinsically linked to Messianic-inspired movements and figures; and Freirean

messages are bound up with spiritual activity and social activism. Consider also the powerful ritual of sharing a meal in the *refeitório*. This is a place where one is 'restored', where dialogue is cultivated, where a sense of collective identity is 'formed'.

102   One can include class, gender, ability, cultural and sexuality conventions.

103   The question thus presents: *To what extent do educators deform learners?*

104   There is indeed much evidence to suggest that learning experiences offer opportunities for learners to positively reconstruct their self-concept and self-esteem and ultimately enable a 'renegotiation of the self' (Walters, 2000).

105   Makarenko is certainly less well known than Lev Semyonovich Vygotsky (1896–1934). The latter is central to the development of sociocultural learning theories and practices (Vygotsky, 1978). In the West, Vygotsky's social-psychology has been somewhat stripped of its Marxist principles which so guided its substance – not an insignificant irony, given Vygotsky's emphasis on the importance of learning-in-context. Specifically, Vygotsky (in parallel with Marx) stresses the importance of relations between human consciousness and the material world. Education and the development of human thought is thus dependent upon the environment and experiences therein. *Normandía*, for example, is already contextualised as, as well as being re-presentative of, an 'other' context. It is this context(s) that so shapes its learners' thoughts and experiences.

106   It is important to remind that the MST *uses* symbolism, ideas and figurative persons/events to create its own identity in opposition to 'other' (dominant) groups. This does not make Marx or Freire, for example, responsible for how it is their ideas are 'used'. Throughout history, as mentioned previously in the main text, many have used and abused 'poverty', 'Marxism', 'revolution'. On a much less impactful social scale, many have used and abused 'Freire' too. Thus, there have been (*and continue to be*) many Freirean approaches in 'use' (*especially in adult education*), much of which was/is not faithful to his (authentic) critical pedagogy approach.

107   Friedrich Wilhelm Nietzsche critiques common-sense notions of morality, charity, Christianity. There appears to be a fundamental difference between enabling 'others' to become empowered (e.g. via critique) and 'commanding' this 'virtue' (of empowerment/critique) *for* 'others'. For Nietzsche, to be 'charitable' (or to 'save' an 'other'; or to 'empower' an 'other') is to command 'virtue' and derive one's own advantage from its powerful authority. Also, the *subjugated* or 'herd' that receive and believe in this 'virtue' are, at once, commanded by it and their 'self-interest' becomes merely a reflection of its power and the 'interest' of those that exercise it (Nietzsche, 1886; 1887). See also Note 75 in Chapter 3.

108   Critique is often fragmented into 'positive' and 'negative' appraisals. *But critique just is.* Perhaps a 'positive' or 'negative' attachment betrays a particular paradigmatic stance (and, alongside it, the views of its proponents). A paradigmatic stance, then, may *ultimately* frame or 'command' critique (see above, Note 10). The question thus presents: *Is critique ever objective?*

109   This interview was produced by The International Literacy Institute in 1997 and was retrieved on 14 November 2014 from www.youtube.com/watch?v=aFWjnkFypFA

110   Note the use of the term 'non-traditional' in this context – here it is used to demonise (not include) difference. Corrupting the youth was a charge levelled against Socrates way back in 399 BC. Presumably the LGBT community is viewed in some contemporary circles as equally 'dangerous'?

111   Of course extraordinary individuals perform courageous, momentous acts of protest, for example, Malala Yousafzai (Pakistan), Anabel Hernández (Mexico), Aung San Suu Kyi (Burma) and Philomena Lee (Ireland). But small acts make a difference too. Indeed, small acts enable protest to take root in wider society. A wonderful example, I think, is the following story told by one man on his Facebook page (the story was circulated in 2014 by Irish gay rights activist Rory O'Neill): This man [identified as Colm] goes into a Dublin supermarket dressed, in his own words, "somewhat flamboyantly in a

big woolly jumper and short shorts." Another man in the line in front of him turns to his girlfriend and says "look at the faggot in the shorts." They both laugh. When it's their turn to be served, the shop assistant refuses their custom. "Why?", 'protests' the offending person. The reply: "I won't serve someone who calls another person a faggot."

112 Any education project that ignores racism, sexism, worker exploitation, and other forms of oppression may do nothing more than affirm/assist inequality and one's status quo position therein. Hence, an education project that ignores inequality is *actively participative* in this state and, subsequent to such choice, loses its (positive) *powerful* force. At the heart of any effective education project, then, is *praxis* – an (informed) transformative rationale that leads to committed action.

113 Note the use of the term 'collective' in this context – the emphasis here is on 'commodifying and exchanging' knowledge for the strategic benefit of the national (and international) *economy*. See also Note 110 that highlights how other terms/concepts (in this case, 'non-traditional') are counter-positioned. In 'capturing' words, educational 'interests' (e.g. neoliberals, conservative elites) seek to capture ideas, values. Hence the *need*, from a protest perspective, *to continually re-name* terms/concepts. In the Freirean sense, we are exhorted to [Re-]'read the word, read the world'.

114 I refer to the Special Assignee Relief Programme (SARP). To qualify, individuals have to earn at least 75,000 euro per annum; 30 per cent of their income in excess of this amount is then excluded for Irish tax purposes. The present scheme is due to finish at the end of 2017. Note how 'knowledge' is conceived here – in powerful 'human capital' terms.

115 See the piece on the *Time* magazine, retrieved on 12 January 2014 from http://time. com/3486048/most-influential-teens-2014/. Signatories to, and supporters of, the Porto Alegre Manifesto (produced at the 2005 World Social Forum; see Note 95) would strongly object to such commercialisation proposals. Under Clause 7, the Manifesto determines that all patenting of knowledge on living things and the privatisation of 'common' goods for humanity (e.g. water, plants) ought to be prohibited. As already highlighted (Note 87): "In Europe, five companies (Monsanto, Dupont, Syngenta, BASF and Bayer) own half the patents on plants" (Berne Declaration and EcoNexus, 2013, 10).

116 A recent Credit Suisse study shows that the richest 1 per cent own almost half (48 per cent) of the world population's wealth, while the richest decile hold 87 per cent of global wealth (Treanor, 2014). Oxfam reports that 85 individuals across the world share a combined wealth of 1 trillion pounds sterling, which equals the total wealth held by the poorest 3.5 billion of the world's population (ibid.).

References

Ahmed, S. (2004). *The cultural politics of emotion*. Edinburgh. Edinburgh University Press.

Altieri, M. A. (1995). *Agroecology: The science of sustainable agriculture*. Colorado. Westview Press.

Amnesty International Report on Brazil. (2013). Retrieved on 19 June 2014 from www.state.gov/j/drl/rls/hrrpt/2008/wha/119150.htm

Apple, M. W. (2000). *Official knowledge: Democratic education in a conservative age*. 2nd edn. New York and London. Routledge.

Apple, M. (2006). *Educating the 'right' way: Markets, standards, God and inequality*. 2nd edn. New York and London. Routledge.

Apple, M. W. and Beane, J. A. (2007). *Democratic schools: Lessons in powerful education*. 2nd edn. Portsmouth, New Hampshire. Heinemann Publishers.

Araujo, B. (2013). The imposition of Brazilian agribusiness and the suppression of family farming, with government support. Article written for the *Americas Program*. Retrieved on 06 November 2014 from www.cipamericas.org/archives/9327

Arendt, H. (1963/2006). *On revolution.* Introduction by Jonathan Schell in the 2006 Edition. London. Penguin Books.

Bacon, F. (1597). *Meditationes Sacrae.* Works 14.95; 79. Cited in José María Rodríguez García (2001). Scientia protestas est – Knowledge is power: Francis Bacon to Michel Foucault. *Neohelicon,* 28, no. 1, 109–21.

Balfour, E. B. (1943/2006). *The living soil: Evidence of the importance to human health of soil vitality, with special reference to post-war planning.* Bristol. Soil Association.

Balfour, E. B. (1977/1991). Organic farming. From E. B. Balfour. (1977). Towards a sustainable agriculture: The living soil. Paper presented at the IFOAM Conference, 1977. In A. Dobson, ed. (1991, 116–20). *The green reader.* London. Andre Deutsch.

Ball, S. J. (1990). *Politics and policy making in education: Explorations in policy sociology.* London and New York. Routledge.

Baudrillard, J. (1981). *For a critique of the political economy of the sign.* St Louis, MO. Telos Press.

Baudrillard, J. (1994). *Simulacra and simulation.* Translated by S. Faria Glaser. Ann Arbor, MI. University of Michigan Press.

Beckett, S. (1951/1956). *Malone meurt/Malone dies.* New York. Grove.

Berne Declaration and EcoNexus. (2013). *Agropoly: A handful of corporations control world food production.* Translated by C. Wittstock, Oxford. Berne Declaration (DB) and EcoNexus Publication. Retrieved on October 28, 2014 from www.econexus.info/sites/econexus/files/Agropoly_Econexus_BerneDeclaration_wide-format.pdf

Bernstein, B. (1977). *Class codes and control.* London. Routledge and Kegan Paul.

Bookchin, M. (1980/1991). Social ecology. From M. Bookchin. (1980). Open letter to the ecology movement in Toward an ecological society. Montreal. Black Rose Books. In A. Dobson, ed. (59–63). *The green reader.* London. Andre Deutsch.

Bourdieu, P. (1977). Cultural reproduction and social reproduction. In J. Karabel & A. Halsey, eds. *Power and ideology in education.* New York. Oxford University Press.

Bové, J. et Dufour, F. (2000). *Le monde n'est pas une marchandise: Des paysans contre la malbouffe.* Entretiens avec Gilles Luneau. Paris. Éditions La Découverte.

Branford, S. and Rocha, J. (2002). *Cutting the wire: The story of the landless movement in Brazil.* London. Latin American Bureau.

Brasileiro, A. (2013). Brazil's child sex trade thrives as world cup looms. Retrieved on 21 July 2014 from http://articles.chicagotribune.com/2013–12–03/features/sns-rt-us-brazil-prostitution-20131202_1_child-prostitution-sexual-exploitation-reais

Brookfield, S. (2006). *The skillful teacher: On technique, trust and responsiveness in the classroom.* 2nd edn. San Francisco. Jossey-Bass.

Butler, J. (1990). *Gender trouble: Feminism and the subversion of identity.* Abingdon. New York.

Butler, J. (2002). What is critique? An essay on Foucault's virtue. Retrieved on 24 October 2011 from http://tedrutland.org/wp-content/uploads/2008/02/butler-2002.pdf

Butler, J. (1997). *The psychic life of power.* Stanford. Stanford University Press.

Caldart, R. S. (1997). *Educação em Movimento: Formação de Educadoras e Educadores no MST.* Petrópolis. Editora Vozes.

Caldart, R. S. (2000). *Pedagogia do Movimento Sem Terra: Escola é mais do que escolar.* Petrópolis. Editora Vozes.

Carter, M. (2011). The landless rural workers movement and democracy in Brazil. *Latin American Research Review,* Special Issue, 186–287. Retrieved on 13 October 2014 from ggjalliance.org/system/files/Miguel%20Carter%20LARR%20Article%20(2011)_0%20(1).pdf

Carter, M. (ed., 2014). *Challenging social inequality: The landless rural workers movement and agrarian reform in Brazil.* Translated by Miguel Carter. Durham, North Carolina. Duke University Press.

Candido, A. (1995). *On literature and society*. Translated by H. S. Becker. New Jersey. Princeton University Press.

Castro, Josué de. (1946/1952). *Geografia da fome*. Rio de Janeiro: O Cruzeiro. Published in English in 1952 as *The geography of hunger*. London. Gollancz.

Chmielewska, D. and Souza, D. (2011). *The food security policy context in Brazil*. Brasília. International Policy Centre for Inclusive Growth, United Nations Development Programme.

Collins, R. (1979). *The credential society: An historical sociology of education and stratification*. New York. Academic Press.

Collins, J. and Selina, H. (2012). *Introducing Heidegger: A graphic guide*. London. Icon Books.

Debord, G. (1967). *La société du spectacle / The society of the spectacle*. Translated by Ken Knabb. 6th edn in 2000. London. Rebel Press.

de Saint-Exupéry, A. (1943/1995). *Le petit prince / The little prince*. Translated by Irene Testot-Ferry. Hertfordshire. Wordsworth Classics.

Dewey, J. (1916/1966). *Democracy and education*. New York. Free Press.

Dobson, A. (1991, ed.). *The green reader*. London. Andre Deutsch.

dos Santos, M. (2014). The landless of yesterday, of today and of tomorrow. Article written in the *Friends of the MST* website on 11 February 2014. Retrieved on 22 September 2014 from www.mstbrazil.org/content/landless-yesterday-today-tomorrow

Fausto, B. (1999). *A concise history of Brazil*. Cambridge. Cambridge University Press.

Freire, P. (1970/1996). *Pedagogy of the oppressed*. Volume 10. London. Penguin.

Freire, P. (1974/2010). *Education for critical consciousness*. London and New York. Continuum.

Freire, P. and Freire, A. M. A. (1994/2004). *Pedagogy of hope: Reliving pedagogy of the oppressed*. Translated by Robert R. Barr. New York and London. Continuum.

Freire, P. (1996). *Letters to Cristina: Reflections on my life and work*. Translated by Donaldo Macedo with Quilda Macedo and Alexandre Oliveira. London and New York. Routledge.

Freire, P. (1998). *Teachers as cultural workers: Letters to those who dare teach*. Commentary by Peter McLaren, Joe L. Kincheloe and Shirley Steinberg. Colorado. Westview Press.

Freire, P. (2000). *Pedagogy of freedom: Ethics, democracy, and civic courage*. Lanham, Boulder, New York and Oxford; Rowman & Littlefield.

Freire, A. M. A. and Macedo, D., eds (2001). *The Paulo Freire reader*. New York and London. Continuum.

Foucault, M. (1977). *Discipline and punish*. Translated by Alan Sheridan. New York: Vintage.

Foucault, M. (1990). *The history of sexuality, Volume 1: An introduction*. Reissue edn. New York. Vintage.

Foucault, M. (1997). What is critique? In Michel Foucault, ed. (23–83). *The politics of truth*. New York. Semiotext(e).

Gillborn, D. (2008). *Racism and education: Coincidence or conspiracy?* Abingdon and New York. Routledge.

Giroux, H. A. (2001). *Theory and resistance in education: Towards a pedagogy for the opposition*. Foreword by Paulo Freire. Preface by Stanley Aronowitz. Westport, Connecticut; London. Bergin & Garvey.

Gliessman, S. R. (1998). *Agroecology: Ecological processes in sustainable agriculture*. Florida. CRC Press.

Global Hunger Index, GHI. (2014). *2014 Global hunger index: The challenge of hidden hunger*. Bonn, Washington DC, Dublin. Published by the International Food Policy Research Institute, Concern Worldwide and Welthungerhilfe.

Goleman, D. (2005). *Emotional Intelligence: Why it can matter more than IQ*. London. Bloomsbury.

Gordon, C. (2005). *Power/knowledge: Selected interviews and other writings of Michel Foucault 1972–1977*. Translated by Colin Gordon, Leo Marshall, John Mepham and Kate Soper. New York. Pantheon Books.

Government of Brazil. (2010). *Constitution of the Federal Republic of Brazil 1988*. Brasília. Documentation and Information Centre.

Grant, C. A. and Sleeter, C. (2011). *Doing multicultural education for achievement and equity*. 2nd edn. Abingdon and New York. Routledge.

Heidegger, M. (1927/1996). *Sein und Zeit/Being and Time*. New York. State University of New York Press.

Hennigan, T. (2014). Grêmio case the latest sign racism no longer accepted in Brazil. Article written for the *Irish Times*, Thursday 20 November 2014. Retrieved on 20 November 2014 from www.irishtimes.com/news/world/gr%C3%AAmio-case-the-latest-sign-racism-no-longer-accepted-in-brazil-1.2007637?mode=print&ot=example.AjaxPage Layout.ot

Horton, M. and Freire, P. (1990). *We make the road by walking: Conversations on education and social change*. Philadelphia. Temple University Press.

Intergovernmental Panel on Climate Change, IPCC. (2014). *Climate change 2014: Impacts, adaptation, and vulnerability*. IPCC 5th Assessment Synthesis Report. Retrieved on 12 January 2014 from ipcc-wg2.gov/AR5/images/uploads/WG2AR5_SPM_FINAL.pdf

Jaynes Chandler, B. (2000). *Bandit king: Lampião of Brazil*. Texas. Texas A&M University Press.

Kassai, L. and Moura, F. (2011). Monsanto sees Brazil soy seed share exceeding 80% on new strain. Article written for *Bloomberg News*. Retrieved on 28 October 2014 from www.bloomberg.com/news/2011–02–18/monsanto-sees-brazil-soy-seed-share-exceeding-80-on-new-strain.html

Kitching, K. (2011). Taking educational risks with and without guaranteed identities: Freire's 'problem-posing' and Judith Butler's 'troubling'. In A. O'Shea and M. O'Brien, eds (2011). *Pedagogy, oppression and transformation in a 'post-critical' climate: The return of Freirean thinking*. London and New York. Continuum.

Kitching, K., O'Brien, S., Long, F., Conway, P., Murphy, R. and Hall, K. (2014, in press). Knowing how to feel about the Other? Student teachers and the contingent role of embodiments in educational inequalities. *Pedagogy, Culture and Society*.

Klein, N. (2014a). *This changes everything: Capitalism versus the climate*. New York. Simon and Schuster.

Klein, N. (2014b). The change within: The obstacles we face are not just external. Article written in *The Nation*. 22 April 2014. Retrieved from www.thenation.com/article/179460/change-within-obstacles-we-face-are-not-just-external

Klein, N. (2014c). Using Ukraine to cook the planet. Article written in *The Guardian*, 10 April 2014. Retrieved on 01 November 2014 from www.naomiklein.org/articles/2014/04/using-ukraine-cook-planet

Kuhn, T. S. (1962/1996). *The structure of scientific revolutions*. 3rd edn. Chicago. University of Chicago Press.

Leopold, A. (1949/1991). A land ethic. From A. Leopold. (1949). *A sand county almanac*. Oxford. Oxford University Press. In A. Dobson, ed. (238–41). *The green reader*. London. Andre Deutsch.

Makarenko, A. (1936). *Road to life*. Translated in English by Stephen Garry. London. Stanley Nott.

Maram, S. (1990). Juscelino Kubitschek and the politics of exuberance, 1956–1961. *Luso-Brazilian Review*, 27, no. 1, 31–45.

Mezirow, J. (2009). An overview on transformative learning. In K. Illeris, ed. (90–105). *Contemporary theories of learning: Learning theorists . . . in their own words*. London and New York. Routledge.

Ondetti, G. (2008). *Land, protest and politics: The landless movement and the struggle for agrarian reform in Brazil*. Pennsylvania. The Pennsylvania State University Press.

O'Sullivan, D. (1995). Cultural strangers and educational reconstruction. *Czech Sociological Review*, 32, 159–73.

O'Sullivan, D. (2005). *Cultural politics and Irish education since the 1950s: Policy paradigms and power*. Dublin. IPA Publication.

O'Sullivan, D. (2008). Turning theory on ourselves: Some resources and constraints for adult educators. *The Adult Learner*, 2008, 13–32. Dublin. AONTAS Publication.

Owen, D. (1980/1991). The science of ecology. From D. Owen (1980). *What is ecology?* Oxford. Oxford University Press. In A. Dobson, ed. (18–24). *The green reader*. London. Andre Deutsch.

Oxfam. (2010). Fighting hunger in Brazil: Much achiveved, more to do. *Oxfam Case Study*. Retrieved on 06 November 2014 from www.oxfam.org/sites/www.oxfam.org/files/cs-fighting-hunger-brazil-090611-en.pdf

Perry, G. (2014). Who are you? A 3-Episode Television Series with Channel 4, 22 October–05 November 2014. Retrieve information from www.channel4.com/programmes/grayson-perry-who-are-you/episode-guide

Rabhi, P. (2008). *Manifeste pour la terre et l'humanisme*. Préface de Nicolas Hulot. Arles. Actes Sud, Babel.

Ramos, G. (1939/1999). *Vidas Secas/Barren Lives*. Translated and introduced by Ralph Edward Dimmick. Illustrated by Charles Umlauf. Austin Texas. University of Texas Press.

Rose, N. (1999). *Governing the soul: The shaping of the private self*. London. Free Association Books.

Rousseau, J. J. (1762/1997). Du contrat social, ou Principes du droit politique. Reprinted in 1997 in *'The social contract' and other later political writings*. Cambridge. Cambridge University Press.

Russell, W. (2000). *Educating Rita*. Harlow, Essex. Longman.

Schaff, K. P. (2004). Agency and institutional rationality: Foucault's critique of normativity. *Philosophy and Social Criticism*, 30, no. 1, 51–71.

Shor, I. and Freire, P. (1987). *A pedagogy for liberation: Dialogues on transforming education*. Westport, Connecticut. Bergin & Garvey.

Shor, I., ed. (1987). *Freire for the classroom: A sourcebook for liberatory teaching*. Afterword by Paulo Freire. Portsmouth, New Hampshire. Heinemann Publishers.

Shor, I. (1999). What is critical literacy? In I. Shor and C. Pari, eds (1–29). *Critical literacy in action: Writing words, changing worlds – a tribute to the teachings of Paulo Freire*. 1st edn. Portsmouth, New Hampshire. Heinemann Publishers.

Slee, R. (2010). *The irregular school: Exclusion, schooling and inclusive education*. Foundations and Futures of Education Series. Abingdon and New York. Routledge.

Stédile, J. P. (2011). Landless battalions. In F. Mulhern, ed. (255–79). *Lives on the left: A group portrait*. London. Verso.

Tavares Correia, J. (1999). Hidden meanings: The mocambo in Recife. *Social Science Information*, 38, no. 2, 297–327.

Treanor, J. (2014). Richest 1% of people own nearly half of global wealth, says report. Article written for *The Guardian*. 14 October 2014. Retrieved on 12 January 2015 from www.theguardian.com/business/2014/oct/14/richest-1percent-half-global-wealth-credit-suisse-report

Vidal, J. (2014). Murder capitals of the world: How runaway urban growth fuels violence. Article written for *The Observer*. 01 November 2014. Retrieved on 07 November 2014 from www.theguardian.com/global-development/2014/nov/01/murder-capitals-world-city-violence

Vygotsky, L. (1978). *Mind in society: The development of higher psychological processes*. Edited by Michael Cole, Vera John-Steiner, Sylvia Scribner and Ellen Souberman. Cambridge, Massachusetts. Harvard University Press.

Wallerstein, I. (2009). Crisis of the capitalist system: Where do we go from here? The Harold Wolpe Lecture, November 5, 2009. University of KwaZulu-Natal, Durban. Retrieved on 01 October 2014 from http://mrzine.monthlyreview.org/2009/wallerstein121109p.html

Wallerstein, I., Collins, R., Mann, M., Derluguian, G. and Calhoun, C. (2013). *Does capitalism have a future?* New York. Oxford University Press.

Walter, R. J. (1987). Literature and history in contemporary Latin America. *Latin American Literary Review*, 15, no. 29, 173–82.

Walters, M. (2000). The mature students' three R's. *British Journal of Guidance & Counselling*, 28, no. 2, 267–78.

Wearn, O. R., Reuman, D. C. and Ewers, R. M. (2012). Extinction debt and windows of conservation opportunity in the Brazilian Amazon. *Science*, 337, no. 6091, 228–32.

Willis, P. (1981). *Learning to labour: How working class kids get working class jobs*. New York. Columbia University Press.

World Development Indicators (2012). *World Development Indicators – Brazil*. Washington. World Bank Publication.

World Health Organization, WHO. (2014). *World Health Statistics 2014*. Geneva. World Health Organization publication.

Youdell, D. (2011). *School trouble: Identity, power and politics in education*. Abingdon and New York. Routledge.

Zweig, S. (1941). *Brazil – Land of the future*. New York. The Viking Press.

INDEX